WORDS AND SHADOWS

Jeff East and Johnny Whitaker as Tom and Huck break into song in the *Reader's Digest*
musical adaptation of Mark Twain's *Tom Sawyer* (1973).

WORDS
AND SHADOWS

Literature on the Screen

By Jim Hitt

A CITADEL PRESS BOOK
Published by Carol Publishing Group

ACKNOWLEDGMENTS

This book could not have been written without the kind assistance of Chuck McCleary of Nostalgia Enterprises of Los Angeles, California, who supplied many of the photographs that made this work possible. Thanks also to the Jerry Vermilye Collection and to Alvin Marill for filling in the photo gaps.

DEDICATION

To Fanchon, my mother, whose patience, persistence, and love helped me to become what I am.

To Vicki, my wife, who helped me to see my potential.

To Holly, my daughter, who showed me how much I could love.

And to Nonnie, who is watching.

A Citadel Press Book

Published by Carol Publishing Group

Citadel Press is a registered trademark of Carol Communications, Inc.

Editorial Offices: 600 Madison Avenue, New York, N.Y. 10022

Sales & Distribution Offices: 120 Enterprise Avenue, Secaucus, N.J. 07094

In Canada: Canadian Manda Group, P.O. Box 920, Station U, Toronto, Ontario M82 5P9

Queries regarding rights and permissions should be addressed to Carol Publishing Group, 600 Madison Avenue, New York, N.Y. 10022

Carol Publishing Group books are available at special discounts for bulk purchases, for sales promotions, fund-raising, or educational purposes. Special editions can be created to specifications. For details, contact: Special Sales Department, Carol Publishing Group, 120 Enterprise Avenue, Secaucus, N.J. 07094

Manufactured in the United States of America

10 9 8 7 6 5 4 3 2 1

Designed by A. Christopher Simon

Library of Congress Cataloging-in-Publication Data

Hitt, Jim, 1939–
    Words and shadows : literature on the screen / by Jim Hitt.
       p.   cm.
    "A Citadel Press book."
    Includes index.
    ISBN 0–8065–1340–3
    1. American fiction—Film and video adaptations.   2. Motion pictures and literature.   I. Title.
PN1997.85.H5   1992
791.43'657–dc20   92–31154
                                                                          CIP

Jennifer Jones and Rock Hudson as Catherine and Frederic, expressing their undying love,
in the color remake of Hemingway's *A Farewell to Arms* (1957).

Jon Hall as Major Heyward, Michael O'Shea as Hawkeye, Ric Vallin as Uncas, and Buzz Henry as Davy
Gamut in *Last of the Redmen* (1947), an adaptation of James Fenimore Cooper's *Last of the Mohicans*.

Val Kilmer as Philippe and George C. Scott as Dupin in the television movie of Edgar Allan Poe's *Murders in the Rue Morgue* (1986).

Ethan Hawke as Jack
Conroy in the Disney
version of Jack London's
White Fang (1991).

Peter Strauss as Dick Diver and Mary Steenburgen as Nicole, the lovers torn apart by their obsessions, in the television miniseries of F. Scott Fitzgerald's *Tender Is the Night* (1985).

CONTENTS

Lars Hanson as Dimmesdale in *The Scarlet Letter* (1926).

ONE

WORDS AND SHADOWS: AN INTRODUCTION

Hollywood loves stories of deals made and deals lost. Among these is the tale of a well-known American author (some say it was Harold Robbins), who in the early 1960s wrote a phenomenal bestseller that stayed at the number one spot on the *New York Times* for a record number of weeks. Since this author already had a good track record with Hollywood—several of his novels had been made into successful films—he sold the rights to a major studio for half a million dollars. The movie adaptation proved to be as sensational as the novel and was among the top three money-makers for the year of its release. This prompted the studio to offer a million dollars for his next novel, only half completed at the time. Of course, the author eagerly accepted.

This novel also proved to be another bestseller, hitting the number-one spot and staying there for fifteen or sixteen weeks. The studio tripled the budget from the previous hit and imported a star from Europe whom it intended to make into a big star in America, too. This film failed to make back its negative cost.

Reasoning that the film's failure lay in a star who had trouble speaking English, the studio shipped the actor back home and, undaunted, offered the author two million dollars for the rights to his next book. At that moment, the author had not written one word and, in fact, didn't even have an idea for a plot. When he told the studio negotiators this, they said, "Never mind. Let us know in a few days."

The author took the money, and now living the good life, proceeded to invest his earnings in luxurious cars, beautiful women, and big parties. Six months later, the negotiators hadn't heard from him and, a bit concerned, called at his house. When they asked for information about the plot, the author excused himself for a few moments and ran off to the bedroom, where he immediately phoned his lawyer.

"Bill," said the author. "These studio guys want to know what my next book is about."

"Well, tell them," responded the lawyer.

"That's just it," the author said. "I still don't have an idea. I can't think of anything. Look, I'm afraid that if I don't give them something, they'll want their money back. What should I do?"

On the other end of the line, the lawyer glanced at the

newspaper that lay unopened on his desk and noticed the headline concerning the current oil crisis. "Tell them it's about oil and the Arabs."

The author hung up, hurried back into the living room, and informed the studio men that his new book would be about oil and the Arabs. Satisfied, they shook hands with the author and left. The author did write the novel, and although he was noted for writing schlock, this was even below his standards. The book never made it to the big screen, although it did become a television movie of the week.

The story is most likely nothing more than a legend, a tall tale Hollywood-style, yet it illustrates the long love affair that the American film industry has had with American literature. Since those early primitive days when motion pictures were in their infancy, filmmakers have adapted thousands of American novels, short stories, and plays. By merging film with the older and more established medium of fiction, early movie makers could claim a legitimacy for a new art form which, at the time, was considered by critics and public alike as nothing more than a novelty. In addition, by basing a film on a literary work, the studios and producers had a ready-made idea. More important, however, by choosing literary works, they had a ready audience, a reason as valid in the time of Griffith as it is today.

The studios have seldom allowed a strict translation of a fictional work to reach the screen. Sometimes they have added, sometimes deleted; sometimes they have changed the title, sometimes kept the title and thrown out everything else. The only thing the studios asked was: Would the film make money? The changes most often found in literary adaptations reflect this attitude. Sad or disappointing endings of books became happy endings in films; failed love affairs in novels succeed on the screen; heroes who die in one medium survive in the other. Films based on literature were sacrificial lambs, offered up for the price of a theater ticket.

Yet, even in the worst adaptation, there is often a magic. Perhaps it lies in the attempt to turn literature into film. How often do we read a book that touches us and hope that the film will do the same? It rarely does. Still, we keep hoping to see the books that live in our head come alive on the screen. Certainly we understand that our minds are far more adept than celluloid at sustaining our fantasies, that most films can never reproduce or replace good books that somehow reach beyond our visceral pleasure to touch our hearts. Yet we long to see the physical reality of a cherished novel or short story, to see the ethereal become solid, touchable.

American filmmakers took the novels and short stories and molded them into shadows that flickered across the silver screen, shadows that were seldom eloquent. But occasionally words and shadows combined in such a way that the magic of the book became magic on the screen, and that magic also touched our hearts.

One final word. Every book must have limitations. This one is no exception. This survey concentrates upon the adaptations of mainstream American fiction, novels, and short stories, from James Fenimore Cooper to Pat Conroy. Zane Grey, Raymond Chandler, Ray Bradbury, Stephen King—these and many more are important writers, certainly, and in today's world, perhaps there is little distinction between their works and mainstream literature. But some sort of line, some demarcation, must be drawn in order to cover such a vast subject. The line is arbitrary but necessary. Hopefully, a later volume will cover genre fiction and include such authors.

Lex Barker as Deerslayer in rear of the canoe in *Deerslayer* (1957). Looking on are Rita Moreno as Hetty Hutter, Cathy O'Donnell as her sister, Judith, and Forrest Tucker as Hurry Harry Marsh.

TWO

CLASSIC AMERICAN

James Fenimore Cooper, Nathaniel Hawthorne, Edgar Allan Poe, Herman Melville

He wasn't much of a writer; his prose was awkward and his novels and short stories have dated badly; today he is seldom read and little remembered. Yet American writers should be forever thankful to Peter B. Kyne (1880–1957), for it was he who changed the structure of the American film industry.

In 1910, the *Saturday Evening Post* published Kyne's "Bronco Billy and the Baby," the story of a "good bad man" who sacrifices his freedom to aid a stricken child. Kyne would later expand the story into a short novel, *Three Godfathers*, a symbolic parable that itself would reach the screen numerous times. G. M. Anderson, who had appeared in *The Great Train Robbery* (1903) and had formed his own production company, read the *Post* story, and, without contacting Kyne, set about filming the story with himself in the lead. The film proved an immediate success, prompting Kyne to pay a visit to Anderson. The author made it clear that while he, too, liked the film, he expected to be paid for his work. Kyne was paid, legal action was avoided, and a great victory was won for authors of source material.

The key word here is *copyright*. Copyrighted material is protected by law. However, there is a great deal of literature where the copyright has expired or which has never been copyrighted. This material is in the public domain, and anyone can use it in any manner he or she sees fit. It was to these authors and works that many studios turned after 1910, authors like James Fenimore Cooper, Nathaniel Hawthorne, Edgar Allan Poe, and Herman Melville, classic figures in American literature whose names and works cost nothing to use.

Among the first American authors to reach the screen was James Fenimore Cooper (1789–1851). His Leatherstocking Tales are the foundation of frontier fiction. In *The Last of the Mohicans* (1826), Major Hayward is escorting Cora and Alice Munro, the daughters of the British commander. Accompanying them are psalm singer David Gamut and the traitorous Huron, Magua, who intends to betray the party to the French. Enter Hawkeye and his brave Indian companions, Chingachgook and his son Uncas, to save the stubborn major and his party. After the fall of Fort William Henry, Cora and

3

Alice are captured by Magua. Pursuit follows pursuit, adventure follows adventure, until, at last, Magua slays Uncas, Cora is killed by another Huron, and Magua falls under Hawkeye's rifle. Alice is returned to the safety of civilization, where she will eventually marry Major Hayward. Hawkeye promises to remain forever with his friend Chingachgook, the last of the Mohicans, and together the two return to the forest.

With all its movement and adventure, the novel was a natural for the silent screen. *Leatherstocking* (Biograph, 1909), directed by D. W. Griffith, and *The Last of the Mohicans* (Pat Powers, 1911) were so short—each ran only about twenty minutes—very little of the novel made it to the screen. It was left to Maurice Tourneur to direct the first full-length American version of *The Last of the Mohicans* (Associated Exhibitors, 1920), an outstanding silent feature and the best adaptation of the novel to date.

Although the film made some key changes, the narrative is swift and lean, consistently striking a balance between romance and adventure. The film follows the first half of the novel very closely, except that Cora Munroe (Barbara Bedford) has a beau, the effeminate Captain Randolf. However, once Randolf betrays Fort William Henry to the French, the film goes its own way until the climax, where the story returns to the fight on the cliff and the deaths of Cora, Uncas (Albert Roscoe), and Magua (Wallace Beery).

In the novel, Hawkeye and Chingachgook are Cooper's central characters, but in the film they play secondary roles, appearing first only after the desertion of Magua. During the attack on Fort Henry and the subsequent chase to save the girls, they are strangely absent, arriving at the last moment like avenging angels to kill Magua and bury the dead lovers. In taking this approach, the directors focused on the love triangle between Cora, Uncas, and Magua. All of this ends badly because these three threatened to break the taboo against racial mixing. Cora goes over a cliff after being stabbed by Magua, Uncas follows her, and Magua falls after being shot by Hawkeye. Their falls are both literal and symbolic.

The *New York Times* thought that except for the actors who portrayed Indians—they looked more like native Africans than American Indians—*The Last of the Mohicans* was "authentic" and captured the "quality of life" of the novel. *Photoplay* said that the director had treated the novel with "dignity" and "reverence" without sacrificing its cinematic possibilities. He also called it "thrillingly true to the spirit of the story."

The next two adaptations, *Leatherstocking* (Pathe, 1924) and *The Last of the Mohicans* (Mascot, 1932), were both serials that had little to do with the Cooper novel, but in the next remake of *The Last of the Mohicans* (United Artists, 1936), a feature film, some of the novel returned. There were the Munro sisters threat-

ened by the evil Magua (Bruce Cabot) and his Hurons; the fall of Fort William Henry, and the deaths of Cora (Heather Angel) and Uncas (Philip Reed). Even the ill-fated love affair between the Indian youth and the white daughter of a British officer was restored. The climax of the film finds Chingachgook (Robert Barrat) and Magua flailing at each other with tomahawks high above the cliff where Uncas and Cora have met their deaths. Magua is struck down and tumbles after his victims. While this ending varies from the novel, it retains the spirit of Cooper's work. However, Major Hayward (Henry Wilcoxon) fails to win the hand of Alice (Binnie Barnes), a task left to Hawkeye (Randolph Scott), whose romantic yearnings cause Chingachgook to utter, "Hawkeye's heart like water."

While this version took liberties with the Cooper novel, they proved minor compared to those in *Last of the Redmen* (Columbia, 1947), in which Chingachgook disappears entirely, and only Uncas accompanies Hawkeye (Michael O'Shea) and the major (Jon Hall). Director George Sherman keeps things moving as Magua (Buster Crabbe) chases Hawkeye and his companions around the countryside, but the film never rises above the level of kiddie matinee.

The Iroquois Trail (United Artists, 1950) claimed to be based on *The Leatherstocking Tales*, and while Hawkeye (George Montgomery) is again the hero, the plot had little to do with Cooper. Hawkeye becomes a scout for the British to avenge the death of his brother, who was killed by the French. In the process, he and his faithful Indian companion Sagamore (Monte Blue) break up a spy ring, rescue a fair maiden, and defeat an Indian rebellion. A "Classics Illustrated" television version of *Last of the Mohicans* (teleplay by Stephen Lord, NBC Schick Sunn Classics Productions, 1977) emphasized its ties to the old comic book more than to Cooper's novel. Another production of *The Last of the Mohicans* starring Irish actor Daniel Day Lewis is planned for release in 1992.

Other Cooper novels were adapted to the screen, none with great success. Republic Studios cranked out an adaptation of *The Deerslayer* (1941) that the New York *Daily News* called "a refugee from a nickelodeon." The next version, *The Deerslayer* (20th Century-Fox, 1957), was a quickie about a frontier scout, the Deerslayer (Lex Barker), who rescues a trapper and his daughter from the Hurons. *The Deerslayer* (teleplay by S. S. Schweitzer, NBC Schick Sunn Classics Productions, 1978) followed the previous year's TV excursion into Cooper, with Hawkeye (Steve Forrest, again) and Chingachgook (Ned Romero, again) rescuing a chief's daughter from the hands of her enemies.

The Pathfinder (Columbia, 1953) in which the Pathfinder (George Montgomery), his sidekick Chingachgook (Jay Silverheels), and a beautiful woman (Helena Carter) help to squelch a French plan to take over the Great Lakes area, played more like a dime novel than James Fenimore Cooper. *The Pioneers* (Monogram, 1941) was a cheap "B" Western vehicle for Tex Ritter without any real connection with *The Leatherstocking Tales*.

In many respects, the novels of James Fenimore Cooper were naturals for the screen. Most were full of action and peopled by red-blooded heroes, maids in distress, and dastardly villains, the kind of cardboard characters that are tinseltown's stock in trade. Nathaniel Hawthorne (1804–64) had no such advantage. Although he did write an occasional science fiction or supernatural story, his work was staid and placid compared to Cooper's.

Although set in Puritan times, Hawthorne's 1850 masterpiece, *The Scarlet Letter*, was an attack on morality and hypocrisy. The heroine, Hester Pyrnne, is married to one man but bears the child of another, and because of her infidelity, the community ostracizes her and forces her to wear across her chest a scarlet letter "A" for adulteress.

The first version of *The Scarlet Letter* (MGM, 1926) was a personal project of Lillian Gish, who suggested the Hawthorne novel to Louis B. Mayer. Mayer balked at the idea because the novel was on the blacklist of many church and women's organizations, but Gish persisted, and the studio put the project in her hands. On a purely visual level, the film succeeded admirably, with the look and feel of Hawthorne's novel, if not its intellectual strengths. The static moments without dialogue often seem to be photographs drawn directly from the novel and placed on the screen. In addition, the sharp black-and-white photography often reached for and captured the stark symbolism of the novel. The darkness of the characters, the stark settings, and the grim fatalism of the plot captured the very essence of the novel.

The problem with the film lay neither in the way it looked, nor in the performances, which were generally excellent, but in the Frances Marion script, which took too many liberties with Hawthorne, going so far as to invent a whole new beginning that romanticizes the relationship between Hester and Dimmesdale. As the story opens, Hester (Lillian Gish) is in the stocks, put there because she was chasing a bird that escaped its cage, making her late for church. Kind Reverend Dimmesdale (Lars Hanson) releases her, and soon the couple is holding hands and cavorting through the woods. At last she tells Dimmesdale that she is married and begs his forgiveness. She explains that she was forced by her father into wedlock with a man much older than herself, a man she never loved and to whom she was never a real wife. Her husband, Roger Chillingworth (Henry B.

Philip Reed as Uncas holds the unconscious Heather Angel as Cora in *The Last of the Mohicans* (1936).

Walthall), has been gone for four years and is presumed killed by Indians. At this point the camera pulls away, leaving the lovers in front of a fire, embracing. Shortly thereafter, Dimmesdale rushes out of the house, guilt lining his face.

These invented scenes damage the integrity of the adaptation. Hester lacks the stoical strength that makes her such a strong character in the novel. In addition, there is no gradual progression of Dimmesdale's guilt and torment, which is the heart and soul of the novel; in the film, he is a sinner by accident, not because, as in the novel, he lacks backbone. Finally, this opening delays the entrance of Chillingworth until two thirds of the movie is completed. He is not a complex character, but a stock villain whose actions are conceived and executed solely out of a need for revenge.

In the early sound remake of *The Scarlet Letter* (Darmour/Majestic, 1934), Colleen Moore played the role of Hester with appropriate humility but none of the cold fire that distinguishes the character in the novel. Henry B. Walthall repeated his role of Chillingworth from the silent version, and once again, the character reacts as a stereotypical villain rather than the three-dimensional character of Hawthorne's masterpiece. Hardie Albright was Dimmesdale in this version.

A West German/Spanish production of *The Scarlet Letter (Der Scharlachrote Buchstabe*, 1972), cowritten and directed by Wim Wenders, rearranges many of the details and invents many others. The result is that while the film has some very interesting moments, a Freudian interpretation of Hester (Senta Berger) and Puritanism is substituted for Hawthorne's story.

The only complete version to date of *The Scarlet Letter* appeared on PBS in 1984 as a four-hour, four-part adaptation by Alvin Sapinsley and Alan Knee. This one dropped all attempts at comic relief, but while extremely faithful to the novel and to the character of Hester (Meg Foster), the film remained cold and distant. (Earlier television versions included one in 1950 on *Studio One* with Mary Sinclair and John Baragrey and another four years later on the *Kraft Television Theater* with Kim Stanley and Leslie Nielsen.)

With *The House of the Seven Gables*, an 1851 Gothic novel with realistic overtones, Hawthorne moved away from the past and forward into his present, but Puritanism still dominates the characters. It is, however, surprising that when Universal decided to make *The House of the Seven Gables* (1940), it chose to concentrate more on the social aspects of the novel rather than the Gothic. This may be due to screenwriter Lester Cole, a man who later became one of the "Hollywood Ten" and landed in jail for being an uncooperative witness before the House Un-American Activities Committee. Cole made changes in plot, which caused Bosley Crowther to write in the *New York Times*, "And for devoted readers of Hawthorne, it is likely to prove a bit of a shock. . . . There have been some changes made in the family of the Pyncheons." While Cole's alterations do not damage Hawthorne's story, the ambiguity that enriches the novel is missing, and the whole pessimistic middle section of the novel is passed over. The curse of Maule is never effectively handled.

This is not to imply that *The House of the Seven Gables* is without merit. On the contrary, the film is often visually fascinating, especially in a courtroom scene involving Clifford (Vincent Price), a man unjustly convicted of murdering his father. In the background, two huge windows filter light into the cavernous courtroom, and, in the foreground, angry townspeople dressed in dark clothes are outlined against white walls. The accused man cries out against the injustice of privilege and power, a speech that seems aimed more at Nazi Germany than at New England courts; nevertheless, it is a powerful, well-directed scene.

The House of the Seven Gables turned up again as the third of three stories in *Twice Told Tales* (United Artists, 1963), which had little to do with the novel. The studio picked "Dr. Heidegger's Experiment" and "Rappaccini's

Daughter" to complete the anthology. However, it showed little faith in the first, substituting for Hawthorne's parable about wasted youth a story of betrayal and revenge. Far closer to its source was "Rappaccini's Daughter," the third of the stories. Rappaccini (Vincent Price) has injected a serum into his daughter (Joyce Taylor) which gives her eternal life but causes anything she touches to wither and die. When she falls in love with a young student (Brett Halsey), he obtains an antidote, but the concoction kills both lovers. Horrified by what he has done, Rappaccini takes his own life.

Twice Told Tales was a low-budget affair whose production values, miniature work, and makeup leave much to be desired. In addition, there are far too many close-ups and far too much expository dialogue, which drag the stories along at an excruciatingly slow pace. Yet despite these faults, the film remains creepily effective, often creating an atmosphere that is reminiscent of Hawthorne's stories.

Three years after Hawthorne's first edition of *Twice Told Tales,* Edgar Allan Poe (1809–49) published *Tales of the Grotesque and Arabesque* (1840), containing twenty-four of his stories.

One of the earliest Poe stories to be adapted was "The System of Dr. Tarr and Prof. Fether" (1845), which became the two-reel French film, *La Système du Docteur Goudron et du Professor Plume* (1912; U.S. title: *The Lunatics*), directed by Maurice Tourneur. It may have been the success of Tourneur's film that influenced D. W. Griffith to attempt *The Avenging Conscience* (Mutual, 1914), a combination of "The Tell-Tale Heart" (1843) and the Poe poem "Annabel Lee" (1849). A young man (Henry B. Walthall) is prevented from marrying the girl he loves (Blanche Sweet) by his iron-willed and tyrannical uncle (Spottiswood Aitken). One evening the nephew reads Poe's "Tell-Tale Heart," and immediately begins planning murder. He strangles the old man and walls up the corpse in the fireplace. Just as in the Poe story, the nephew begins to hear the beat of the old man's heart—"It grew louder-louder-louder!" Overcome with guilt, he hangs himself, and his girl throws herself off a cliff. At this point, Griffith, who also wrote the screenplay, used a plot device that must have been a cliché even in 1914. The boy awakes to discover it has all been a dream induced by reading Poe.

Two decades later, the British *Bucket of Blood* (Clifton-Hurst/Fox, 1934, aka *The Tell-Tale Heart*) attempted to transfer "The Tell-Tale Heart" to the screen. Using a spareness of dialogue and relying on camera work and atmosphere, the production stayed relatively close to Poe's story. The *New York Times* said the production proved that it was "not absolutely necessary to distort a great author's work in order to create a fascinating motion picture."

Manfish (United Artists, 1956) also claimed to be

Margaret Lindsay as Hepzibah Pynchon watches while Vincent Price as her husband, Clifford, is threatened by George Sanders as his black-hearted brother, Jaffrey, in *The House of the Seven Gables* (1940).

Sebastian Cabot as Dr. Heidegger and Mari Blanchard as his wife in Hawthorne's "Dr. Heidegger's Experiment," one of the three episodes in *Twice Told Tales* (1963).

Vincent Price as Dr. Rappaccini is concerned over the conduct of Joyce Taylor as his daughter, Beatrice, cradling a fallen Brett Halsey as Giovanni Guastconti in the "Rappaccini's Daughter" segment of *Twice Told Tales* (1963).

based on "The Tell-Tale Heart" and "The Gold Bug" (1843), but the story of three men searching for pirate treasure in the West Indies offered little atmosphere or mood. At one point, a character named Professor (Victor Jory) kills one of his partners (John Bromfield) and ties the body to an oxygen tank. Soon he comes to believe he hears the beating of the dead man's heart. The soundtrack included several calypso numbers, which further distanced the film from Poe.

Restoring the original title, the British production, *The Tell-Tale Heart* (Danziger/Brigadier-Union, 1962, aka *The Hidden Room of 1,000 Horrors*), bears a striking resemblance to *The Avenging Conscience* in terms of resolution. Here a young writer (Laurence Payne) fantasizes falling in love with a woman, killing her lover, and burying the body under the floorboards of a house. When the beating of the unquiet heart drives him crazy—it sounds like faulty plumbing—he digs up the body, cuts

Karloff and Lugosi are featured on this lobby card for *The Black Cat* (1934).

out the heart, and reburies it in the woods. The film concludes when the young writer awakens and discovers it has all been a dream. The *New York Times* lamented, "Poor Poe."

"The Fall of the House of Usher" (1839) may well be Poe's crowning achievement in the short story form. Within the confines of this single story are all the stock trappings of Gothic romance; and from first sentence to last, the single effect is consistently powerful and mesmerizing.

In 1960, Roger Corman had been making films for nearly a decade, yet he had never made one with a shooting schedule longer than two weeks. Most were shot in half that time. But with *House of Usher* (American International, 1960), he moved his career to new artistic and commercial heights, and in the process revitalized the American horror film, which had been supplanted by Hammer productions from England.

Corman conceived the house itself as the monster, and

it was on this basis that Corman sold the idea to AIP head Samuel Z. Arkoff. It was also the slant that Richard Matheson took when writing the screenplay. The opening scene, filmed in a burned-out section of the Hollywood Hills, was the only location work; the remainder of the movie was filmed on a studio set.

Matheson's script took certain liberties. In the short story, the narrator comes to visit Roderick Usher, a friend since boyhood, but in the screenplay, Philip Winthrop (Mark Damon) has come to visit Madelene (Myrna Fahey), his fiancée. He is greeted with an icy hostility by Roderick (Vincent Price), her brother, who makes plain his objections to a marriage between Philip and Madelene, claiming that both he and his sister suffer from a form of madness and that his sister is dying from the disease.

Later, Philip is almost killed during a tour of the tombs when a flying coffin barely misses him; Madelene faints and must be taken to her room. When Philip finds

Broderick Crawford (left) as Hubert Smith tries to stop an altercation with the help of Gladys Cooper as Myrna Hartley in the first remake of *The Black Cat* (1941).

The mob led by Leo Gordon (center) as Edgar Weeden prepares to do in Vincent Price as Charles Ward in *The Haunted Palace* (1963).

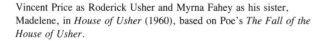

Vincent Price as Roderick Usher and Myrna Fahey as his sister, Madelene, in *House of Usher* (1960), based on Poe's *The Fall of the House of Usher*.

John Bromfield being restrained by Victor Jory and Lon Chaney Jr. in *Manfish* (1960), a very loose adaptation of "The Tell-Tale Heart."

her draped across her bed, apparently dead of a heart attack, Roderick seals her in a coffin and entombs her. However, the next morning, Bristol the butler informs Philip that Madelene suffered from cataleptic seizures, and the visitor realizes that they have buried Madelene alive. That night, Philip goes down into the crypt, where he discovers a trail of blood leading from the coffin. Madelene has clawed her way free, and Philip runs after her. Totally insane now, she eludes Philip and goes after Roderick. Outside, a storm is raging, and lightning strikes the house. In horror, Philip watches as Madelene and Roderick are both crushed under a falling beam. The house begins to crumble around Philip, and only Bristol's timely arrival to drag him free of the house saves his life. Bristol rushes back into the house just as it collapses and sinks into the tarn.

"Poe's classic horror tale has been fixed on film in fine style," said the *New York Herald Tribune*. "Far above the human gadgetry of most current movies in this category, it concentrates on atmosphere, makes no bones about its necessary artifices and, most crucial, walks conscientiously in Poe's stylistic steps."

A "Classics Illustrated" *Fall of the House of Usher* (teleplay by Stephen Lord, NBC Schick Sunn Classics Productions, 1982) introduced several new plot lines to the story, none of which were very original, and the production sank under a heavy dose of clichés and cheap production values.

The House of Usher (21st Century Productions, 1990) updated the story to the present. Roderick (Oliver Reed) imprisons his nephew's fiancée in order to make her his unwilling bride. In the end, the house sinks into the tarn. The nephew and his sweetheart are the only survivors, but Poe expires under this modern treatment, written by Michael J. Murray.

Few tales have ever been as influential as Poe's "Murders in the Rue Morgue" (1841), which marks the birth of the detective story. It introduced C. Auguste Dupin, who solves the case of a mother and daughter who were murdered in their locked room several stories above the street. By deductive reasoning, he proves that the women were killed by an "Ourang-Outang" which escaped from a sailor who had brought the beast back from Borneo.

Murders in the Rue Morgue (Universal, 1932) was an attempt by Universal Studios to capitalize on the success of the previous year's *Dracula* and *Frankenstein*. Poe's name was used in connection with this film to sell the horrific elements of the story. There is a character named Pierre Dupin (Leon Waycoff [Ames]), a romantic fellow who hardly fits the qualifications of a master detective. There is also a gorilla which kills various people at the command of Dr. Mirakle (Bela Lugosi), a mad scientist who wants to find a bride for his monster. Unfortunately,

there is no Poe. As the *New York Times* said, "Poe, it would seem, contributed the title and the Messrs. [Tom] Reed and [Dale] Van Every thought up a story to go with it."

The first remake, *Phantom of the Rue Morgue* (Warner Bros., 1954), was given color and 3D. In the script by Harold Medford and James R. Webb, the ape is sent out to kill women who refuse the amorous advances of the mad scientist (Karl Malden). French actor Claude Dauphin is Dupin, an inspector for the police rather than a private citizen who helps the police solve crimes. As in the previous version, when the mad scientist orders his simian to go after one particular lady, the ape develops a crush on her and kills its master instead.

The story resurfaced once again as *Murders in the Rue Morgue* (American International, 1971), and once again the only connection was Poe's name. In this version, written by Christopher Wicking and Henry Slesar, Dupin has disappeared completely. A young woman (Christine Kaufmann) gets mixed up with the man (Herbert Lom) who murdered her mother, and the climax finds him, dressed in an ape's costume, chasing her around a Parisian theater, owned by Jason Robards.

In *The Murders in the Rue Morgue* (teleplay by David Epstein, CBS, Robert Halmi; Productions, 1986), Dupin (George C. Scott) is a retired detective who investigates a hideous double murder. Despite all the embellishments, some of Poe filtered through.

The character of Dupin returned in *The Mystery of Marie Roget* (Universal, 1942, aka *Phantom of Paris*). As usual, the film had little to do with Poe's story. A music hall star, Marie Roget (Maria Montez), plans to kill her younger sister (Nell O'Day) but is instead murdered herself. When another woman is also killed and horribly mutilated, Dr. Paul Dupin (Patric Knowles) attempts to discover the identity of the "phantom mangler of Paris."

Even further afield from Poe are the various film adaptations of "The Black Cat" (1843). This Poe story concerned a murderer who, suffering from "perverseness," kills his wife and seals up her body within the walls of his house, then goes crazy and confesses his crime.

The first *Black Cat* (Universal, 1934) became a bizarre vehicle teaming Boris Karloff and Bela Lugosi in an effort that the *New York Times* said was "not remotely to be identified with Poe's short story." As helmed by cult director Edgar G. Ulmer, the film, with a screenplay concocted by Peter Ruric, presented a strange story of revenge, necrophilia, and satanism, all wrapped up in an Art Deco package. The climax has Lugosi peeling the skin from Karloff's naked chest and then pulling a switch that blows up the castle full of people celebrating a black mass.

Seven years later the studio released another *Black Cat* (Universal, 1941), which it claimed was "suggested" by the Poe story. This one not only chose to ignore the story, but also violated the spirit of Poe by turning it into a comedy. (It was tossed together by a committee of four: Robert Lees, Fred Rinaldo, Eric Taylor, and Robert Neville.) The action takes place at a mansion where a wealthy old lady is murdered by one of her greedy relatives. When the will is read, the inheritance is tied up until the dead woman's cats have also died, and the killer begins knocking off other relatives as well as the cats. Basil Rathbone, Gale Sondergaard, Broderick Crawford (as the bumbling hero), and soon-to-be-star Alan Ladd (in a minuscule part) carry along the story, what there is of it; Bela Lugosi shows up again, this time as a sinister acting caretaker who has little to do except make other people twitch nervously.

When Roger Corman released his fourth film based on the works of Poe, *Tales of Terror* (American International, 1962), he and screenwriter Richard Matheson constructed it along the lines of the British classic *Dead of Night*. Corman took four of Poe's tales and compressed them into three story lines, each bearing little resemblance to its source. The first was based on "Morella" (1846), an overt horror tale in which a woman rises from the dead and takes possession of the body of her daughter (Maggie Pierce) to wreak vengeance on her husband (Vincent Price) who had murdered her twenty-six years earlier.

The second tale, full of sardonic humor, included elements from "The Black Cat" and "The Cask of Amontillado" (1846). Montresor (Peter Lorre) prefers wine to his wife (Joyce Jameson), and she falls in love with Fortunato (Vincent Price). When Montresor discovers the duplicity of his friend and wife, he entombs both behind a cellar wall, and when the police come to investigate, he confidently allows them to inspect the house; but he has inadvertently walled up his wife's pet cat with the bodies. Hearing the intruders, the animal sets up quite a howl. The police tear down the wall and discover the bodies.

The final tale was taken from "The Case of M. Valdemar" (1845). Here a dying man, Valdemar (Vincent Price), is kept alive by an evil hypnotist (Basil Rathbone) whose sole purpose is to force Valdemar's beautiful wife (Debra Paget) to marry him. As Valdemar is released from the spell and his body begins to liquefy and dissolve, he rises up and kills the hypnotist, thus setting his wife free to marry the young man whom she really loves.

All three of these stories reappeared on the screen. "Morella" returned as *The Haunting of Morella* (Concorde, 1990) with Roger Corman acting as producer. Unfortunately his influence appears minimal. This is a

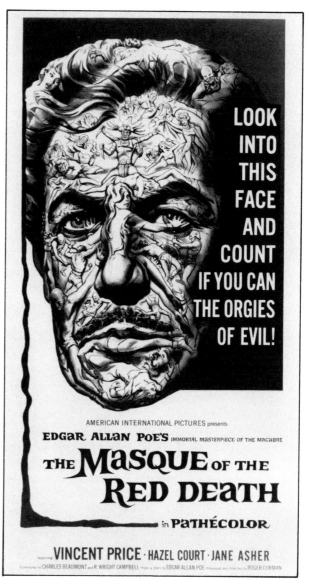

LOOK INTO THIS FACE AND COUNT IF YOU CAN THE ORGIES OF EVIL!

AMERICAN INTERNATIONAL PICTURES presents
EDGAR ALLAN POE'S IMMORTAL MASTERPIECE OF THE MACABRE

THE **MASQUE** OF THE **RED DEATH**

in PATHÉCOLOR

starring VINCENT PRICE · HAZEL COURT · JANE ASHER
Screenplay by CHARLES BEAUMONT and R. WRIGHT CAMPBELL · From a Story by EDGAR ALLAN POE · Produced and Directed by ROGER CORMAN

The face of Vincent Price is a portrait of evil for *The Masque of the Red Death* (1964).

Sidney Fox as Camille L'Espanaye has her bonnet confiscated by a simian admirer in *Murders in the Rue Morgue* (1932). Behind the ape is Leon Waycoff (later Ames) as Pierre Dupin and leaning on the cane is Bela Lugosi as sinister Dr. Mirakle.

Jason Robards as Cesar Charon collars Herbert Lom as Marot, the phantom killer, in *Murders in the Rue Morgue* (1971).

shoddy remake, with a script by R. J. Robinson, more interested in buxom beauties, lesbianism, and soft-core sex than Poe. "The Truth About the Valdemar Case," written and directed by George Romero, and "The Black Cat," written and directed by Dario Argento, were used in *Two Evil Eyes* (aka *Due Occhi Diabolici,* Gruppo Bema/ADC Production, 1990), an Italian production with a largely American cast. The Romero episode is effectively chilling and comes closest to capturing the spirit, if not the substance, of Poe.

Two other versions of "The Black Cat" reached American screens. In *The Black Cat* (Falcon/Hemisphere, 1966), a man (Robert Frost), believing that his father has been reincarnated as a black cat, plucks out the eye of the cat and then kills it. Later, he kills his wife and others in various assorted manners, until his deranged mind at last leads him to his own doom. *The Black Cat* (Selenia/World Northal, 1984) returned to the tactic of using Poe's name but dispensing with the story. A woman

Michael Dunn as Pierre is finally about to get the point from a very insistent Jason Robards as Charon in *Murders in the Rue Morgue* (1971).

Maria Ouspenskaya (seated), Nell O'Day, Edward Norris, John Litel, Patric Knowles, and Lloyd Corrigan in *The Mystery of Marie Roget* (aka *The Phantom of Paris*, 1942).

reporter (Mimsy Farmer) investigates the mysterious death of several villagers and follows a trail that leads to a researcher (Patrick Magee) who is trying to contact the dead through his cat.

Supposedly based on the short story "The Pit and the Pendulum" (1843) and the poem "The Raven" (1845), *The Raven* (Universal, 1935) was made to capitalize on the studio's success the previous year with *The Black Cat* by again uniting Karloff and Lugosi. In this tale, adapted to the screen by David Boem, Richard Vollin (Bela Lugosi) is a demented doctor, who because of his obsession with Poe, constructs a torture dungeon decorated with various devices mentioned in the author's stories. The conclusion finds Edmound Bateman (Boris Karloff), a criminal whom the doctor has disfigured, placing the doctor in a chamber where the walls close in to crush him. The *New York Times* labeled the production an "amazing effrontery" and lamented "the indignity being visited upon the helpless Edgar Allan Poe."

In Roger Corman's production of *The Pit and the Pendulum* (American International, 1961), the second of his adaptations of Poe, he ventured much further from the source than his previous Poes.

The original story takes place during the Inquisition, and the action is confined entirely to a dungeon, but Corman and screenwriter Richard Matheson dropped all references to the Inquisition and opened up the action. In an effort to discover the facts concerning the death of his sister, Elizabeth (Barbara Steele), Francis Barnard (John Kerr) travels to the castle of her husband, Spanish nobleman Nicholas Madina (Vincent Price). Obsessed with the idea that he has buried his wife alive, Madina is rapidly going mad, believing that he hears her voice throughout the castle.

It turns out that Elizabeth is not dead. She and her lover, Dr. Charles Leon (Anthony Carbone), have hatched a scheme to drive Madina mad in order to gain his wealth. Madina truly goes insane when he discovers the truth. He traps the lovers in his dungeon, tosses the guileful doctor into the pit and locks his faithless wife in an iron box. When Barnard innocently intrudes, the mad Madina places him on the table and sets the pendulum in motion. Set free by Madina's sister, Catherine (Luana Anders), Barnard escapes just as Madina trips and falls into the pit. The sister closes the door to the dungeon, vowing to seal the door to the evil chamber, while trapped within the iron box is the still very much alive wife.

The Pit and the Pendulum was even more successful at both the box office and in critical acclaim than its predecessor, *House of Usher*. Writing in the *New York Times*, Howard Thompson said, "Don't expect Poe," but he praised the film for its rich atmosphere and the ironic script. *Time*, in a play on words, called the film "a

literary hair-raiser that is cleverly, if self-consciously, Edgar Allan poetic."

The latest remake of *The Pit and the Pendulum* (Full Moon Entertainment, 1990) has a baker and his wife imprisoned and tortured by Torquemada (Lance Henriksen). The story (with a screenplay by Dennis Paoli) offers a great deal of sex and sadism but little Poe.

Next Corman made *The Premature Burial* (American International, 1962) which proved to be a problem for screenwriters Charles Beaumont and Ray Russell, who discovered that the "story" was not really a story but an essay on being buried alive. In its place, they constructed a plot of a man, Guy Carrell (Ray Milland), who is buried alive by his greedy wife and her lover but who escapes when released by grave robbers, exacting his revenge before finally meeting his own doom.

When Corman came to make his version of *The Raven* (American International, 1963), he again used screenwriter Richard Matheson, who agreed to do the film as a comedy. As the story opens, a sixteenth-century good wizard, Erasmus Craven (Vincent Price), sits alone in his study lamenting the death of his wife, Lenore (Hazel Court). His thoughts are interrupted by a raven of whom he asks the whereabouts of his lost Lenore. "How the hell should I know?" replies the raven.

The raven turns out to be Dr. Bedlo (Peter Lorre). He was changed into one by the evil sorcerer, Dr. Scarabus (Boris Karloff), and now asks Craven to help him out of his fix. Craven agrees because he learns that Lenore faked her death to be with Scarabus, and the climax comes when the two wizards battle one another in a wild melee filled with flying axes, disappearing floors, floating chairs, and bombs filled with confetti. Getting the upper hand, Craven brings the castle down around the heads of Scarabus and Lenore. As Craven and his cohorts, including Bedlo, fully restored to his rotund little body, drive off in a carriage, Scarabus and Lenore emerge from the dusty remains of the castle. Brushing himself off, Scarabus mutters philosophically, "I guess I just don't have what it takes anymore."

As usual with these Corman productions, the film had little to do with Poe or his poem, but the results were hilarious. *Time* called it "a snappy little parody of a horror picture" and singled out Matheson's script for special praise. *Variety*, too, said, "The screenplay is a skillful, imaginative narrative and Corman takes the premise and develops it expertly as a horror-comedy. . . ." One of the few negative reviews came from Bosley Crowther in the *New York Times*, who, parodying Poe's poem, said, "Edgar Allan Poe's Raven might well say 'Nevermore' to appearing in Hollywood films after taking a look at the movie called *The Raven*. . . . Strictly a picture for the kiddies and the bird-brained, quote the critic."

After *The Raven*, Corman suffered an artistic setback with *The Haunted Palace* (American International, 1963), which was the title of a poem Poe used in "The Fall of the House of Usher." In actuality the film was based on H. P. Lovecraft's *Strange Case of Charles Dexter Ward* (1941). However, Corman returned to form with *The Masque of the Red Death* (American International, 1964), a combination of "The Masque of the Red Death" (1842) and "Hop Frog: or, The Eight Chained Ourang-Outangs." Filming on location in England, from a script by Charles Beaumont and R. Wright Campbell, Corman generated an eerie Poe-like atmosphere from beginning to end.

In twelfth-century Italy, a Satan-worshipping Prince Prospero (Vincent Price) rules his kingdom with sadistic cruelty when the Red Death strikes. Prospero flees to the protection of his walled castle to give a ball. Among the guests there suddenly appears a man clad in red, and as he passes through the throng of people, whoever he touches dies. In an effort to escape, Prospero goes from one bedroom to another, but at last he comes face to face with the man in the red mask; when the man removes it, Prospero finds himself staring into his own face.

The conclusion, reminiscent of Ingmar Bergman's *Seventh Seal*, finds the Red Death playing cards with a young boy and having a conversation with a Yellow Death, a Green Death, and others. "Each man makes his own heaven," says the Red Death, "and his own hell."

The film polarized critics. Some, like *Time*, found the film pretentious and overblown; others, such as the *New York Herald Tribune*, waxed poetic. "Gather 'round, my kiddies,' said critic Robert Salmaggi, "and you shall hear of the midnight bloodbath of Vincent Price, Edgar Allan Poe's first cousin, in *The Masque of the Red Death* and does Price revel in it!"

The only remake to date of *Masque of the Red Death* (21st Century Productions, 1990) sets its story in present-day Bavaria. A dying millionaire (Herbert Lom) gives a lavish costume party, but his real goal is to kill off unsuspecting guests. Unfortunately, in this adaptation by Michael J. Murray, Poe was not invited.

For his final excursion into Poe, Corman chose "Ligeia," a Gothic story that the author believed was his finest tale. Like the earlier "Morella," which Corman had used to open *Tales of Terror*, Poe dealt with the idea that the human spirit is strong enough to survive the death of the body. Previously, the screenwriters in the Poe series had been recognized names in the science fiction–fantasy genre, but on this project, Corman used Robert Towne, who would later pen *Chinatown*. The result, a love story set in twelfth-century England, with supernatural overtones, was *Tomb of Ligeia* (American International, 1965), the most subtle of all Corman's films based on Poe.

Towne retained the basic idea of the story. When Verden Fell (Vincent Price) buries his wife, Ligeia (Elizabeth Shepherd), a black cat becomes guardian of her grave. A few months later, Fell marries a Ligeia lookalike, Lady Rowena (also Elizabeth Shepherd), but things are not well at their ancestral abbey. At a dinner party, Fell hypnotizes Rowena, but the voice that speaks to the visitors is that of Ligeia. Soon after, Rowena begins to have dreams about Ligeia and the black cat and, half mad, begins to believe that the dead woman is taking possession of her soul.

The climax occurs when Rowena discovers that Fell has been keeping the body of the dead Ligeia in a secret crypt where he visits her every night. Attempting to break Ligeia's hold over Rowena, Fell turns on the black cat, believing that within the animal lies the soul of his departed wife. A lantern topples, the tomb catches fire, and Fell and the cat die in the blaze.

In his script, Towne maintained the ambiguity of Poe's story, and in the final scene, as the inferno rages, it is impossible to determine whether the cat is, in reality, Ligeia. Perhaps all of the happenings are brought on by Fell, who may not be under a spell cast by Ligeia, as he claims, but only mad.

Although Corman was finished with Poe—"I stopped because I was tired of doing them," he said—American International was not. It produced two more features using Poe's name. The first was *The Conqueror Worm* (American International, 1968, aka *Edgar Allan Poe's Conqueror Worm* aka *Witchfinder General*, its British title), but as had happened so often before, Poe had nothing to do with any of this. The studio threw his name over the title but based the script on *Witchfinder General* by Ronald Bassett. *The Oblong Box* (American International, 1969) harked back to *Premature Burial* for part of its plot, but it was nothing more than a studio concoction capitalizing on Poe's name. With this feature, the Poe series at American International concluded.

Various other Poe films reached American screens in the 1960s and 1970s, but these were only dubbed imports of varying quality. Many of the films based on the master's works are second-rate programmers meant to make a small profit and play the bottom half of double bills, but Poe has also inspired some topflight directors and screenwriters who admired Poe and attempted, within the confines of motion pictures, to capture the spirit and essence of his stories even when they did not always stick to the exact plot lines.

A surrealist adaptation of Poe's "Hop Frog" using a combination of life-size puppets and live actors appeared as *Fool's Fire* (PBS, American Playhouse, 1992). This rather bizarre version captured much of the feeling of Poe, causing the television critic for the *Los Angeles Times* to comment that writer-director Julie Taymor "has

Vincent Price as Julian
Markham keeps a vigil over
a coffin in Poe's *The Oblong
Box* (1969).

Vincent Price as Nicholas Medina stands watch over John Kerr as Francis Barnard as
the blade descends in *The Pit and the Pendulum* (1961).

Ray Milland as Guy Carrell shows his specially prepared coffin to his wife (Heather Angel) and her lover in *The Premature Burial* (1962).

Lobby card from *The Raven* (1935) in which both Karloff and Lugosi appear to be threatening Irene Ware.

Vincent Price as Fortunato and Peter Lorre as Montresor in "The Black Cat" segment of *Tales of Terror* (1962).

Leona Gage as Morella wreaks long-delayed vengeance on Vincent Price as her husband, Locke, in "Morella," one segment of *Tales of Terror* (1962).

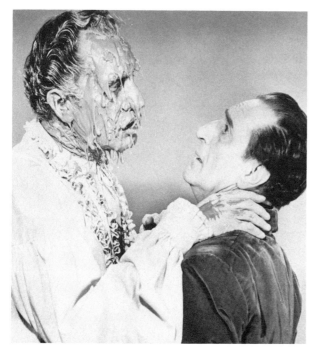

In "The Facts in the Case of M. Valdemar," a segment of *Tales of Terror* (1962), Vincent Price as M. Valdemar attacks Basil Rathbone, his tormentor.

Laurence Payne embraces Adrienne Corri, the woman he would kill for, in *The Tell-Tale Heart* (1962).

Vincent Price as Vernon Fell
agonizes over his dead wife, Ligeia,
in Poe's *Tomb of Ligeia* (1965),
based on his short story.

dared to visualize Poe's dark, symbolist mind, leaving all prior Poe adapters in the dust."

The same year that Poe died, 1849, Herman Melville (1819–91) published his fourth novel, *Redburn*. Two years later came his masterpiece, *Moby-Dick; or, the Whale* (1851), an epic of a literal and a metaphysical quest. Melville's contemporaries found the novel not to their liking, and it was not until the 1920s that the American literary establishment began to reevaluate his importance.

Hollywood's first try at Melville was *The Sea Beast* (Warner Bros., 1926), a very loose adaptation of *Moby-Dick*, which turned the story into a love triangle, and the whale was not part of the triangle. Ahab Ceeley (John Barrymore) and his half brother, Derek (George O'Hara), are both passionately in love with Esther Harper (Dolores Costello). When they go off on a long whaling trip, Derek pushes Ahab off the ship just as Moby-Dick attacks, tearing off Ahab's leg. Blaming the whale for the loss of Esther's love, Ahab becomes possessed with destroying the creature. As captain of his own ship, Ahab searches the Seven Seas until, just before he confronts the beast, he learns it was his brother who pushed him overboard, and it is really Derek who is to blame for his disfigurement. Nevertheless, Ahab goes out to meet the beast and conquers it, driving a harpoon deep into its mighty heart. During the fight, Derek falls overboard and drowns, and the story ends with Esther

and her father being shipwrecked and rescued by Ahab, thus reuniting the two lovers.

The whale is usually seen as only a large tail occasionally flapping out of the water, but when the beast finally surfaces, it fools no one. It was made out of a bar of soap with buttons for eyes, hastily carved by a technician after a full-scale model sank on its first trial.

The love scenes between Barrymore and Costello—they would later marry—were so convincing that director Millard Webb had trouble choosing which ones to use; so, for the conclusion, he used them all, splicing them together to make one long embrace filled with steamy passion. Although beautifully edited, they did not belong in this story. In addition, John Barrymore, who often regarded his screen work as secondary to his stage career, frequently overacted, giving a performance that critics would not soon let him forget. To say that *Moby-Dick* has been trivialized is an understatement. It was a silly adaptation with an unbelievable plotline that turned the whole proceedings into a lark. John Grierson in *Motion Picture News* said, "*The Sea Beast* had a magnificent story (the greatest story in American literature, *Moby-Dick*) but the telling made it nothing at all."

The studio remade the film as a sound feature, restoring the original title, *Moby-Dick* (Warner Bros., 1930), but keeping the 1926 plot. Although (thanks to scriptwriter J. Grubb Alexander) it was no closer to Melville the second time around, Barrymore, again as

18

Ahab, improved on his performance, prompting the *New York Times* to say, "Words bring out his true talent, whether he is affording humor or delivering a grim impression of a man who wants to even matters with a white whale." In this version, the white whale was a full-scale rubber model, not convincing, but better than a bar of soap with button eyes. There is no doubt that this film (with Joan Bennett as Esther and Lloyd Hughes as Derek) looked and sounded much better than the 1926 one, but Melville, his mad captain, and his symbolic sea beast were still missing.

They appeared at last in *Moby-Dick* (Warner Bros., 1956), directed by John Huston, who managed to convey the powerful and obsessive drive of Melville's greatest work. If, in the end, much of the philosophical complexity of Melville is missing, the essential story of Ahab's insane struggle to wreak vengeance on the white whale remains intact.

Using a voice-over narration, the film opens, as does the novel, with the words: "Call me Ishmael." Ishmael (Richard Basehart) has come to New Bedford to sign on with the whaling ship *Pequod*, and on his first night in the town he shares a room and bed with Queequeg

Dolores Costello as the love interest for John Barrymore as Ahab in *The Sea Beast* (1936), an adaptation of *Moby Dick*.

Gregory Peck as the obsessed Captain Ahab prepares to harpoon his nemesis, the great white whale, in *Moby Dick* (1956).

(Friedrich Ledebur), a tattooed Polynesian whose mystical antics and stories of Captain Ahab (Gregory Peck) cause him to be apprehensive. The next day, in a scene lifted almost intact from the novel, Ishmael visits the church of Father Mapple (Orson Welles), who warns his congregation of the dire consequences if man tampers with God's will. His sermon is a portent.

Once the ship is at sea, Ahab gathers his crew about him, and in another scene lifted straight from the novel, nails a gold doubloon to a mast. He who first sights Moby-Dick and gives the cry will be awarded the Spanish coin. As the crew gets caught up in Ahab's mad lust for the whale, Ishmael turns to first mate Starbuck (Leo Genn) for counsel, and it is he who tells Ishmael the story of how Ahab lost his leg to the whale.

The whale is sighted, and the longboats give chase. In the pursuit, Moby-Dick destroys each of the longboats, and Ahab is entangled in harpoon lines and carried to his death on the back of the whale. In one last apocalyptic act, Moby-Dick rams the *Pequod*, sinking her. Only Ishmael is left to tell the tale, saved when a coffin built by one of the crew pops to the surface, providing a raft.

"Here was the story of a man who shook his fist at God," said John Huston. Certainly the mad captain dominates the film. It is his hatred that drives the ship and sends the men to their doom, as well as he to his, and it is the picture of Ahab entangled in the lines and lashed to the whale's back, his arms waving as if beckoning his men to embrace death with him, that remains with the viewer long after the film has ended.

The success of the film, adapted by Huston and science-fiction writer Ray Bradbury, was asserted by critic Bosley Crowther when he wrote, "This is the third time Melville's story has been put to the screen. There is no need for another, because it cannot be done better, more beautifully or excitingly again."

A few other adaptations of Melville reached the screen, but most were unsuccessful in approaching the complexities of his works. *Last of the Pagans* (MGM, 1936), which claimed to be based on *Typee* (1856), told the story of a pair of romantic Polynesians who find true happiness after overcoming a rampaging shark and imprisonment by evil white traders and withstanding a mine cave-in and a hurricane. Only the location had anything to do with Melville. *Enchanted Island* (RKO, 1958), also based on *Typee*, had two American sailors jumping ship for a South Seas island, but that was the only resemblance to the novel. *Omoo Omoo, the Shark God* (aka *Omoo-Omoo* aka *The Shark God*, Screen Guild, 1949), supposedly based on *Omoo* (1847), was turned into a silly South Seas adventure wherein a sea captain plucks out the pearl eye of a shark sea god and is put under a curse for his sacrilege.

With the exception of Huston's *Moby-Dick*, these adaptations failed to take Melville seriously. This approach changed with *Billy Budd* (Allied Artists, 1962), based on Melville's posthumously-published short novel, *Billy Budd, Foretopman* (1924), one of the author's true masterpieces. The novel was first dramatized as a very successful stage play in 1956, and when Peter Ustinov came to the project, he and fellow screenwriter DeWitt Bodeen used the play as a basis for their script.

The H.M.S. *Avenger*, a British man-o'-war during the Napoleonic Wars, has sailed shorthanded from England. In order to bring its crew up to standard, it stops another ship, *Rights-of-Man*, and impresses a young sailor, Billy Budd (Terence Stamp). Despite his stammering when he gets excited, Billy is well loved by all, and his mates hate to see him go. As he waves from the longboat to his friends, he cries out prophetically, "And goodbye to you, too, old *Rights-of-Man!*"

Captain Vere (Peter Ustinov) of the *Avenger* immediately takes to Billy as if the impetuous young sailor were the son he never had. But also on board is Master-at-Arms Claggart (Robert Ryan), who is as evil as Billy is good, and Claggart sets out to destroy the young foretopman. When accused of mutiny by Claggart, Billy strikes him and kills him. Claggart dies with a smirk of victory on his lips. Seeing no alternative, Vere convenes a court-martial and forces his officers to find Billy guilty. At the execution, Billy accepts his fate, putting the noose around his own neck and just before he is hanged,

20

Dana Andrews as the sailor returning to his ship with the help of Jane Powell as the native princess in *Enchanted Island* (1958), an adaptation of Melville's *Typee* and one of the last pictures made by RKO before the studio shut down production.

Terence Stamp in the title role is about to be hanged in *Billy Budd* (1963).

Robert Ryan as Claggert and Peter Ustinov as Captain Vere in *Billy Budd* (1963), based on Melville's *Billy Budd, Foretopman*. David McCallum (center) looks on.

Lilleo and Mala, two Polynesians, played the leads in *Last of the Pagans* (1936), supposedly based on Melville's *Typee*.

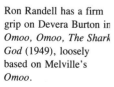

Ron Randell has a firm grip on Devera Burton in *Omoo, Omoo, The Shark God* (1949), loosely based on Melville's *Omoo*.

shouts, "God bless Captain Vere!" Unexpectedly a French warship appears on the scene and fires upon the ship, sinking her.

Somerset Maugham advanced the theory that Claggart was a latent homosexual who first became attached to Billy and then fell in love with him. However, if Claggart were to give in to this passion, he would face rejection by Billy and loss of control over the crew. In order to avoid his own destruction, he set out to destroy Billy. One scene in the film supports this idea. Claggart accidentally drops his stick, which is retrieved by Billy. As their fingers touch, Claggart withdraws in horror.

Although the film found instant admirers, it died at the box office. Bosley Crowther in the *New York Times* said, "The classic conflict of good and evil, drawn in Herman Melville's *Billy Budd* with the story of a pure young British sailor tormented by a vicious master at arms, is trimly battened down and rendered shipshape in a splendid film based on the book and on a recent play."

Before we quit this period, mention must be made of Harriet Beecher Stowe (1811–96). Even though as an artist she does not rank with Cooper, Hawthorne, Poe, and Melville, her importance cannot be denied. *Uncle Tom's Cabin* (1852), the novel of slavery and the Old South, changed the course of American history. President Lincoln, upon meeting the author, remarked that here was the little lady who started the great big war.

The melodramatic story first became a long-running play and was made several times as a silent. The first, from Edison Studios, was a two-reel film composed of a prologue and fourteen individual scenes linked by title cards. In 1910, Vitagraph produced a three-reel version of *Uncle Tom's Cabin,* releasing one reel each month for three months, much like a theatrical serial. In 1913, Harry Pollard directed a version for Imp, but it failed to generate any excitement with the critics or public.

The first full-length *Uncle Tom's Cabin* (Paramount, 1918) proved a real audience-pleaser. Marguerite Clark portrayed both Little Eva and Topsy, Little Eva's naughty black playmate. The story faithfully followed Ms. Stowe's novel. Uncle Tom (Frank Losee) and Eliza (Florence Carpenter), both slaves, are sold, but Eliza escapes across the icy Ohio River with her child. En route south, Tom saves Little Eva, and as a reward, her parents buy him. Everyone is happy until Little Eva and her father die, and Tom is once again sold, this time to dastardly Simon Legree (Walter Lewis), who tortures the poor slave to his death. Legree in turn is killed by a mistreated slave girl. This was an efficient adaptation that did its best to wring every tear possible from the melodrama. *The Moving Picture World* praised the film, saying that "the different elements of suspense, pathos, humor, and strongly drawn characters are handled with great skill."

22

James Lowe as Uncle Tom and Mona Ray, playing Topsy in black face, in *Uncle Tom's Cabin* (1927).

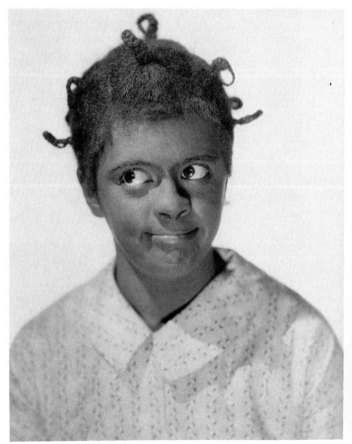

Two versions of the novel were made in 1927. The first (Universal, 1927) cost a whopping $1.5 million to produce. Harry Pollard, who directed the three-reel 1913 *Uncle Tom's Cabin*, overplayed many scenes, especially the death of Little Eva (Virginia Grey) and the flogging of Uncle Tom (James Lowe) by Simon Legree (George Siegmann). The running time was a lengthy 141 minutes

Lobby card and original ads for *Uncle Tom's Cabin* (1918).

Vivian Duncan as Eva (lying in bed) and her sister, Rosetta Duncan, in black face as Topsy in *Topsy and Eva* (1927), based on *Uncle Tom's Cabin*.

Czech-born British screen villain Herbert Lom as Simon Legree in the German-made *Uncle Tom's Cabin* (1965).

and incorporated many scenes not found in the novel, including Lincoln reading the Emancipation Proclamation, a historical event that happened eleven years after Stowe wrote her novel. The year's second production, although not released until 1929, was entitled *Topsy and Eva* (United Artists, 1927), a strange version in which the Duncan sisters, both white, played Topsy and Eva. Director Del Lord, who would later direct Three Stooges comedies, introduced some odd humor. As the story opens, two storks are delivering babies. The white stork delivers Little Eva (Vivian Duncan), the black stork drops Topsy (Rosetta Duncan) into a barrel.

Only one theatrical sound version of *Uncle Tom's Cabin* has appeared, a 1965 international production shot in Yugoslavia with a multinational cast, none of whom, even in blackface, looked particularly like slaves. In addition, the story added all sorts of extraneous events not found in the novel and a plethora of historical inaccuracies. A laughable performance by Herbert Lom as Simon Legree highlighted an otherwise atrocious film. An ambitious if revisionist made-for-television version of the Stowe story appeared in 1987 with a basically black cast. Edward Woodward was the vile Simon Legree. The adaptation was by prolific screenwriter John Gay.

Mary Pickford as M'liss speaks out at a town meeting in defense of Thomas Meighan as schoolteacher Charles Gray in *M'liss* (1918).

THREE

NEW BOYS OUT WEST

Bret Harte, Mark Twain, Jack London, Willa Cather

As the United States expanded westward, it was only natural that new and important writers should emerge. While their material was regional, these authors—and most particularly Bret Harte, Mark Twain, and Jack London—reached audiences far beyond their particular area, and they influenced a whole generation of American writers. Their stories and novels told compelling tales filled with interesting characters and, for the most part, packed with movement and adventure. They were ideal for adaptation to the motion pictures.

At age nineteen, Francis Bret Harte (1836–1902) left his home in New York and journeyed to California, working there as a schoolteacher and later a journalist. While he had little firsthand knowledge of the gold camps, he knew the men and women who inhabited them. Most of his stories are often rather shallow, lacking verisimilitude because he romanticized his characters, but in his best work, he imbued an atmosphere that lifted the material above the banal.

The first time Harte used the narrative technique and subject matter that were to make him famous was in "M'liss," in which a local schoolmaster attempts to civilize Melissa Smith, a half-wild girl, only to discover that the task is beyond his abilities. The first screen *M'liss* (World, 1915) was a minor silent, and another adaptation followed only three years later. In this second version (Paramount, 1918), Mary Pickford starred as the wild girl who is never quite wild enough to offend the paying public. She allows herself to be taken under the guidance of the schoolmaster with whom she falls in love and whom she eventually marries, but not before he is falsely accused of murder and almost lynched. A third silent version, *The Girl Who Ran Wild* (Universal, 1922), starred Gladys Walton as M'liss.

The only sound version, *M'liss* (RKO, 1936), also bore little resemblance to the Harte story. The turbulent old mining camp of Smith's Pocket, full of saloons and sin, has been replaced by a small midwestern town squabbling over its new schoolteacher, Stephen Thorne (John Beal). The relationship between Thorne and M'liss (Anne Shirley) blossoms into an idyllic love, and Harte's story expires under an overdose of romanticism. (A television version in the early 1950s starred Rita Moreno.)

Other Harte stories were also adapted by silent filmmakers. "Salomy Jane's Kiss" was filmed twice as *Salomy Jane* (Alco Films, 1914, and Paramount, 1923).

25

"In the Carquinez Woods" became *The Half Breed* (Triangle, 1916) with a miscast Douglas Fairbanks as the noble savage saddled with a script that completely obliterated the Harte story. The short novel *Cressy* became *Fighting Cressy* (Pathe, 1919), an action-oriented "B" Western that filled the second half of double bills.

In the late 1800s, Bret Harte published his most famous stories, "The Luck of Roaring Camp" (1868) and "The Outcasts of Poker Flat" (1869). The former revolved around the child of a camp follower in a remote mining camp who dies in childbirth. The miners find prosperity in the communal decision to rear the child born in their midst, but tragedy strikes when winter floods swamp the camp, and the child drowns. *The Luck of Roaring Camp* (Monogram, 1937) reached the screen only once, a penny-ante production that tacked on a happy ending for audience consumption.

Harte's other classic told of a group of undesirables who are kicked out of a miners' town and forced to cross the Sierras in winter. Trapped by a storm, most die from cold and exposure, except for the gambler Oakhurst, who, "at once the strongest and yet the weakest of the outcasts of Poker Flat," shoots himself.

The first adaptation of *The Outcasts of Poker Flat* (Universal, 1919) was directed by John Ford and bore little resemblance to the Harte story. Using the plot-within-a-plot technique, the principal actors playing dual roles, Ford told of a gambling-hall owner in Arizona (Harry Carey) who cannot make up his mind whether to sacrifice his love for his pretty ward (Gloria Hope), who he believes is in love with his best friend, or tell her of his true feelings. Coming across a copy of Harte's story, he sees that Oakhurst had the same problem. Closing the book, the gambling-hall owner decides to fight for the girl, and it turns out that she has been in love with him all along.

In the first sound version of *The Outcasts of Poker Flat* (RKO, 1937), screenwriters John Twist and Harry Segall took ingredients from the original story and threw in a few from "The Luck of Roaring Camp." Oakhurst (Preston Foster) drinks, a habit he repudiates in the story because he doesn't want liquor to cloud his judgment. Helen (Jean Muir), the schoolmarm, is out to reform Oakhurst, and when she fails and Oakhurst dies, the Reverend Samuel Woods (Van Heflin) is around to comfort her. The *New York Times* reviewer mused, "An interesting experiment, but is it Harte?"

The last version to date of *The Outcasts of Poker Flat* (20th Century-Fox, 1952) attempted to add psychological insight to Harte's characters. Ryker (Cameron Mitchell) and his henchmen rob the assay office–bank and flee with the money. Frustrated and angry, the townspeople take out their aggressions by exiling four individuals of dubious character: Oakhurst (Dale Robertson); Jake (Billy Lynn), the town drunk; Duchess (Miriam Hopkins); and Cal (Anne Baxter), who also happens to be Ryker's wife.

When a snowstorm catches the small party high in the Sierras, they take shelter in a cabin when Ryker bursts in and holds them at gunpoint. After killing two of the travelers, Ryker jumps Oakhurst and is himself killed. The film ends on a happy note with Cal and Oakhurst riding off to a better future.

A "Classics Illustrated" production, *California Gold Rush* (teleplay by Tom Chapman and Roy London, NBC, Schick Sunn Classics, 1981), incorporated both "The Luck of Roaring Camp" and "The Outcasts of Poker Flat." The stories were linked by the character of Harte (Robert Hays), an aspiring young writer in the 1840s who goes west in search of adventure.

One of Harte's favorite themes, loyalty, is characteristically exaggerated in "Tennessee's Partner" (1875). The partner is like a faithful dog in his dumb devotion to Tennessee, making him a comic figure and, simultaneously, pathetically appealing. In *Tennessee's Partner* (RKO, 1955), Tennessee (John Payne) is a slick gambler in the town of Sandy Bar, where his lady friend, the Duchess (Rhonda Fleming), runs the local saloon. When a disgruntled prospector tries to kill Tennessee, Cowpoke (Ronald Reagan) saves his life, and the two become fast friends. Cowpoke has come to Sandy Bar to marry his girl, Goldie (Coleen Gray), appropriately named since she is a golddigger and unworthy of Cowpoke. At first, Tennessee tries to talk some sense into his friend, but when Cowpoke refuses to listen, Tennessee woos Goldie, much to Cowpoke's consternation. Despite the conflict between the two men, when Tennessee is accused of murder, Cowpoke comes to his rescue and is gunned down. The grateful Tennessee gives his partner a fine funeral, then marries the Duchess, who understands the ruse employed by Tennessee to save Cowpoke from Goldie.

The best parts of the film, and where it comes closest to Harte, are the scenes in the mining camp, rampant with gold fever, excitement and shady characters. Still, this is no more Harte than any of the other films based on his stories. In each case, the filmmakers settled for the romantic West, turning the centers of their works soft and missing Harte's hard edge and his artistry.

Perhaps the most famous of the writers from the West was Samuel Langhorne Clemens (1835–1910), better known as Mark Twain, who made humor a necessary ingredient in the lives of many Americans. When Twain died in 1910, the movies were in their infancy, and the first adaptation of one of his books still seven years away. It was just as well, for he would have been mightily disappointed.

The first of Twain's works to reach the screen was *The*

Prince and the Pauper (1882), the story of two boys who live at the opposite end of the social spectrum in sixteenth-century London. One is the Prince of Wales and the other is Tom Chanty, a guttersnipe and the son of a thief.

The first film of *The Prince and the Pauper* (Famous Players–Paramount, 1915), in which Marguerite Clark played the dual roles, contained some exciting action, especially in the scene where Miles Hendon and the Prince fight off a gang of brigands in the ruins of a castle. The *New York Times* called it "a costume picture that is infinitely superior in every way to the average photo drama." The reviewer, however, failed to note that the film missed the biting humor of the novel.

The first sound version of *The Prince and the Pauper* (Warner Bros., 1937) starred Errol Flynn as Miles Hendon, but he took a back seat to twins Billy and Bobby Mauch as Tom Canty and Prince Edward. Screenwriters Laird Doyle and Catherine Chisholm Cushing made several changes in Twain's plot that was, according to Frank Nugent of the *New York Times*, "a friendly adaptation."

The boys switch roles as a lark, and inadvertently Prince Edward is kicked out of the palace. At first he doesn't protest, but once he has experienced enough poverty and filth, he asserts that he is the true heir to the throne. Miles overhears him, and although he believes the boy is mad, he is amused by the claims. In the meantime, the conniving Earl of Hertford (Claude Rains) learns the truth and sends an assassin (Alan Hale) to kill Prince Edward, but Miles kills the assassin. Miles then rushes the Prince to the court. There the boy proves that he is the rightful heir by revealing the location of the hidden royal seal.

Despite Erich Wolfgang Korngold's rousing musical score, the film lacked the excitement usually associated with swashbucklers. William Keighley's direction missed any sense of fantasy; at best, it was leisurely functional. The one area that made this adaptation closer to Twain was its gentle sense of humor.

Disney released a British-made theatrical version of *The Prince and the Pauper* (Buena Vista, 1962) in Europe, but in America it showed up as a three-parter on *Walt Disney's Wonderful World of Color*. The film's many close-ups and the use of Guy Williams, a TV actor noted for his role as Zorro, to play Miles made it obvious that television had been its original destination. Young British actor Sean Scully had the title roles.

The next adaptation of *The Prince and the Pauper* (Storyland/Childhood Productions, 1969) was filmed in Ireland, and the lush scenery was highlighted by some superb color photography. However, the film's appearance worked against Twain's story; the world of the urchin appeared far too beautiful. The basic story re-

Jacqueline Logan in the title role in *Salomy Jane* (1923), based on Bret Harte's *Salomy Jane's Kiss*.

Owen Davis Jr. and fellow miners display their gold finds in *The Luck of Roaring Camp* (1937), based on the Harte short story.

Anne Shirley as M'liss and John Beal as Stephen Thorne, the teacher she loves, in *M'liss* (1936).

Preston Foster as Oakhurst and Jean Muir as his love interest in the first sound version of *The Outcasts of Poker Flat* (1937).

Cameron Mitchell as Ryker has a hold on Anne Baxter as Cal, his wife, in *The Outcasts of Poker Flat* (1952).

mained the same—young Prince Edward wanders the countryside while Tom suffers the agonies of being a king—but this adaptation was aimed strictly at the kiddie set.

The Prince and the Pauper resurfaced once again as *Crossed Swords* (Warner Bros., 1978), a remake that was standard on all counts. This version was adapted by novelist George MacDonald Fraser, who had scripted *The Three Musketeers* and *The Four Musketeers,* both of which displayed wit and charm, but Fraser did not seem to grasp Twain's American sense of humor. However, there was one directorial touch by Richard Fleischer that Twain would have admired. Once outside the palace, Prince Edward discovers the streets of sixteenth-century London are littered with beggars and garbage. Mark Lester (of *Oliver!* fame) plays the titular parts. Ernest Borgnine as John Canty and George C. Scott as Ruffler look as if they have never taken a bath. Oliver Reed as Miles Hendon appears grubby and unkempt, a far cry

Ronald Reagan (far left) as the Partner watches as John Payne (seated right) as Tennessee plays his cards while Rhonda Fleming as the Duchess and Leo Gordon (center) as the sheriff also show some interest in *Tennessee's Partner* (1955).

Jack Pickford (left) as Tom Sawyer and Robert Gordon as Huck Finn in *Huck and Tom* (1917).

from the dashing figure cut by Errol Flynn in the 1937 version.

Adolescent adventure was also the cornerstone of *Tom Sawyer* (1876), Twain's first full-length novel, which must be regarded as one of the greatest—if not the greatest—boys' books ever written, one that has become the American boyhood idyll. Two interrelated silent films attempted to tackle Twain's single novel. *Tom Sawyer* (Famous Players–Lasky, 1917) carried the story from the fence painting through the fake deaths of Tom and Huck Finn. *Huck and Tom* (Famous Players–Lasky, 1918) completed the story, as the boys witness the murder by Injun Joe, bring the culprit to justice, and find the buried treasure, all in a swift fifty minutes. Seen together, the two films (both directed by William Desmond Taylor from Julia Crawford Ives's adaptation) represent a unified whole; unfortunately both were weakest where they could least afford to be. Jack Pickford, already twenty-one, was too large and too old for the part of Tom.

The first sound version of *Tom Sawyer* (Paramount, 1930) had no such problem: Jackie Coogan, only fifteen at the time, was an excellent choice to play Tom, and Junior Durkin, who was killed in a fatal car accident five years later, was a capital Huck. Even the supporting roles were uniformly excellent, especially Clara Blandick, who made a history of playing "auntie" roles, as Aunt Polly, and Charles Stevens, a grandson of the real Geronimo, as Injun Joe. Added to this was the finely restrained direction of John Cromwell and a relatively faithful screenplay by Grover Jones, Sam Mintz, and William Slavens McNutt.

While there are some omissions, the main incidents are all here in one single version. The story opens when Tom, in an effort to avoid punishment for stealing crabapples, convinces his friends to give up their prized possessions to help him whitewash the fence. In a long

29

Lobby card for *Huckleberry Finn* (1931).

Mickey Rooney as the screen's best Huck Finn, relaxing with his fishing pole and dog in *Huckleberry Finn* (1939), and then inspecting stolen loot with William Frawley as the Duke and Walter Connolly as the King.

shot, the audience sees both sides of the fence with the boys busily painting. When Aunt Polly comes to inspect his work, she is justly amazed that Tom has completed his job so quickly and is forced to allow him to go off to play. The run-in with Joe Harper (Dick Winslow) and

30

the romance with Becky Thatcher (Mitzi Green) quickly follow, including Tom's antics to get himself seated next to her in school.

The funniest scene in the film remains the funeral. As the preacher gives the eulogy for the "dead" boys, he happens to look up at the gallery, and there they sit, listening in rapture to every word. Soon afterward, the film briefly turns dark as Tom and Huck witness Injun Joe's murder of a man in the graveyard. The climax finds Tom fleeing through the caves with Injun Joe in close pursuit. Here the novel and film diverge. The novel has Injun Joe getting lost in the cave and dying of starvation. The film needed a more immediate and action-filled climax, so Injun Joe falls into a black hole, his body thudding far below against an inky bottom.

Eight years later, producer David O. Selznick tried his hand with *The Adventures of Tom Sawyer* (Selznick, 1938). The script by John V. A. Weaver maintained a delicate balance between the episodic structure of the novel and the more dramatic structure of the 1930 film; and, like the preceding screenplays, this one incorporated all the important characters and incidents from the novel—the whitewashing of the fence, Tom's courting of Becky Thatcher (Ann Gillis), the murder in the graveyard, and the flight through the caves. Once again, Injun Joe (Victor Jory) meets his death in a far more melodramatic fashion than in the novel. Tom (Tommy Kelly) kicks the killer from a precipice and sends him screaming to his death. Then, just before he and Becky are rescued, Tom discovers a cache of pirate gold. While the ending is not quite the one given to us by Twain, it works well enough on the screen.

The negative cost was $1.5 million, a whopping sum for 1938. Not only did the film fail at the box office, but it turned out to be artistically disappointing. While tasteful and faithful, *The Adventures of Tom Sawyer* was basically dull. Due to the censorship of the times, most of Twain's language was watered down, and scenes such as Huck introducing Tom to pipe smoking were deleted, a regrettable decision that limited some humorous insights into Twain's characters. In addition, several slapstick episodes were added. In one running gag, Sid Sawyer is pelted with whitewash, tomatoes, and cake. While such scenes are not strictly at odds with the novel, they add nothing to the story. Entertaining as the film was, audiences familiar with the book had to be disappointed; Twain's novel had been scrubbed too clean. "David O. Selznick's color-candy version of *The Adventures of Tom Sawyer* should make Mark Twain circulate in his grave like a trout in a creel," critic Otis Ferguson wrote in *The New Republic*. "These people follow the story, parading its episodes stiffly, squeezing each character and episode for more emotional pulp than Twain ever conceived."

A TV production of *Tom Sawyer* (teleplay by Jean Holloway, CBS, Universal Television, 1973) proved to be memorable for the performance of Vic Morrow, who instilled a menace in Injun Joe often lacking in other productions, but while the film (with Josh Albee as Tom) covered most of the main incidents of the novel, the overabundant use of close-ups destroyed all flavor of the period and setting.

The last theatrical version to date of *Tom Sawyer* (United Artists, 1973) was a musical financed by *Reader's Digest*, which believed that the public would flock to good family movies (then in short supply). The music and script were done by brothers Richard and Robert Sherman, who previously had written scores for Disney's *Mary Poppins* and *Bedknobs and Broomsticks*. Although the Shermans' score was nominated for an Oscar, it failed to produce one memorable number. Within their bag of lyrical tricks, they created such deeply philosophical lines as "Sooner or later, just like a patater, man's planted in his grave." Not only were the songs meaningless excursions into mediocrity, but they also slowed the narrative and forced many important elements of the novel to be altered or omitted.

The film, directed by onetime actor Don Taylor, looked good, having been shot on location in Missouri, but like the previous version, this *Tom Sawyer* was too clean and too sanitized. From the opening shot, we know that Tom is on the side of the angels as the camera swoops down from a long shot of the exuberant lad as he runs through a cornfield. At the same time, a heavenly choir intones its acceptance and appreciation of his free spirit. The entire film is brimful of such sentimental manipulation. As a result, even the wonderfully classic scenes have been remodeled and reduced to pure schmaltz. Perhaps the most famous scene in the novel, the whitewashing of the fence, has been transformed into a musical number, "Gratification." It is not that the film has left out the exciting parts—the corrupting influence of Huck Finn (Jeff East) on Tom (Johnnie Whitaker), the murder in the graveyard, Becky (Jodie Foster) and Tom's getting lost in the cave, the death of Injun Joe (Kunu Hank)—but all their suspense and tension have been muted to make the story safe for family consumption.

Tom and Huck also reached the screen in *Tom Sawyer, Detective* (Paramount, 1938), a little "B" aimed at the younger set, but it took too long to introduce and develop characters whom the audience already knew, and events drag as Tom (Billy Cook) and Huck (Donald O'Connor) engage in their usual antics before settling down to the business of clearing a preacher accused of murder.

Tom Sawyer was a book for boys. Not so *The Adventures of Huckleberry Finn* (1885), which is a

Eddie Hodges and Archie Moore as Huck and Jim float down the Mississippi in *The Adventures of Huckleberry Finn* (1960).

Archie Moore as Jim disguised as an African chieftan, Andy Devine as Mr. Carmody, Eddie Hodges as Huck, and Buster Keaton as the lion tamer in the forth version of *The Adventures of Huckleberry Finn* (1960) and the first in color.

Tommy Kelly and Jackie Moran as Tom and Huck in the graveyard scene in *The Adventures of Tom Sawyer* (1938).

deeply rewarding and enduring classic that can be read on any number of levels. As befits its status, it has been adapted for the screen more times than any other Twain work. Unfortunately, all the versions have major flaws; most fail even to rise above mediocre.

The character of Huckleberry Finn initially came to films in *Tom Sawyer* (Paramount, 1915), but the first true screen adaptation of *The Adventures of Huckleberry Finn* wasn't until *Huckleberry Finn* (Paramount, 1920). It opens and closes with an appearance by an actor impersonating Mark Twain, which was a nice touch, especially since the player managed to look a great deal like the author. Many subtitles are drawn straight from the book, but only a small fraction of the observations and reflections of Huck show up on the screen. These deletions are far less crucial than the changes made in the story by adapter Julia Crawford Ives. Young Huck (Lewis D. Sargent) falls in love with nineteen-year-old Mary Jane (Esther Ralston), and the conclusion finds

Billy Cook as Tom Sawyer has the villain (William Haade) collared and is about the administer a finishing blow in *Tom Sawyer, Detective* (1939). Looking on are Howard Mitchell and Dorothy Vernon at the left, and Phillip Warren, leaning over Haade.

Myrna Loy as Morgan Le Fay uses her wiles on Will Rogers as Hank, the stranger from another time, in *A Connecticut Yankee* (1931).

him intending to return to her rather than striking out for the Territories.

The first sound version of *Huckleberry Finn* (Paramount, 1931) was also made in response to the success of an earlier *Tom Sawyer* (Paramount, 1930) and again starred Jackie Coogan as Tom and Junior Durkin as Huck. However, the changes in Mark Twain's story were monumental. (Screenwriters Grover Jones and William Slavens McNutt did the adaptation.) An early incident has Huck at school where all the pupils are far younger than he. He struggles with geography and is not only unable to comprehend the term "bounding Pennsylvania," but also incapable of spelling the state's name. While this scene is not in the novel, it is in the spirit of Twain. Not so with the temporary falling out between Huck and Tom over Becky Thatcher (Mitzi Green). Later, Huck transfers his interest to Mary Jane Wilks (Charlotte Henry). While these incidents stray from the novel, the most damaging change involves Jim (Clarence

Muse). The relationship between Jim and Huck is the heart and soul of the novel, but here it is only a minor subplot. The character of Jim was so unimportant in this version that the film critic for the *New York Times* failed to mention him in the review.

Huck and Tom set sail on their journey down the Mississippi, but even with Jim aboard, the ironic meaning of the voyage—their descent deeper into slave territory as they are trying to win Jim's freedom—is diluted, since the emphasis is on the boys and their pranks. The Duke (Eugene Pallette) and the King (Oscar Apfel), two gamblers, are tossed off a riverboat and the boys haul them aboard their raft, but after an attempted con by the river rats, Tom and Huck desert them. The entire last sequence from the novel involving Aunt Sally and mistaken identities has been omitted, replaced by a segment in which Huck saves Jim from a lynch mob.

In 1939 came the most entertaining version of *Huckleberry Finn* (aka *The Adventures of Huckleberry Finn*, MGM, 1939), a slick and fast Mickey Rooney vehicle, but it still was not Mark Twain's novel. Many characters from the novel were simply dropped, including Becky Thatcher and her father, the Judge. Tom Sawyer is never even mentioned. Susan has lost her harelip and is really quite attractive. Dr. Robinson has become Captain Brandy, a steamboat captain. Once again, the whole last episode with Aunt Sally and Uncle Silas has been deleted.

Huck (Mickey Rooney) is being raised by two old maids who want to civilize him, but when his drunken father (Victor Killian) comes to take him back, Huck heads downriver with Jim (Rex Ingram). Before going, Huck manufactures evidence that he has been murdered so that no one will come looking for him. Once again, the Duke (William Frawley) and the King (Walter Connolly), two gamblers, are thrown off a steamboat just in time for Huck and Jim to haul them out of the river. When the crooked pair try to pass themselves off as brothers of a dead man in an attempt to swindle a couple of beautiful but helpless girls, Huck informs kindly Captain Brandy (Minor Watson), who has the Duke and the King tarred and feathered.

In the meantime, Huck learns that the law is after Jim because it is believed he murdered Huck. As the two flee toward the river, Huck is bitten by a cottonmouth, and at the expense of his freedom, Jim carries him back into town to a doctor. Jim is captured and returned home to face charges of murder. A mob gathers and rushes the jail, but, with the aid of Captain Brandy, Huck manages to arrive in time to save his friend. Jim is set free to join his wife and child up North, and Huck promises Miss Watson (Clara Blandick) he'll wear shoes and quit smoking.

In this version, Huck's world is filled with adults who exist only as comic foils. Although the Duke and the King are humorous scoundrels, they are cardboard characters, more fit for comic opera than Mark Twain's world. Mary Jane and Susan (Lynne Carver and Jo Ann Sayer) are bland ingenues, and Captain Brandy is a compassionate, intuitive old riverboat man. Among the subordinate characters, there is not one made of flesh and blood.

However, Mickey Rooney is perhaps the best of all the screen Huck Finns, exhibiting just the right amount of rascality and naïve intelligence. If there is a drawback to his character, it lies in Hugo Butler's script rather than Rooney's performance. For some inexplicable reason, Huck becomes a sentimental abolitionist, even persuading the Widow Douglass (Elizabeth Risdon) to free Jim because "it ain't right for one human being to own another." In the novel, one of Huck's character flaws is that he is unable to transfer his feelings about Jim to all blacks who are slaves. In fact, Huck's biggest revelation regarding Jim is when he "knowed he [Jim] was white inside."

As created by screenwriter Butler, Jim is an inferior creature because of the color of his skin. At one point, Captain Brandy defends his abolitionist views by citing a speech by a young lawyer-congressman from Illinois, Abraham Lincoln, who said that the white man should not take away rights from the Negro just because God made the Negro inferior. This appears to be the attitude of the film. Jim and Huck become friends but not equals; and like a good, subservient black man, Jim saves Huck when the latter is bitten by the snake. When the mob comes for the lynching, Jim cowers behind the bed. When Huck arrives just in time to save his friend, he throws his arm over the slave's shoulder as if to say that he will protect Jim since Jim is incapable of protecting himself. Even the placement of the characters within the frame adds to this impression. Jim huddles on the floor submissively, and Huck stands over him, his arm around Jim's shoulder. In the novel, Jim becomes Huck's symbolic father, but the film reverses the roles. Huck is the "father" saving his "son" and finally setting him free.

To coincide with the seventy-fifth anniversary celebration of Mark Twain's book came a remake of *The Adventures of Huckleberry Finn* (MGM, 1960), and while this may have been the most beautiful version of all, it was bland and boring. The technical aspect of the film helped to make it look good, but the story was changed (by adapter James Lee) to lessen the more harrowing aspects of the novel. A far more serious drawback was the character of Huck (Eddie Hodges), who even in the smallest of difficulties has to be rescued and is incapable of being the independent adventurer that Twain created.

Nepotism reared its head in *Huckleberry Finn* (teleplay

by Jean Holloway, ABC Circle Films, 1975), in which Ron Howard and various members of his real family made up a good portion of the cast. Although Tom Sawyer (Donny Most) was retained, the story dropped the whole last section of the novel and tried to squeeze the rest of the material into a ninety-minute time slot that included commercials. Much was omitted.

Louisa May Alcott once said of *Huckleberry Finn*, "If Mr. Clemens cannot think of something better to tell our pure-minded lads and lasses, he had better stop writing." It would be safe to say that Ms. Alcott would have approved of the last theatrical version of *Huckleberry Finn* (United Artists, 1974), a *Reader's Digest*–financed follow-up to its *Tom Sawyer*. The writers and director (J. Lee Thompson) made a perfect little gentleman out of Huck. A year before, the script and songwriting team of Robert and Richard Sherman had put together the excruciating *Tom Sawyer*, and not satisfied with one triumph of mediocrity, they tackled *Huckleberry Finn* and produced another plethora of forgettable songs. The scenery looks as if it were imported from Disneyland; so does the script. Huck takes right to the concept of the Brotherhood of Man. "Why, Jim!" he exclaims when he sees that his friend is injured. "Your blood's red the same as mine!" Soon he has become a real homespun civil-rights worker.

For the first hour or so, the film plods along from one incident—and one song—to another. Then Huck (Jeff East) meets the King (Harvey Korman) and the Duke (David Wayne), and for a short time, the screen comes alive. All too soon the pair is languishing in Jackson's Landing Jail, and with them languishes all the film's energy. Aside from the King and the Duke putting on airs, fleecing yokels, and facing lynch mobs—and for that matter, putting up with the dullards around them—this version of Twain's classic is a monumental bore, the kind that gives family entertainment a bad name.

The most complete *Adventures of Huckleberry Finn* (teleplay by Guy Gallo, PBS, Great Amwell Co., 1985) was a 240-minute version done for *American Playhouse*. While the film drags in spots, it retains much of the humor and Swiftian satire of the novel, but in an effort to integrate as many stars as possible, screenwriter Gallo had characters come and go with surprising speed, seldom allowing the audience to get involved with the individual stories. A 105-minute version was released theatrically.

No one should ever mistake the *Huckleberry Finn* films with the Twain classic. Every theatrical version sanitized the events and emasculated the violence until Twain almost disappeared. These films watered down Huck and made him a better boy, and therefore less independent and weaker. Every version was smothered by good taste, which is exactly what Huck would have hated. Let it be said, you still do not know Huck Finn

without having read a book by the name of *The Adventures of Huckleberry Finn*.

Just as *Tom Sawyer* was a rehearsal for *Huckleberry Finn*, so *The Prince and the Pauper* was a rehearsal for *A Connecticut Yankee in King Arthur's Court* (1889), which is far more than an adventure novel. To Twain, the Age of Chivalry was one of squalor and superstition. In fact, Twain's attack on chivalry was in reality an attack on Christian religion and civilization that had enslaved people's minds for thirteen centuries. But to the movies, the Age of Chivalry was still the Age of Romance. While the studios saw the humor in the contrasting cultures—they never failed to contrast the days of King Arthur with the modern world and its values—the films concentrated on adventure and romance.

In the age of screen innocence, *A Connecticut Yankee in King Arthur's Court* (Fox, 1921) was pretty good fun, with Harry Myers starring. There are some rough-and-tumble pratfalls. A few incidents and characters from the book manage to survive; many others including a motorcar, motorcycles, slang, and references to World War I and Prohibition were added. Studio publicists claimed that if Twain were alive, he would have liked this version of his novel. Certainly he might have laughed at the film, for it is indeed funny in spots, but he would have laughed at a piece of work independent of his novel, which was used only as a jumping-off place. Once in King Arthur's Court, the film goes its own slapstick way, and Twain's content is lost in a cloud of motorcycle dust.

The novel returned as *A Connecticut Yankee* (Fox, 1931) with homespun comic Will Rogers as Hank. Once again, the contents of the story were updated (this time by screenwriter William Conselman). Now Hank—or Sir Boss as he is known at Arthur's Court—introduces helicopters, radios, and cars to Medieval England.

This story opens with radio operator Hank Martin of Hartsdale, Connecticut, besieged by a crazy radio enthusiast who claims to be listening to discussions between King Arthur and his knights. A suit of armor topples over and knocks Hank unconscious, and when he awakens, he is in the land of Arthur. When captured, Hank tries to extricate himself by showing a cigarette lighter to the King (William Farnum, who also appears as the mad radio operator), and after snapping it and showing the flame, Hank challenges Merlin (Mitchell Harris) to do the same. Now Merlin insists that the foreigner be burned at the stake, but just as the torch is about to be applied, Hank correctly predicts a total eclipse of the sun. The King pleads with Hank to restore the light, and Hank chants until the eclipse is over. Hank is freed, and King Arthur knights him Sir Boss.

Sir Boss quickly finds that his modern knowledge can

Bing Crosby as Hank feels the pike prod of one of the king's soldiers (Art Foster) as William Bendix as armor clad Sir Sagamore looks on in the third adaptation of Twain's *A Connecticut Yankee in King Arthur's Court* (1948).

Dennis Dugan as Tom, the accidental time traveler, receives a feather for good luck from Sheila White as Alisande as he makes ready for a joust in Disney's *Unidentified Flying Oddball* (1979), a space age version of the Twain story.

be converted to power. In the jousting scene with Sir Sagamore (Brandon Hurst), Hank comes into the arena wearing a cowboy outfit and twirling his lariat. He rides circles around his heavily armored opponent. When he rebuffs the romantic advances of the King's evil sister, Morgan Le Fay (Myrna Loy), she tries to have both Sir Boss and Arthur hanged, but Hank's sidekick Clarence (Frank Albertson) arrives with a host of mail-clad knights to save the day. In the attack on Morgan Le Fay's castle, Hank employs airplanes, a helicopter, and automobiles. The explosion that brings the castle's bricks crumbling down also awakens Hank, and he discovers himself back in Connecticut with the mad radio operator. Clarence turns out to be a modern lover who wishes to wed Alisande (Maureen O'Sullivan), and Hank loans them his car so they can run off to the nearest minister.

On its own terms, *A Connecticut Yankee* is an excellent film. Will Rogers proved to be an ideal choice to play Hank. He drawls his lines and scratches his head in typical Rogers fashion; he is funny, warm, and convincing. However, this film was made during the depths of the Depression, and many of his jokes are contemporaneous with the times and therefore may be lost on much of today's audience. Rogers's physical antics have no such drawbacks. His jousting contest with Sir Sagamore is as funny today as when it was filmed. In addition, Fox spent a great deal of money on this production, especially considering the economic conditions of the times, and it showed on the screen as a colorful, enjoyable romp.

But Twain never meant his story as a colorful,

36

Lobby card picturing Errol Flynn as Miles Hendon protecting Bobby Mauch as Tom Canty in *The Prince and the Pauper* (1937).

Mark Lester as Prince Edward masquerading as the urchin is detained by Oliver Reed as Miles Hendon in *The Prince and the Pauper* (aka *Crossed Swords*, 1977).

enjoyable romp. Farce is certainly part of the novel, but the novel also contains some very intense moments. Two scenes in it are particularly grueling. In a smallpox hut, the King and Hank encounter a woman who is glad her husband and daughters are dead. It doesn't matter whether they are in heaven or hell; they are out of England. Soon after, Hank and Arthur come upon a young mother hanged for stealing a small piece of cloth, hanged so that the concept of property in England might be safe. As good as this film is, nothing like these two scenes appear in *A Connecticut Yankee*, a sanitized, Hollywood version of Twain's classic.

The same problems that afflicted the 1931 *Connecticut Yankee* also afflicted *A Connecticut Yankee in King Arthur's Court* (Paramount, 1949), a pleasing and lavishly mounted production, tailored to its affable star,

Edgar Buchanan as Jim Smiley holding a rabbit, Anna Lee as his wife, Gary Gray as their son, Bob, and Robert Shayne as Judge Carter in *Best Man Wins* (1948), an adaptation of Twain's "The Celebrated Jumping Frog of Calaveras County.

37

Wilfrid Hyde-White as Roderick Montpelier converses with a skeptical Gregory Peck as Henry Adams in *Man With a Million* (1954), an adaptation of Twain's "The Million Pound Note."

Reginald Denny as Pat Glendon grasps the hand of Julienne Scott as Maude Sangster while confronting George Stewart as her disapproving father in Jack London's *The Abysmal Brute* (1923).

Bing Crosby, beautifully filmed in Technicolor, and blessed with a tuneful score of songs by James Van Heusen and Johnny Burke. This version (adapted by Edmund Beloin and directed by Tay Garnett) eschews the use of most of the modern inventions thrown into the earlier films. There are no cars or airplanes or helicopters introduced into Arthur's kingdom, although Hank does manufacture a pistol that he uses to kill a knight. With the exception of a few "miracles," he relies upon his own ingenuity to survive. However, this change alone does not make the film closer to the novel. Just as in the previous versions, there is no mention of the Church, and there is not a priest to be seen. If one did not know better, one would think that Arthur's world existed without religion.

Although superb entertainment, the film contains only one reference to the very things that Twain attacked. At one point, a young girl comes to Hank asking for help for her plague-stricken father. When Hank goes to her home, the mother informs him that her husband is dead now, and that her two sons have been unjustly accused of a crime and languish in a dungeon. While Hank persuades the King (Sir Cedric Hardwicke) to find out what is really happening to his people, a few other woes are mentioned but never seen. Even though the film makes a feeble attempt to introduce an element of conscience, the afflictions of the kingdom are undercut by the musical numbers—as the King, Hank, and Sagamore (William Bendix) wander along a country road investigating the people's complaints, they sing "Busy Doing Nothing"—and the lush Technicolor makes things much too pristine. Even the hovel where the dead man lies appears amazingly clean and roomy.

Thirty years later, *A Connecticut Yankee in King Arthur's Court* returned updated as a curious Disney oddity entitled *Unidentified Flying Oddball* (Buena Vista, 1979) in which astronaut Tom Trimble (Dennis Dugan) and his robot double are knocked through a time warp back to Camelot when their space shuttle is struck by lightning. This time, the hero introduces into Camelot a laser pistol, a moon buggy, a space suit, and a rocket-powered ejection seat, and at each point when the villains try to do him in, our hero pulls out one of his futuristic tricks to save the day.

A television production of *A Connecticut Yankee* (teleplay by Pulitzer Prize–winner Paul Zindel, NBC, NBC Productions, 1989) changed the sex, age, and race of the Yankee ten-year-old (Keshia Knight Pulliam). In the first three minutes, when Tom Cruise, Disney World, and *Attack of the Killer Tomatoes* are all mentioned, it is quite clear that this version, while carrying Twain's title, bears little resemblance to the novel.

To date, Twain's Camelot of farce and realism has never shown up on the screen. What *have* shown up are films that emphasize the farce and throw out the realism. Each in its own way is pleasant entertainment—in fact, the 1930 and the 1949 versions are excellent—but each uses Twain's basic plot and neglects his bitter, antiromantic, antireligious content.

Various short stories of Twain also have made it to the screen. *Best Man Wins* (Columbia, 1948), based very loosely on "The Celebrated Jumping Frog of Calaveras County" (1865), revolves around the efforts of the young son (Gary Gray) of Jim Smiley to help his wandering father (Edgar Buchanan) win back his wife (Anna Lee), who is about to marry another man. A jumping frog contest is the climax of the film, but Twain's story is missing in this adaptation by Edward Huebsch.

Another of Twain's less acerbic short stories, "The Million Pound Bank-Note" (1893), became *Man With a Million* (J. Arthur Rank/United Artists, 1954), with Gregory Peck and an all-British cast. Like Twain's story, the film (adapted from Twain by Jill Craigie) is an amiable little tale that pokes fun at British traditions and man's worship of money. At times, the story of the pauper who becomes a prince may seem a little less than fresh, but it is only a variation of an idea that uncounted writers had already used, including Twain himself.

On *American Playhouse* and *Great Performances*, PBS has offered a number of top-notch television adaptations of Twain, through a production company called Great Amwell. *Life on the Mississippi* (teleplay by Philip Reisman Jr., 1980) and *The Innocents Abroad* (teleplay by Dan Wakefield, 1983) were both culled faithfully from nonfiction works in which Twain himself was the central character. *The Private History of a Campaign That Failed* (teleplay by Philip Reisman Jr., 1981) was taken from a short story, as were *The Mysterious Stranger* (1982), based on Twain's last work, and *The Man Who Corrupted Hadleyburg* (1984). Perhaps the most successful of these adaptations was *Pudd'nhead Wilson* (teleplay by Philip Reisman Jr., 1984) with Ken Howard, mainly because it was a tightly structured novel that emerged almost intact on the screen.

Twain was also portrayed numerous times on stage (primarily, of course, by Hal Holbrook) and on television: by Dan O'Herlihy in *Mark Twain: Beneath the Laughter* (1979), by McLean Stevenson in the 1985 *Mark Twain and Bret Harte in the Wild West* (a speculative bit of entertainment about the two writers meeting in San Francisco in 1869 over supper), and by Jason Robards in *Mark Twain and Me* (1991), about an elderly Twain's friendship with an eleven-year-old Dorothy Quick, who would grow up to write a popular children's novel about their meetings.

Not one Hollywood adaptation had the courage to do *Tom Sawyer* or *Huckleberry Finn* or *A Connecticut Yankee in King Arthur's Court* or even *The Prince and the Pauper* as Mark Twain wrote it. Even the film biography, *The Adventures of Mark Twain* (Warner Bros., 1944), written by Harold Sherman, Alan Le May, and Harry Chandler, with Fredric March as Twain, while occasionally entertaining, was full of biographical inaccuracies and overlooked most of the dramatic possibilities of his life.

The studios had the money and the know-how to make the films, but they never had the guts to do them right. Twain's musings on courage seem a fitting epitaph for Hollywood's treatment of his films. "It is curious," he said, "that physical courage should be so common in the world, and moral courage so rare."

At one time dubbed "the Kipling of the Klondike," Jack London (1876–1916) was in the forefront of the movement toward naturalism and realism. The author of over sixty published works, London was a master of many fields. Best known as a novelist and short story writer, he was also an outstanding journalist and essayist. In addition, he wrote three plays and, although the film industry was still in its infancy, a screenplay, *Hearts of*

Pauline Stark is held captive by Wallace Beery (left) and Raymond Hatton in Jack London's *Adventure* (1925).

Hobart Bosworth (left), whose production company made several silents based on Jack London short stories, here with Walter James in a scene from *Blood Ship* (1927).

Jean Rogers on the phone but more interested in boxer John Wayne in *Conflict* (1936), a remake of *The Abysmal Brute*.

Slim Summerville relates a fishy tale to Michael Whalen in *White Fang* (1936), billed by the studio as the sequel to its hugely successful *Call of the Wild*.

Malcolm McGregor (left) and Roy Stewart in *Stormy Waters* (1928), based on London's "Yellow Handkerchief."

40

Jack Oakie as Shorty watches in consternation as friend Clark Gable as John Thornton turns on the charm for Loretta Young as Claire Blake in *Call of the Wild* (1935).

Edward G. Robinson as Wolf Larsen threatens John Garfield as George Leach in London's *The Sea Wolf* (1941).

Charles Bickford saves a woodland friend from a forest fire in *Romance of the Redwoods* (1939), which claimed to be based on Jack London's "The White Silence."

Ruth Roman as Judith Burns is ministered to by Robert Douglas as hostage Aubry Milburn while Dane Clark as Bob Peters looks on in *Barricade* (1950), *The Sea Wolf* remade as a Western.

Gita Hall as Ruth watches as Barry Sullivan as Wolf teaches a lesson to Peter Graves as Van Weyden in *Wolf Larsen* (1958), the third screen version (of four) of *The Sea Wolf*.

Three. However, when the movies came to adapt Jack London, his realism seldom found its way into the finished products as the studios opted for adventure over social commentary.

London's most enduring and popular novel, *The Call of the Wild* (1903), the story of the dog Buck, was the first of his works to reach the screen. In 1908, D. W. Griffith adapted the novel for a Biograph production, but the twenty-minute running time could hardly tell the whole story of Buck. At least the narrative concentrated on the dog, an accomplishment that later versions could not claim. A full-length silent version, *The Call of the Wild* (Pathe, 1923), appeared fifteen years later, with Jack Mulhall as Thornton.

Few film adaptations of London's work can be called classic, but the first sound version of *Call of the Wild* (20th Century-Fox, 1935) comes close. Producer Darryl F. Zanuck instructed his screenwriters, Gene Fowler and Leonard Praskins, to cut down the role of Buck and put in a romantic angle, and they obliged by adding two romantic interests, one for John Thornton and one for Buck. They also threw in a few incidents from *White Fang* for good measure.

After prospector John Thornton (Clark Gable) loses his stake at a gambling table, he buys a huge dog, Buck, believed by most to be too vicious to pull a sled. Thornton uses love with training, and the dog responds. Another man, Smith (Reginald Owen), had tried to buy Buck earlier because the dog had almost chewed off his hand. Smith is incensed when he sees Thornton with the dog, and he maneuvers Thornton into wagering a hefty sum that Buck cannot pull a thousand pounds one hundred yards. Buck helps Thornton win the bet and enough money for Thornton and his friend Shorty (Jack Oakie) to set out for the gold country. Along the way they come across the beautiful, unconscious Claire Blake (Loretta Young), who has been deserted by her prospector husband (Frank Conroy). With Claire in tow, they proceed to her husband's mine, where they work the claim. While Shorty is off for supplies, Thornton and Claire proceed to fall in love. At the same time, Buck hears the call of the wild in the form of a female wolf howling for a mate. Off the dog goes to find her. Soon after, Smith and his henchmen appear, having learned of the mine from Blake, whom they knocked on the head and left for dead. They steal the gold, but as they are making their escape, their canoe tips over and the heavy bags drag them to the bottom of the river. Buck finds the injured Blake, and Thornton carries him back to the cabin, where he and Claire nurse him back to health. Once Blake is again healthy, Claire tells Thornton that she will always love him but that she must go with her husband. Not long after they have departed, Shorty reappears with provisions.

The Call of the Wild explored the Darwinian concept of the survival of the fittest. Despite the message failing to make the screenplay, which concentrated on romance and villainy among humans, the story was fascinatingly told.

The Call of the Wild resurfaced once more—as a German-Italian-Spanish-French production (MGM, 1972). Despite some beautiful location photography in Finland, it proved to be a big, boring movie, thanks primarily to the adaptation by Peter Welbeck, Wyn Wells, and Peter Yeldman. This time Thornton (Charlton Heston) roams the countryside looking for gold, and once again Buck is relegated to a secondary role. As usual, the real Jack London is set aside for romantic adventure.

The next *Call of the Wild* (teleplay by James Dickey, NBC, Charles Fries Productions, 1976) had the advantage of the noted American poet's script. While Dickey took liberties with the story, he managed to retain much of the novel's feeling as well as its theme of survival of the fittest.

A Canadian production called *Klondike Fever* (CFI Investments, 1980) related the fictional adventures of a young Jack London (Jeff East) in the wild north. Among the characters he encounters is John Thornton (Barry Morse), and many of the events sound suspiciously like *The Call of the Wild*.

As a piece of fiction and as a cornerstone in the works of Jack London, *The Call of the Wild* is extremely important, but the author's greatest work is probably *The Sea Wolf* (1904), telling of the survival of Humphrey Van Weyden, who unavoidably finds himself abroad *The Ghost*, a schooner on its way to hunt seals in Japanese waters. Van Weyden soon discovers that the captain of the schooner, Wolf Larsen, has created a hell aboard his ship based on brutality and sordidness, where the only purpose is to survive. Van Weyden survives because, like Buck in *The Call of the Wild*, he is able to adapt. In the end, Wolf Larsen dies because he cannot adapt.

In 1913, actor Hobart Bosworth, who himself had run away to sea at the age of twelve, formed his own production company and proceeded to make a number of films based on the works of London. The first was *The Sea Wolf* (Bosworth, 1913). Shot in California, it included some footage at sea, about which *The Moving Picture World* said, "No praise can be too high for the settings and the photography." The film contained some exciting moments—Larsen (Hobart Bosworth) going blind, his attempt to ravish Maude (Viola Barry), and his eventual death at the hands of Van Weyden (Herbert Rawlinson).

The first remake of *The Sea Wolf* (Paramount/Artcraft, 1920), with Noah Beery as Wolf Larsen, failed to make any improvements on the earlier film, causing the

Ian MacDonald as Butch Ragan administers a beating to Glenn Ford as Martin Eden, who later is caught between two women, Evelyn Keyes as Ruth Morley and Claire Trevor as Connie Dawson in *The Adventures of Martin Eden* (aka *High Seas*, 1942).

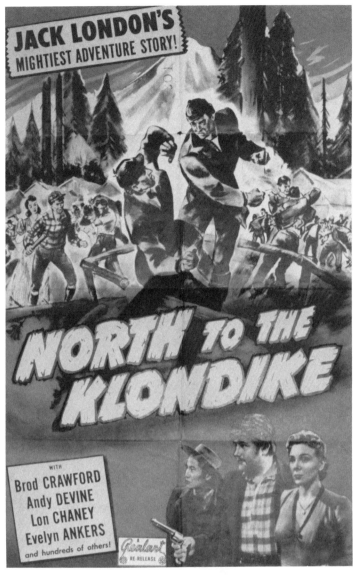

Poster for *North to the Klondike* (1942), one of the many "B" films using Jack London's name but not his fiction.

Screenwriter Robert Rossen made several important and interesting changes in *The Sea Wolf* (Warner Bros., 1941). First, London used Van Weyden as the narrator of the novel, but Rossen chose an omniscient viewpoint. Next, although all the previous versions had followed London's novel in making Van Weyden the central character, Rossen divided the heroics. The intellectual jousting with Larsen (Edward G. Robinson) fell to Van Weyden (Alexander Knox), a weakling who grows stronger as the story progresses. The action and romantic interest was turned over to George Leach (John Garfield), a character who drowns halfway through the novel but survives in the film. Finally, the studio forced Rossen to include a romance, and he constructed one with far more substance than could be expected.

Some critics thought the scenes between Van Weyden and Larsen too talky, but generally speaking, the reviews ranged from good to outstanding. The *New York Times* said that the film "rolls along ruthlessly and draws a forbidding picture of oppressive life at sea." The verdict of time has shown the 1941 version of *The Sea Wolf* to be a classic, though not because of Jack London's story, which was all but discarded by the studio. Rather the classic stature of the film lies with Robert Rossen's script, the direction of Michael Curtiz, and the acting of

reviewer for *Photoplay* to remark, "*The Sea Wolf* is another picture that is forced to hold its audience by the picturesque quality of its scenes rather than the plausible grip of its story." Will Rickey wrote the screen adaptation. *The Sea Wolf* (Producers Distributing Corp., 1925) was soon remade with Ralph Ince producing, directing, and starring.

The initial sound version of *The Sea Wolf* (Fox, 1930) made drastic changes in London's story, but the *New York Times* said, "The flavor of Jack London's sea-swept tale permeates *The Sea Wolf*." Milton Sills starred in this adaptation by Ralph Bloch and, of all people, S. N. Behrman. However, it wasn't until 1940 that a classic film was made from the classic novel.

Dean Jagger gets the drop on Kent Taylor in *Alaska* (1944), which claimed to be based on Jack London's "Flush of Gold."

all the participants, especially Robinson, in one of his great roles. This version remained true to the spirit if not the letter of London.

Several inferior versions of *The Sea Wolf* followed. *Barricade* (Warner Bros., 1950) was a Western disguised as London's novel, notable as an almost scene-by-scene remake of the 1941 film in buckskins. William Sackheim did the adaptation. *Wolf Larsen* (Allied Artists, 1958) restored Van Weyden (Peter Graves) to the dual role of intellectual hero and man of action. Larsen (Barry Sullivan) is the crazed captain who controls his ship like some malevolent despot, but the script by Turnley Walker and Jack DeWitt deleted the Nietzschean overtones, the absence of which destroys the whole point of London's story.

Larsen, Wolf of the Seven Seas (aka *Wolf Larsen* and *Legend of the Sea Wolf*, 1975) was a made-on-the-cheap Italian version with Chuck Connors chewing up the scenery in the title role.

The silent period saw other London adaptations of generally inferior quality. Director Victor Fleming, who would later direct *The Wizard of Oz* and *Gone With the Wind*, kept *Adventure* (Paramount, 1925) moving at a brisk pace, but except for the title, the film (with Pauline Stark and Wallace Beery) had little to do with the

Richard Conte as Felipe Rivera listens to Frank Silvera's stories of outrage, together with Vanessa Brown, Paul Fierro, and Margaret Padilla in *The Fighter* (1952), based on Jack London's "The Mexican."

London novel. The adaptation of *Burning Daylight* (Paramount, 1928) was so bad that the *New York Times* said, "Jack London's story trudged across the screen . . . punctuated only by the soft footfalls of persons quietly leaving before the appointed time." London's "Yellow Handkerchief" was one of the stories in *Tales of the Fish Patrol*, a book written for boys, but by the time it reached the screen as *Stormy Waters* (Tiffany, 1928), the story had changed to that of a prostitute (Eve Southern) who tries to steal the affections of a young seaman.

A number of London's novels were made as silents and later redone as sound films. *The Abysmal Brute* (Universal, 1923) emerged as only a simple tale of romance, with Pat Glendon, Jr. (Reginald Denny) becoming a successful boxer known as "The Abysmal Brute," and after winning the biggest fight of his life, retiring to the backwoods with socialite Maude Sangster (Mabel Julienne Scott). The social commentary of the novel disappeared in an inane story. Remade as *Conflict* (aka *The Abysmal Brute*, Universal, 1936), the story was even sillier. This time Pat (John Wayne) is a crooked boxer who takes dives for the reigning champion (Ward Bond) before finding true love with a beautiful blonde (Jean Rogers).

Like *The Call of the Wild*, London's *White Fang*

45

(1906) was a story about a dog, and the first film version was an inconsequential silent (FBO, 1925) that concentrated on the human story. The sound remake of *White Fang* (20th Century-Fox, 1936) was no different. Sylvia Burgess (Jean Muir) and her brother Hal (Thomas Beck), heirs to a rich vein of gold, are assisted to their isolated mine by Yukon guide Weedon Scott (Michael Whalen). Unable to withstand the rigors of the trail, Hal commits suicide. An evil band of thieves led by Beauty Smith (John Carradine) try to wrest the mine from Sylvia by planting the suspicion that Scott murdered Hal. There is gunplay, and White Fang pulls off some daring rescues before Sylvia finds Hal's diary, which clears Scott.

The next version of *White Fang* (Italian-Spanish-French, 1972) added color, but that didn't help. This international production, a scenic but needlessly violent remake starring Franco Nero, tells the badly dubbed story of a boy and his dog in the wilds of Alaska, but any connection to the novel reposes primarily in the title. The latest version of *White Fang* (Buena Vista, 1991) was a beautiful Disney film about a boy and his wolf, but with a script by Jeanne Rosenberg, Nick Thiel, and David Fallon, it had little connection to the London novel other than the title.

The sound period also had its share of cheapies based on London's fiction. Somehow scriptwriter George Satre turned *Torture Ship* (Producers Distributing Corp., 1939), based on "A Thousand Deaths," into a weak imitation of H. G. Wells's *Island of Dr. Moreau*. The same year's *Romance of the Redwoods* (Columbia, 1939) claimed to be based on "A White Silence," but London's story is nowhere to be found in the Michael J. Simmons screenplay. (This *Romance of the Redwoods* had nothing in common with the one Mary Pickford did in 1917.) *Wolf Call* (Monogram, 1939), *Queen of the Yukon* (Monogram, 1940), and *Sign of the Wolf* (Monogram, 1941) all claimed to be based on novels by Jack London, but each was only a "quickie" from a Poverty Row studio in which the sources were not London but studio hacks. *North to the Klondike* (Universal, 1942) claimed "Gold Hunters of the North" as its source, but it was only a "B" Western set north of the border. In *Alaska* (Monogram, 1944), any connection to London's "Flush of Gold" disappeared as soon as the credits ended. Even the film biography, *Jack London* (United Artists, 1943), written by Ernest Pascal, was little more than an adventure in which London (Michael O'Shea) discovers the Japanese threat to the world. These "B" films all had one thing in common. They used Jack London for the value of his name, not for the value of his stories.

In 1907, while sailing around the world on his yacht *Snark*, London began writing *Martin Eden* (1909), a work that has been called both his best and worst novel.

A young seaman, Martin Eden, a stand-in for London himself, yearns for sophistication and knowledge, and he discovers that social betterment lies through his writing. In the end, he loses all reason for living and commits suicide.

The only film version to date of *The Adventures of Martin Eden* (Columbia, 1942) eschews London's story for a contrived story of Eden (Glenn Ford) serving on a hellship, enduring brutal treatment, and finally escaping. He writes his memoirs in which he exposes the cruelty toward his fellow seamen and helps to free an imprisoned buddy (Stuart Erwin) wrongly accused of mutiny. In the end, Martin does not commit suicide but finds happiness in the arms of the poor girl (Claire Trevor) from the wrong part of town. When the film dealt with the cruel merchant marine system, it came closest to the novel, evoking a real sense of life aboard ship.

Somewhat atypical of London is "The Mexican," a story of the Mexican Revolution, which became *The Fighter* (United Artists, 1952), a rather glum adaptation that depended on too many ringside clichés. In 1910, Filipe Rivera (Richard Conte) joins the patriots trying to overthrow Diaz and falls in love with another member of the revolutionaries, Kathy (Vanessa Brown). A flashback tells how Rivera's family, sweetheart, and village were destroyed by Diaz's soldiers. Rivera becomes a prizefighter to raise money for the cause, and in a fight against a top contender, wins a big purse that he turns over to guerrilla leader Durango (Lee J. Cobb).

The Assassination Bureau, Inc., the last fictional work of Jack London, which was completed by Robert Fish in 1963, was also atypical of the author. The film version (Paramount, 1969) turned out to be a black comedy, removing it even further from the main body of London's work. A group of international assassins are roaming around Europe knocking off various dignitaries. Intrepid woman reporter Sonya Winter (Diana Rigg) tracks down the leader of the assassins, Ivan Dragomiloff (Oliver Reed), and a chase across Europe ensues, climaxing in a spectacular scene aboard a Zeppelin.

Much of Jack London's fiction captured the frontier spirit of the westward expansion, and it is a credit to him that as a writer he saw no romance in the way men hacked and tore at the land and at each other. He also saw little romance in the sea; life aboard ship was often cruel and demeaning. However, the films adapted from his works invariably softened the viewpoint until little of London remained. It wasn't his content, though, that so often failed to translate to the screen; rather, it was his view of the content.

Before we leave the boys out West, we must mention the lady out West, Willa Cather (1876–1947), whose stories and novels displayed a high regard for the courage and industry of the pioneers. Only one of her works has thus far been adapted for the screen, *A Lost Lady* (1923), the story of a Californian woman in the 1880s who is transplanted to Nebraska, although *two* versions of her *O, Pioneers!* were produced for television in 1991—one for PBS's *American Playhouse* with Mary McDonnell and one for *Hallmark Hall of Fame* with Jessica Lange.

The first film of *A Lost Lady* (Warner Bros., 1924) updated the material to the 1920s to tell the story of Marian Forester (Irene Rich), who leaves her older husband (George Fawcett) to run off with a younger man (John Roche). This adaptation, so truncated in plot and character and so saddled with confusing flashbacks, had little to do with the Cather novel. Yet it was far closer to its source than the second version, *A Lost Lady* (aka *Courageous*, Warner Bros., 1934), which became the story of Marian Ormsby (Barbara Stanwyck), who marries an older man (Frank Morgan) out of loyalty, then discovers that she is in love with a younger man (Ricardo Cortez). Her marriage causes her all sorts of misery, but the script by Gene Markey and Kathryn Scola provided a happy ending. The film pleased neither the fans of the novel nor the general paying public.

Irene Rich as Marian Forester pledges her love to John Roche as Frank Ellinger in Willa Cather's *A Lost Lady* (1924).

Barbara Stanwyck as Marian Forester with Frank Morgan as her much older husband, Daniel, in *A Lost Lady* (aka *Courageous*, 1934), and with Ricardo Cortez as Frank Ellinger, her real love.

Lee Remick as Eugenia in *The Europeans* (1979).

FOUR

THE RISE OF REALISM

Henry James, Stephen Crane, Edith Wharton, Ellen Glasgow,
Theodore Dreiser, Frank Norris, Booth Tarkington

If the studios turned to Harte, Twain, and London for outdoor adventure rather than their more esoteric qualities, the same is not true of Henry James, Stephen Crane, and the other realists. When the studios chose to adapt one of these authors, it was often their themes and social commentary the filmmakers embraced. Even though there were many failures and insignificant adaptations, a number of important movies did emerge from the group, and in a few cases, true works of art.

The first of these realists, Henry James (1843–1916), not only was a critic and a short-story writer but also became a major figure in the history of the novel. He was the first to employ the point of view that allowed the reader to share the experiences and perceptions of his characters, a technique that William James, the American philosopher and teacher, and Henry's brother, described as "stream of consciousness."

The first of the author's works to be adapted, *The Aspern Papers* (1888), was inspired by the story of Claire Clairmont, a mistress of Lord Byron, who clung to the poet's letters long after his death; but *The Lost*

Moment (Universal, 1947), after a promising start, soon deteriorates into second-rate Poe and trivializes a beautiful story. Bosley Crowther in the *New York Times* called it "a thriller injected with romance of a sort that Mr. James never dreamed." It may be that the director and producer believed that to adapt the real Henry James would mean death at the box office, but if so, it proved to be an unwise choice. The film, adapted by Leonardo Bercovici, directed by Martin Gabel, and starring Susan Hayward, Robert Cummings, and Agnes Moorehead, failed to generate much enthusiasm among either critics or paying public.

While *The Lost Moment* was an artistic and financial failure, the next James adaptation, *Washington Square* (1881), has become a true classic of the cinema. *The Heiress* (Paramount, 1949) was the screen version of a stage play that appeared on Broadway under James's original title, and when director William Wyler came to the story, he had playwrights Ruth and Augustus Goetz do their own film adaptation. In the hands of Wyler, their script took on a fluidity and intimacy that the stage play could not match. Wyler also insisted on one important change in character. In the play, when Townsend (Montgomery Clift) first comes to the Soper house, he begins inquiring about the value of the expensive paintings and vases, thus telegraphing his intentions. Wyler wanted the audience to believe Townsend just as Catherine (Olivia de Havilland) believes him, so that when he doesn't show up on the night the couple is to elope, the audience will be shocked and hurt just as Catherine is. Later, when she takes her revenge on him, the audience will revel in the act just as she does.

In James's version, as Catherine changes, she does not move from innocence to bitterness; rather, she grows from a naïve young woman to one who understands the disappointments of life. But in the Goetzes' play and the film, Catherine settles for revenge. Throughout her life, her father (Ralph Richardson) resented and abused her, believing her responsible for her mother's death, and as he lies dying, she sits in the park across from the house. When a servant comes to tell her that Dr. Sloper wants to see her, she replies, "I know he does. Too late, Maria."

Later, when Townsend returns after five years and pleads his case, explaining that he left because it was best for her, she pretends to believe him, agreeing to elope, just as they had planned once before. But when he goes for his luggage, she tells her Aunt Lavinia (Miriam Hopkins), "He has grown greedier with the years. The first time, he only wanted my money; now he wants my love, too." When her aunt accuses her of being cruel, she replies, "Yes, I can be very cruel. I have been taught by masters. . . . He came twice—I shall see to it he never comes a third time." When Townsend arrives that evening, she has her maid bolt the door, and she slowly ascends the dark stairs.

It may be that Catherine in *The Heiress* is less complex than Catherine in *Washington Square*, that Wyler, in having his heroine imitate her torturers, has allowed plot to dominate rather than character. If so, his achievement is still one that Henry James might have admired. Among the major figures of American literature of the nineteenth century, perhaps it was Henry James who best understood that adapting a novel for another medium required certain compromises and changes. James himself adapted two of his own novels for the stage—*Daisy Miller* and *The American*—and in both cases, he substituted happy endings for characters who had originally suffered tragic fates.

In his preface to the New York edition of *The Turn of the Screw* (1898), Henry James labeled his novel "essentially a potboiler." This was the generally accepted view of the slim novel until in 1934 critic Edmund Wilson reevaluated the work, suggesting that the governess-narrator, who is sexually repressed, imagines the events.

Since then, the reputation of the novel has grown until some critics now point to it as the finest ghost story ever written.

The script of *The Innocents* (20th Century-Fox, 1961) by Truman Capote and William Archibald eschewed shock and gore, the type being churned out in the popular horror films from England's Hammer Studios, and chose instead to incorporate the ambiguities inherent in James's novel. Director Jack Clayton took his time weaving together the various threads until at last the screen is pervaded with a sense of evil, an evil that may or may not exist in the mind of the governess, Miss Glidens (Deborah Kerr).

There are minor variations. The film makes it clearer that the relationship between Quint (Peter Wyngarde) and the former governess was sadomasochistic in nature and definitely had a negative effect on the children. Also, the apparitions that haunt the governess are seen by the audience, and since the viewpoint of the film is basically omniscient, this pushes the audience closer to believing her. The ambiguity lies in the sound track where the viewer has trouble identifying certain sounds that are purposely hidden by echoes or electric music or other overlapping ones. At other times, sounds such as scissors plopping into the water or flies buzzing in the tower are amplified. This subjective, distorted sound track forces the audience to question the governess's perception of reality.

Ten years after *The Innocents*, a "prequel" appeared, *The Nightcomers* (Avco Embassy, 1971), a piece of Freudian schlock full of graphic sex and bad language that was devoid of taste and wit. This film (with a screenplay by Michael Hastings) focuses on Peter Quint (Marlon Brando) and his relation with the governess, Miss Jessel (Stephanie Beacham). There is no hint of the supernatural, only overt perversity. *The Nightcomers* is an attempt, and a very weak one at that, to cash in on Henry James and his classic of the supernatural.

Two television adaptations were also made from Henry James's psychological horror tale. The first *Turn of the Screw* (teleplay by William F. Nolan, ABC, Dan Curtis Productions, 1974) added characters and incidents to flesh out the story of the governess (Lynn Redgrave) in charge of her two precocious but strange charges. The result was a bloated production that missed many of the subtleties of the novel. The newest *Turn of the Screw* (teleplay by Robert Hutchinson and James Miller, Showtime, Think Entertainment, 1990) was beset by a script that removed the horror from the mind of the governess (Amy Irving) and made it more tangible, thus eviscerating much of James's story.

Henry James's most popular success was *Daisy Miller: A Study* (1878). When Peter Bogdanovich came to direct the film (Paramount, 1974), from a screenplay by

Olivia de Havilland as heiress Catherine Sloper tries to reason with Ralph Richardson as her unbending father while Montgomery Clift as her beau, Morris Townsend, awaits the outcome and later comforts her in *The Heiress* (1949), an adaptation of Henry James's *Washington Square*.

Frederic Raphael, he announced, "What James meant to say with the story doesn't really concern me. . . . I think all that [social-cultural] stuff is based on some other kind of repression anyway." Although the director remained faithful to the main story line, he wasn't above making changes in the plot and in the tone. At one point, while Daisy (Cybill Shepherd) and her family reside at a posh Swiss hotel, her brother mixes up the shoes outside the doors of the rooms and then slides down a banister.

While comedy and irony are present in James's *Daisy Miller*, sight gags more in keeping with the Penrod novels of Booth Tarkington certainly are not. Bogdanovich was also not above changing motives. In the novella, Mrs. Walker is the main spokesperson for the American establishment, and it is she who ostracizes Daisy from Roman society because Daisy outrages etiquette. Bogdanovich, however, found her "heavily motivated sexually." It is jealousy rather than misguided social conscience which causes her to drive Daisy away.

In the initial review in the *New York Times,* Vincent Canby wrote, "*Daisy Miller* transfers to the screen simply and elegantly." But this judgment proved to be in the minority. Other critics, including those who wrote for the *Times*, attacked the movie viciously. Fifteen days later, in the same newspaper, Michael Sragow wrote, "Bogdanovich's film reduces James's complex love

Deborah Kerr as the governess is threatened by Peter Wyngarde as Peter Quint in *The Innocent* (1961), taken from Henry James's *The Turn of the Screw*.

Stephanie Beacham as the prim but passionate Miss Jessel and Marlon Brando as the masochistic Quint in *The Nightcomers* (1971), a prequel to *The Turn of the Screw/The Innocents*.

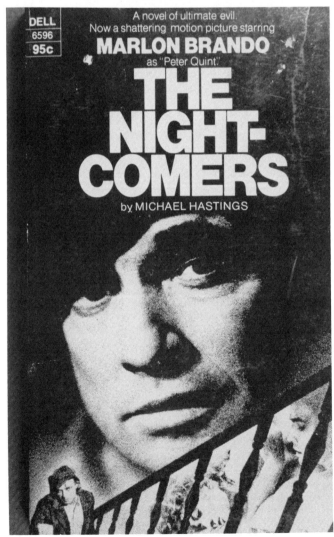

Paperback tie-in to the 1971 film of The *Nightcomers* showing Marlon Brando as Quint.

Madeleine Potter as Verena Tarrant and Vanessa Redgrave as Olive
Chancellor in *The Bostonians* (1984).

Barry Brown as Winterbourne, Cybill Shepherd in the title role, and Cloris Leachman as her mother in James's *Daisy Miller* (1974).

story to a simple flirtation. The sliding, conflicting emotions of James are reduced to simple-minded confrontations."

The Europeans (1878), written the same year as *Daisy Miller*, is a study of a Europeanized brother and sister returning to America to visit cousins in New England. Even less than *Daisy Miller*, this was not the stuff of which movies are made, but nevertheless director James Ivory gave it a try, and *The Europeans* (Levitt-Pickman, 1979) became a quite literal translation (by Ivory's frequent collaborator, Ruth Prawer Jhabvala) of the novel. Critic Vincent Canby found much to admire here. "The screenplay has the sound of the novel, which is James at his most lucidly comic," he wrote. Like any stream of consciousness novelist, Henry James is a difficult writer to translate to the screen, and that is why his later works have never been filmed. Most directors and producers have looked toward his more easily accessible material. This is not a surprise; the surprise is that several of the adaptations of James's works have been intelligently and faithfully transferred to the screen.

Henry James's concern about the rights of women surfaced again in *The Bostonians* (1886). When she came to adapt the material to film (Merchant Ivory, 1984), screenwriter Ruth Prawer Jhabvala followed rather closely the story of suffragette Olive Chancellor (Vanessa Redgrave), who, because of her involvement in female emancipation issues, wrecks her relationship with Basil Ransome (Christopher Reeve). The slow-moving film fared poorly with the critics, most of whom complained that director James Ivory had little grasp of Henry James's material despite his previous encounter with James.

Another James novel, *The Wings of the Dove* (1902),

was never filmed, but had two major productions on live television in the fifties. Charlton Heston, Stella Andrew, and Felicia Montealegre starred in the version on *Studio One* in 1952, and Dana Wynter, James Donald, and John Baragrey were the stars in the 1959 *Playhouse 90* production, adapted by Meade Roberts.

Although the output of Stephen Crane (1871–1900) was relatively small due to an untimely death, his *Red Badge of Courage* (1895) has been hailed by critics as the first modern war novel. Crane abandoned the romantic trappings of historical fiction and shifted the emphasis to the ordeal of the common soldier as he faces battle.

When John Huston wrote the screenplay to and directed *The Red Badge of Courage* (MGM, 1951), he captured the mood of the novel in a very literal translation. However, disastrous sneak previews forced the studio to cut the film while Huston was off in Africa shooting *The African Queen* and, in order to explain gaps in the action, to add a narration culled from passages from the novel.

Most of the major incidents of the novel are intact: the trial of battle; Henry's cowardice and retreat from the battlefield; the death of Jim Conklin, the tall soldier; the fleeing soldier who strikes Henry with the rifle, thus giving him his "red badge of courage"; and finally, Henry redeeming himself in his own eyes through the baptism of battle. The only significant omissions are Henry coming across the rotting corpse in the woods and the death of the Tattered Man.

Audie Murphy does a credible job as Henry, and his grim expressions and erratic attitudes suggest what is going on in his mind, but the film fails to deliver the same emotional punch of the novel because it cannot duplicate the stream of consciousness technique used by Crane, a technique that works well on paper. What it does deliver is the total re-creation of a battle—the din and dust, the marches, the battlefields, the confusion. Especially effective is the scene where the enemy soldiers, like ghosts, materialize out of clouds of smoke, then mysteriously vanish back into them. Furthermore, Huston captured the sense of the soldiers—the way they talked and the way they felt, their looks, their attitudes, their fears. There is one marvelous scene where he also captures the feel of Crane's prose. After Henry has fled the battlefield, he comes upon a line of wounded soldiers as they stumble toward the rear. He encounters Jim, who has been gutshot, but is afraid to lie down for fear that one of the artillery wagons will run him over. Wandering out into an open field, he collapses and dies with Henry by his side.

A new version of *Red Badge of Courage* (teleplay by John Gay, ABC/20th Century-Fox Television, 1974) added color, but the small screen for which it was produced diminished the battle and made it seem far less imposing. Like Huston's film, a narration linked the episodes.

In "The Bride Comes to Yellow Sky" (1898), Stephen Crane used the setting and characters that Harte might have used, but almost everything that Harte would have played up, Crane played down. This lighthearted yet bitter meditation on the death of the Old West made the second half of an anthology film, *Face to Face* (RKO, 1952), the first being an adaptation of Joseph Conrad's "Secret Sharer" (1912). Sticking close to the Crane original, screenwriter James Agee captured the essence of the story as well as the events.

One of Crane's most interesting works is the novelette "The Monster," the tale of Dr. Trescott, whose black servant rescues the doctor's son from a fire but suffers horrible burns, resulting in mutilation and brain damage. As long as the town believes the black man is going to die, there is a great romantic exaltation at his heroism, but gradually the town's sentiment turns to revulsion against the poor man because of his disfigurement.

Based on "The Monster" (1898), *Face of Fire* (Allied Artists, 1959) erased all traces of Johnson's being black. The film begins much as Crane's story did. Monk

Audie Murphy as Henry Fleming lies to Bill Mauldin as the Loud Soldier about how he received his wound in *The Red Badge of Courage* (1951).

Robert Preston as the sheriff takes his new bride (Marjorie Steele) back home in "The Bride Comes to Yellow Sky," the Stephen Crane story that made up half of the two-part *Face to Face* (1952).

WHO WOULD DARE TO LIFT THE MASK?

WHO COULD LOOK AND BE THE SAME?

CAMERON MITCHELL   JAMES WHITMORE

FACE OF FIRE

FROM Stephen Crane's CLASSIC SHOCKER!

ROYAL DANO

MIKO OSCARD · BETTYE ACKERMAN · ROBERT SIMON · Featuring RICHARD ERDMAN · HOWARD SMITH

Produced by ALBERT BAND and LOUIS GARFINKLE in Association With GUSTAF UNGER · Directed by ALBERT BAND · Screenplay by LOUIS GARFINKLE

AN ALLIED ARTISTS PICTURE

One-sheet for *Face of Fire* (1959), an adaptation of Stephen Crane's (unnamed) story, "The Monster."

Johnson (James Whitmore) rescues a young boy from a raging fire, only to be horribly burned, and after the accident, the townspeople, who once adored Johnson, slowly begin to turn against him because of his grotesque appearance. His mind snaps with almost murderous results. While this adaptation by coproducer Louis Garfinkle was potentially interesting, and in some ways faithful to the Crane story, it was wrongly promoted as a horror film and quickly died at the box office.

Like Crane, Frank Norris (1870–1902) lived a short life—he was only thirty-one when he died—but he produced three relatively important naturalistic novels, of which one, *McTeague* (1899), came to the screen as *Greed* (Metro Goldwyn, 1923). The infamous film, directed by Erich von Stroheim, was savagely edited by the studio from forty-two reels—ten-and-a-half hours—to ten reels—two-and-a-half hours. However, what remains is amazingly faithful to both the plot and the naturalistic intent of the novel. Some subtleties that might have been introduced had sound been available and a few scenes that reiterated the theme were omitted, but in their places Stroheim added touches that were strictly his. In the novel, Norris had a ten-sentence passage that referred to McTeague's parents. In the original script, Stroheim increased this section to a whopping twenty-five pages, and even in the edited film the prologue is of a far greater length than in the novel.

Stroheim intended to call the film *McTeague*, but studio executives changed the title and, in the editing process, altered the basic character of McTeague (Gibson Gowland) himself. In the novel, McTeague was content with his life, but environment and heredity were too strong to overcome, and in the end it was Trina's avarice that drove her husband to kill her. The film opens with the quote, added by studio editors: "Gold, gold, gold, gold . . . Hard to get and light to hold, / Stolen, borrowed, squandered, doled." Here it is greed that drives McTeague to kill Trina (ZaSu Pitts). Yet, despite the mutilation by the studio and the changes by Stroheim, much of the story remains intact.

In a career that began in the late nineteenth century and extended well into the twentieth, Edith Wharton (1862–1937) produced over forty books and numerous short stories. Today, with a few exceptions, most notably *Ethan Frome* (1911), her work seems quaintly dated. Yet her novels were consistent best-sellers, and in 1921 she won the Pulitzer Prize.

Her first novel to reach the screen was *The Children* (aka *The Marriage Playground*, 1928), which was an attempt to delve into the world of preadolescents. Plotwise, the film *The Marriage Playground* (Paramount, 1929) remained close to the novel, telling the story of eighteen-year-old Judith Wheater (Mary Brian) who is forced to raise a horde of brothers and sisters while her rich parents party their way through Europe. In Italy, Judith encounters Martin Boyne (Fredric March), with whom she falls in love. The children love him, too, but he has a fiancée back in Switzerland. He leaves only to return a free man. The film relied more heavily on romance than the novel, but otherwise it was a decent adaptation (by J. Walter Ruben and Doris Anderson).

One of Wharton's most popular and enduring novels is *The Age of Innocence* (1920), for which she won the Pulitzer Prize. Except for the conclusion, the first film of *The Age of Innocence* (Warner Bros., 1924), adapted by Olga Printzlau, followed the novel rather closely. After Archer (Elliot Dexter) marries the blue-blooded May Welland (Edith Roberts), he meets and falls in love with the Polish countess Ellen Olenska (Beverly Bayne). The

affair becomes quite intense, and when May hears of it, she goes to the countess and informs her that she is expecting a child. The countess then does the right thing by leaving Archer and returning to Poland.

When *The Age of Innocence* (RKO, 1934) returned as a talkie with John Boles and Irene Dunne, the studio chose to make a version similar to the stars' earlier *Back Street*. In surface details in Philip Moehler's screen adaptation, there were similarities to the Wharton novel. Newlan Archer (Boles) is engaged to the dull but socially acceptable May Welland (Julie Haydon). Into his life drops Countess Ellen Olenska (Dunne), who is in the process of getting a divorce, flying in the face of Victorian society. Although desperately in love with the countess, Archer is forced to marry May. But he continues to see the countess, and it is she who finally breaks off their relationship. This romantic claptrap that the *New York Times* reviewer called "curiously cold and detached" had little to do with Wharton's fine novel.

In the mid-thirties, *Strange Wives* (Universal, 1935) appeared, a comedy supposedly based on an Edith Wharton short story "Bread Upon the Waters," a trifle

ZaSu Pitts as Trina hoards her money in Erich von Stroheim's *Greed*, adapted from Frank Norris's *McTeague*, and later demands that Gibson Gowland as McTeague return it after taking it.

Elliot Dexter as the philadering husband and Edith Roberts as the long-suffering wife in *The Age of Innocence* (1924).

John Bowles as Newland Archer and Irene Dunne as Countess Ellen Olenska in the first remake of *The Age of Innocence* (1934).

written for *Cosmopolitan*. A rather somber story became a lighthearted tale of an American (Roger Pryor) who marries a Russian woman (June Clayworth) with a large family and an ex-lover. Gladys Unger wrote the screenplay, with additional dialogue by Barry Trivers and James Mulhauser.

Perhaps the best Wharton adaptation of its time was *The Old Maid* (1924), a powerful and poignant tale that first was adapted by Zoë Akins into a successful Broadway play. *The Old Maid* (Warner Bros., 1939) embellished the novella, taking much of its action from the stage play. Civil War Southern belle Delia Lovell (Miriam Hopkins), engaged to marry Clem Spender (George Brent), who has been away at the front for two years, gets tired of waiting and instead weds the rich Jim Ralston (James Stephenson). Feeling badly for the jilted Clem, Delia's sister Charlotte (Bette Davis) spends the night with him just before he returns to the front. He is killed, and she discovers that she is pregnant. With the help of her family doctor (Donald Crisp), Charlotte rushes off to Arizona and has the baby. When she returns home, she sets up an orphanage for children who have been left homeless by the war, and in this way she disguises her attempts to raise her child.

After a period of time, Delia's brother-in-law, Joe Ralston (Jerome Cowan), expresses interest in Charlotte, but Delia discovers the truth about the illegitimate child, and, furious at Charlotte for having a liaison with Clem, she convinces Joe that her sister is too ill to marry. The daughter, Tina (Jane Bryan), grows up, falls in love, and becomes engaged, and although Charlotte is determined to tell Tina the truth, she can not bring herself to do so. Tina goes off with her new husband, Lanning Halsey (William Lundigan), and Charlotte is doomed to spend the rest of her life with Delia, who hates her.

Much of the action in the latter half of this film, adapted by Casey Robinson, is determined by the struggle of the two sisters for the love of Tina. Here the film mirrors the novella. However, the character of Delia, although often strident and vindictive, is less dark than the character created by Wharton. Otherwise, this is an extremely faithful film in spirit and content, a film that the *New York Times* said had "come to the screen unimpaired." It was a tearjerker in the best sense of the word—the *National Board of Review* magazine called it "just about perfect"—where the emotional experiences come from the characters and not from contrived situations.

As this is written (spring 1992), another remake of *The Age of Innocence* (directed by Martin Scorsese from a script by Scorsese and Jay Cocks and starring Daniel Day Lewis, Michelle Pfeiffer, and Winona Ryder) and a first *Ethan Frome* (with Liam Neeson) were in produc-

Fredric March as Martin Boyne and Mary Brian as Judith Wheater in *The Marriage Playground* (1929), an early adaptation of Edith Wharton's *The Children*.

Roger Pryor as Jimmy King shakes hands with Claude Gillingwater as Guggins as (from left) Leslie Fenton, Valerie Hobson, Hugh O'Connell, June Clayworth, and Ralph Forbes look on in *Strange Wives* (1935), based on Edith Wharton's "Bread Upon the Waters."

59

Bette Davis as Charlotte Lovell dances with George Brent as Clem Spender in *The Old Maid* (1939).

tion. (In the forties, Warners was planning an *Ethan Frome* with Bette Davis and Henry Fonda, but abandoned the venture.)

Like Edith Wharton, Ellen Glasgow (1873–1945) began writing before the turn of the century; she was rather prolific, but only one of her works was made as a film. In John Huston's *In This Our Life* (Warner Bros., 1942), adapted by Howard Koch from Glasgow's 1941 novel, Stanley Timberlake (Bette Davis) is the selfish and spoiled daughter of a genteel but impoverished Virginia family. Only a week before Stanley is to marry the gentle lawyer Craig Fleming (George Brent), she seduces Peter (Dennis Morgan), the doctor husband of her warm and loving sister, Roy (Olivia de Havilland). This leads to Peter's suicide. Roy forgives Stanley's indiscretion, but when Craig, her ex-finance, falls in love with Roy, Stanley stops at nothing to woo him back. Spurned by Craig, Stanley, in a rage, jumps into her car and speeds away. This results in her running over and killing a boy, but rather than accept the consequences, she blames the deed on the son of the family cook (Hattie McDaniel). The police fail to believe Stanley's story, and once again, she drives off wildly, this time crashing the auto and ending her own life.

Bette Davis chewed up the scenery as Stanley, rearranging the character so that she could throw in all the mannerisms usually associated with her performances, the twitching, the eye-rolling, the frenetic energy. In addition, the film suffered from Production Code restrictions that called for a more concrete form of punishment than Stanley received in the novel. After the movie's release, Bette Davis met with Ellen Glasgow, who expressed her disgust at the film's outcome. "I couldn't have agreed with her more," said the actress.

While Henry James and others wrote of the upper and upper-middle classes, Theodore Dreiser (1871–1945) turned his attention to the lower classes to find his characters. Dreiser's greatest novel, *An American Tragedy* (1925), was an ironic reversal of the Horatio Alger myth, the story of Clyde Griffiths, who attempts to win the American dream for himself.

Dreiser based his novel on an actual case, the drowning in 1906 of Gracie Brown by her lover, Chester Gillette. The author had attended the trial, personally noting that Gillette sold photos of himself to admiring young ladies to raise money for catered meals on death row. Dreiser had investigated a number of similar cases and found a pattern: a poor boy impregnated a girl from the lower class, saw a chance for a more advantageous marriage, and killed his sweetheart. *An American Tragedy* is a distillation of these investigations, a gloomy picture of the American success story.

When Paramount expressed an interest in bringing the novel to the screen, Dreiser demanded $100,000 for the rights. His agent attempted to persuade him to settle for $25,000, but Dreiser held out, and after personally negotiating with Jesse Lasky, he emerged with a contract that gave him $90,000. The studio immediately approached the great Russian director, Sergei Eisenstein, to write and direct the feature. Eisenstein produced a script, but its proletarian views so shocked studio heads—Clyde is shown as a youth victimized by a society of capitalistic tyrants—that they dumped Eisenstein and his script, and Josef von Sternberg was brought in to save the project. Screen credit for the script eventually went to Samuel Hoffenstein, although von Sternberg took a personal hand.

The film opens with Clyde (Phillips Holmes) working in a hotel, but soon he has a factory job and is visiting the home of a rich relative, whose daughter Sondra (Frances Dee) takes a liking to him. In the meantime, he is dallying with another factory employee, Roberta (Sylvia Sidney), whom he gets pregnant. In order to extricate himself from his predicament, Clyde takes Roberta to a small upstate lake where he intends to kill her. While rowing on the lake, Roberta becomes insistent that Clyde marry her and an argument ensues. The boat capsizes, and Roberta is drowned. Clyde later is arrested, put on trial, and found guilty.

The film condensed a novel of more than eight hundred pages into a running time of ninety-six minutes, forcing Hoffenstein to pare down certain scenes and delete others, including most of the early ones involving Clyde's boyhood and his escape from his parents. Hoffenstein also changed the character of Clyde. In seducing Roberta, he threatens her with her job, and when he receives a note from her, his smug smile indicates that he has broken her will. In doing so, he places the sympathy of the audience on the side of the girl, showing her as the one who was victimized rather than Clyde. Fully one-third of the film, far greater proportionally than the amount of time Dreiser spent in the novel, was the trial, which the *New York Times* said was "emphatically stirring" and the one part where von Sternberg "fires his film with feeling."

Upset at Eisenstein's dismissal and the subsequent version of *An American Tragedy*, Dreiser sued the studio. He lost the case, but kept in touch with Eisenstein and, as late as 1938, was still begging the director to consider remaking the story. Nothing ever came of this, but a decade later, a new version did appear: George Stevens's *Place in the Sun* (Paramount, 1951), a film that not only proved to be a huge financial success but also garnered universal critical acclaim.

The story opens with George Eastman (Montgomery Clift) trying to hitch a ride on the highway. A beautiful, dark-haired girl drives past him in a flashy sports car, honking her horn flirtatiously, and George is struck by

Bette Davis and Olivia de Havilland as sisters Stanley and Roy Timberlake in Ellen Glasgow's *In This Our Life* (1942).

her stunning looks. When he arrives in an unnamed city to find work at his uncle's bathing-suit factory, he discovers that the girl, Angela Vickers (Elizabeth Taylor), is a distant cousin. George gets the job and is quickly captivated by the nearness of wealth and luxury, symbolized by the glorious Angela, who of course is far above him socially. To combat his loneliness, George begins to see Alice Tripp (Shelley Winters), a coworker at the factory. But as he becomes increasingly involved with Alice, he also becomes more deeply enmeshed with Angela and her upper-crust life. Then Alice announces that she is pregnant. Confused and embittered, Clyde takes a drastic step by plotting to kill her. He takes her boating on a lonely lake, but he cannot bring himself to murder. He begins to explain how he really feels and about his plans to marry Angela. They argue, the boat capsizes, and Alice drowns. George is arrested for

Lobby card showing Sylvia Sidney as Roberta Alden, Phillips Holmes as Clyde Griffiths, and Francis Dee as Sondra Finchley in Dreiser's *An American Tragedy* (1931).

Shelley Winters as working girl Alice Tripp and Montgomery Clift as social climbing George Eastman in *A Place in the Sun* (1951), based on *An American Tragedy*.

Rita Hayworth as Sally Elliott and Victor Mature as songwriter Paul Dresser in *My Gal Sal* (1942), a very loose adaptation of Dreiser's autobiographical *My Brother Paul*.

murder, convicted, and sentenced to death. Just before his execution, he tells a priest, "I wanted to save her, but I just couldn't." He and Angela meet one final time and he tells her, "I know something now I didn't know before. I'm guilty of a lot of things—of most of what they say I am."

Almost all of the early parts of the novel have been omitted, but what remains is consistent in capturing the naturalism of Dreiser. Some critics complained that the film gave only surface treatment to the society that propels George to his tragic fate, but director Stevens and scriptwriters Michael Wilson and Harry Brown, who the *New York Times* found "have distilled [from the novel] the essence of tragedy and romance that is both moving and memorable," took pains to show that while George is an intelligent man, he is attracted to the opulent lifestyle of his rich relatives and, finally, is pushed by forces beyond his control to commit the violent act that dooms him.

The one area where the film diverges from the spirit of Dreiser is in the characterization of its protagonist. In the novel, Clyde Griffiths is a scheming, grasping youth, much as Phillips Holmes portrayed him in the 1931 film. But George Eastman of *A Place in the Sun* is far less calculating and far more restrained, a mama's boy in need of love and attention, a pitiful little man who has, by the end of the film, grown brave enough to admit his guilt. If George is not exactly Dreiser's Clyde Griffiths, he is nevertheless a finely realized, credible character, who is inevitably drawn toward his fate.

Theodore Dreiser's second novel—his first had been *Sister Carrie* (1900)—was *Jennie Gerhardt* (1911), a story about a girl who is known for fidelity to those she loves, but who, because of her selflessness, is doomed to be victimized. *Jennie Gerhardt* (Paramount, 1933) took four screenwriters (Josephine Lovett, Joseph M. March, S. K. Lauren, and Frank Portos) to remove Dreiser's social commentary and concentrate on the tears.

After losing her first lover, Senator Brander (Edward Arnold), in an accident, Jennie Gerhardt (Sylvia Sidney), left pregnant and abandoned, takes a job as a housemaid. She meets and falls in love with Lester Kane (Donald Cook), a young man whose rich family objects because of Jennie's child. The lovers separate, and Lester marries socialite Letty Pace (Mary Astor). Later, when Jennie encounters Lester, he admits that he still loves her, which offers her some small satisfaction. With the social commentary removed, all that remained was a tearjerker, and Dreiser's naturalism disappeared under overt sentimentality.

The 1940s saw only one attempt at adapting Dreiser, *My Gal Sal* (20th Century-Fox, 1942), which was based on an autobiographical memoir, "My Brother Paul." At an early age, Theodore's older brother Paul Dreiser had joined a minstrel show and gone on to vaudeville, changing his last name to Dresser. Before he died in 1906, Paul penned a number of songs, including the evergreen, "My Gal Sal," which became the title of this affectionate tribute to Tin Pan Alley. The film (written by Seton I. Miller, Darryl Ware, and Karl Tunberg) had little to do with reality. Paul Dresser (Victor Mature) has run away to New York, where he meets and falls in love with Sally Elliott (Rita Hayworth), a Broadway star whom he eventually marries. The casting of the slim, muscular Mature is ironic in that Dresser was a hefty 250-plus pounds.

The silliest adaptation of a Dreiser work is *The Prince Who Was a Thief* (Universal, 1951), based on a 1927 short story of the same title. It is all swords and sorcery wherein a young prince is given by his wicked uncle to a thief to be killed, but the thief raises the child as his own. The young man (now Tony Curtis) grows up to take back the kingdom from his wicked uncle and marry the commoner (Piper Laurie) with whom he has fallen in love. An Arabian Nights adventure, the film (written by Gerald Drayson Adams and Aeneas MacKenzie) played more like a Western set in ancient Tangiers.

Dreiser's first novel, *Sister Carrie*, met with mixed critical reviews upon its appearance. Some thought it an honest and searing portrait of American life, and others lambasted it because it flouted social propriety. Dreiser used his own experiences as a worker in Chicago and also drew upon those of one of his sisters, who eloped to Montreal with the cashier of a Chicago bar who stole money from his employer's safe.

Carrie (Paramount, 1952) is a sentimental version by Ruth and Augustus Goetz of Dreiser's ironic tale. The film presents Carrie Meeber (Jennifer Jones) as an innocent, self-sacrificing girl who is seduced by traveling salesman Charlie Drouet (Eddie Albert) before meeting and falling in love with unhappily married George Hurstwood (Laurence Olivier), manager of a swank saloon. Once the two run off together, their fortunes decline. When Carrie finally leaves him, it is because she believes that he has the chance to move in with his rich brother. After becoming famous and wealthy herself, she tries unsuccessfully to save the now destitute Hurstwood, but by then it is too late and he dies.

Carrie is a young girl who is lured into a life of sin with first Drouet and then Hurstwood. In neither case does she precipitate the action; it is the men who corrupt her, use her. By having Carrie moved by impulses of affection and trust, by portraying her as the true innocent, the film misses all the social implication and ironies that Dreiser intended. In the novel, Carrie destroyed people and relationships to get her way. Where Dreiser turned the standard girl-gone-wrong tale upside down by having her go unpunished in the end, the film rewarded her for

Tony Curtis as the prince and Everett Sloane as the thief who raises him in *The Prince Who Was a Thief* (1951), based on the Dreiser short story.

remaining basically good but mistreated. As Bosley Crowther pointed out, "it isn't *Sister Carrie* and it isn't a realistic show. It is a lush and resplendent romance that ends in a tear and a drop to Skid Row."

Both Henry James and Theodore Dreiser were artists of the first magnitude, writers whose serious work is among the most important that America has produced. In their best work, they pushed fiction beyond its limits, and because of their seriousness, few adaptations of their writings have reached the screen. On the other hand, Booth Tarkington (1869–1946), a contemporary of theirs, not only was more prolific and popular than either, but had more film adaptations of his work than James and Dreiser combined.

Tarkington took his characters from the vast American middle class, usually in a midwestern setting during the first decades of the twentieth century. His earliest works leaned heavily toward romanticism, as exemplified by *The Man From Home* (Lasky, 1914), based on his 1908 play, in which good old American virtue triumphs over European duplicity.

Other silent film adaptations of Tarkington followed the same general pattern. The plot of *The Gentleman From Indiana* (Pallas, 1915) was so sketchy as to bear little if any resemblance to the 1899 novel. *Springtime* (Life Photo Film/Alco, 1915), taken from one of Tark-

Laurence Olivier as Hurstwood, Jennifer Jones as Carrie, and Eddie Albert as Charlie Drouet share a moment together in *Carrie* (1952), an adaptation of Theodore Dreiser's *Sister Carrie*.

63

ington's short stories, tells of a young girl who breaks up with her fiancé to marry the boy she really loves, the son of the man who is trying to destroy her father, thus providing a happy ending for all concerned. Marie Walcamp, playing the title character of *The Flirt* (Bluebird Films, 1916), released as a five-part serial, falls for a con artist, forges her father's name to some checks, then confesses all in time for the law to nab the crook. She is rewarded by having a newcomer to town fall madly in love with her. This was remade under the same title (Universal, 1922) six years later, with Eileen Percy in the lead.

Four adaptations of Tarkington works appeared in a single year. *Clarence* (Paramount, 1923) told the story of a drifter who turns around the lives of a wealthy family. *Boy of Mine* (Associated First National, 1923) mixed pathos with drama to tell of a boy (Ben Alexander) who turns his strict and uncompromising father into a warm and loving human being. *Gentle Julia* (Fox, 1923) was a Bessie Love vehicle about a young woman who follows an older man to Chicago; discovering he is married, she returns to her midwestern home to the boy who still loves her. *Cameo Kirby* (Fox, 1923) was a John Gilbert comedy set on a riverboat in 1850.

Departing from his usual brand of fiction, Booth Tarkington made a successful sortie into romantic history with *Monsieur Beaucaire* (1900). Later in his career, Tarkington spoke lightly of such "trifles," but the fact remains that it is a well-constructed, charming short story set in eighteenth-century England in which the Duke of Orleans, while stopping at Bath, poses as a barber to expose the snobbery and duplicity of the period.

Monsieur Beaucaire (Paramount, 1924) became a Rudolph Valentino vehicle. Here the story, adapted by Forrest Halsey, was one of a French duke donning the disguise of a coiffeur to avoid marrying a persistent lady love. The tale surfaced again six years later as *Monte Carlo* (Paramount, 1930). Directed by Ernst Lubitsch, it displays some of his deft comedy in an updated story (by Ernest Vajda) about a count (Jack Buchanan) who poses as a barber while pursuing an impoverished countess (Jeanette MacDonald). Several songs are thrown into the gossamer plot, including "Beyond the Blue Horizon." In addition, the film includes an operatic sequence also based on "Monsieur Beaucaire." In Bob Hope's *Monsieur Beaucaire* (Paramount, 1946), writers Norman Panama and Melvin Frank threw out most of the Tarkington story and concentrated on burlesquing costume romances.

Tarkington's best-loved fiction—*Penrod* (1914), *Penrod and Sam* (1916), and *Penrod Jashper* (1929)—depicted the lively adventures and misadventures of Penrod Schofield, a boy patterned somewhat along the lines of Huckleberry Finn but without the hardheaded

reality displayed by Twain's character. Despite being a little too long at almost ninety minutes, the first film version of *Penrod* (Associated First National, 1922), proved to be popular silent comedy wherein the mischievous Penrod (Wesley Barry) plays a number of humorous pranks. The high point occurs when he captures a couple of crooks and becomes the hero of the town. *Penrod and Sam* (Associated First National, 1923) finds Penrod (Ben Alexander) and his friend Sam (Joe Butterworth) having problems with a couple of snooty kids who momentarily get the upper hand. The remake of *Penrod and Sam* (Warner Bros., 1931) used the same story of sissies trying to horn in on Penrod's club. It was slim fare, so when it again was remade (Warner Bros., 1937), the boys turned into sleuths to solve a crime. The *New York Times* felt that "little but the title of Booth Tarkington's story remains." This fairly successful "B" film was followed by two quick sequels, *Penrod and His Twin Brother* (Warner Bros., 1938) and *Penrod's Double Trouble* (Warner Bros., 1938), neither of which had much connection with Tarkington's novels.

A popular 1923 play, *Magnolia,* was also filmed several times, the first, *The Fighting Coward* (Paramount, 1924), leaning heavily on comedy, turning the story into a satire on the Southern code of honor. Two sound versions subsequently reached the screen. *River of Romance* (Paramount, 1929), retaining the basic plot, dropped most of the comedy and concentrated on romance and melodrama, a move designed to shape the film to Charles "Buddy" Rogers. *Mississippi* (Paramount, 1935), was a musical comedy built around the talents of Bing Crosby as a dapper gambler and W. C. Fields as a riverboat captain.

Filmmakers of the sound period continued to pursue the romantic Tarkington. *Bad Sister* (Universal, 1931), a remake of *The Flirt*, was the old story of a girl (Sidney Fox) who is abandoned by a con artist but finds true love despite her foolishness. In *The Millionaire* (Warner Bros., 1931), a rich man (George Arliss) disguises himself as a poor gas station attendant only to learn that he can be happy and rich at the same time. It was remade as *That Way With Women* (Warner Bros., 1947) with Sidney Greenstreet in the role. *Business and Pleasure* (Fox, 1932), based on *The Plutocrat*, a minor Tarkington novel, was tailored for Will Rogers, showcasing his "aw, shucks" style of acting and turning the whole thing into a comedy. *Cameo Kirby* (Fox, 1930), *Clarence* (Paramount, 1931 and 1937), and *Gentle Julia* (20th Century-Fox, 1936) were all remakes of silent films.

When it wasn't Tarkington the romantic that Hollywood was filming, then it was Tarkington the juvenile. *Father's Son* (Warner Bros., 1931) examined a young boy (Leon Janney) who plays pranks on family and friends, runs away from home, and returns to loving

A romantic scene filmed in Italy by Cecil B. DeMille from Tarkington's *The Man From Home* (1914).

Two photographs from an edition of Booth Tarkington's *Monsieur Beaucaire* as a tie-in with the 1924 Rudolph Valentino screen version: the frontispiece clearly stating that the book is the Valentino edition, and a scene opposite the frontispiece with the star as the French duke posing as a barber to avoid marrying one of his lady loves, here planting a delicate kiss on the lips of Doris Kenyon.

Rudolph Valentino romancing Doris Kenyon in *Monsieur Beaucaire* (1924).

arms. The first version was romantically wistful, but the remake, also called *Father's Son* (Warner Bros., 1941), was so bad that the *New York Times* said, "Even if it is based on Tarkington—hard to believe, but true—it is still one of the feeblest parables to which this corner has been subjected this or any other season." The title character in *Little Orvie* (RKO, 1940) is told by his parents that he cannot have a dog, but in the end, he bends their wills to his. Made first in 1916 with Jack Pickford in the lead, *Seventeen* (Paramount, 1940) returned to feature Jackie Cooper as William Baxter in a film that captured much of the spirit of the novel. Baxter is an average young high school student worrying about

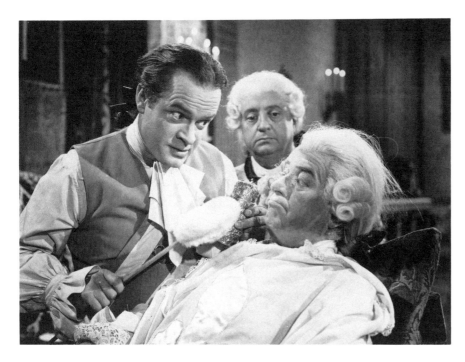

Bob Hope in his own specially-tailored version of *Monsieur Beaucaire* (1946), here pampering Reginald Owen.

Florence Vidor and Vernon Steele in the first version of *Alice Adams* (1924).

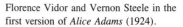

Ben Alexander about to get a taste of the strap from Rockliffe Fellowes in Booth Tarkington's *Boy of Mine* (1923).

Katharine Hepburn in the title role welcomes a visit from Fred MacMurray as Arthur Russell in *Alice Adams* (1935).

Buddy Rogers and Mary Brian in *The River of Romance* (1929), based on the Tarkington play, *Magnolia*.

getting into college until a sophisticated girl, Lola Pratt (Betty Field), arrives on the scene to make him forget about everything else.

While Tarkington's fiction often tended to be light-weight, his best work, produced between 1914 and 1924, forsook elaborate plotting for a more dispassionate view of life in his native Indiana. Among the best of these works is his Pulitzer Prize–winning *Alice Adams* (1921), an unsentimental depiction of an American girl brought up by a socially ambitious mother who fills her with expectations far beyond her reach.

Alice Adams (Encore, 1923) first reached the screen with Florence Vidor as Alice, bringing to the role a nice mixture of humor and pathos. The film, adapted by director Rowland V. Lee, stuck close to Tarkington's novel, including the downbeat ending in which Alice, realizing the futility of pursuing Russell (Vernon Steele), gets a job to help her father (Claude Gillingwater), who has fallen upon hard times.

The sound version of *Alice Adams* (RKO, 1935) retained each of these scenes. Alice (Katharine Hepburn) wants to escape her middle-class surroundings, but her cloddish family keeps dragging her back. Her rich friends tolerate her because she amuses them, but she is real where they are fake, deep where they are shallow. Arthur Russell (Fred MacMurray) is attracted to her, and she convinces him that her family is financially well off, but when she invites him to dinner, he sees that it is all a lie. By the night of the dinner, her father (Fred Stone) has gone broke in an ill-advised business venture that he

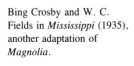

Bing Crosby and W. C. Fields in *Mississippi* (1935), another adaptation of *Magnolia*.

was pushed into by his manipulative wife (Ann Shoemaker), and Alice's brother, Walter (Frank Albertson), has been caught stealing from his employer. Both the novel and the 1923 film ended with Russell, her prince charming, leaving Alice and going back to his own world, but at this spot, the RKO version has Russell forgive her. In addition, a millionaire backs the father's new business and the employer forgives the brother when he returns the money.

Hepburn's Alice is straight out of the novel, a klutzy wallflower who is thoroughly likable, touching, and vulnerable. Unfortunately, the film (written by Dorothy Yost and Mortimer Offner from Jane Murfin's adaptation), which tried so hard to be honest throughout, loses courage at the end because studio heads feared that such a downbeat ending would turn away audiences. In the novel, Alice finally takes responsibility for her own life and is a much stronger individual than when the story began. In the film, she wins her man, but has failed to become a fully realized person. Although stripped of many of her illusions, Alice is still a child who, it might be assumed, will remain dependent upon Russell for her happiness.

In 1915, Tarkington began a trilogy of novels entitled

Norma Terris watches while J. Harold Murray squares off against Douglas Gilmore (right) in *Cameo Kirby* (1930), an adaptation of the play by Booth Tarkington and Leon Wilson.

Lewis Stone appears rather put out that his son (Leon Janney) has brought his pal (Grover Liggon) home in *Father's Son* (1931), based on Tarkington's *Old Fathers and Young Sons*.

Margaret Marquis, Billy Lord, Junior (Frank) Coghlan, and Leon Janney in *Penrod and Sam* (1931).

Eileen Percy as Cora Madison and George Nichols as her father in *The Flirt* (1932), based on Tarkington's short story.

Growth, not completed until 1924, of which one was *The Magnificent Ambersons* (1918), a tale of the decline of a socially prominent dynasty. It won for the author his first Pulitzer Prize. A personal theme of Tarkington's was the regeneration of the individual through work, which he explores through the character of George Minafer, the last scion of Amberson stock, following him from infancy to manhood, from incorrigible brat to humble suitor.

The Magnificent Ambersons first reached the screen as *Pampered Youth* (Vitagraph, 1925), which, while it neither reached the heights nor probed the depths of Tarkington's material as did Orson Welles sixteen years later, tried hard to remain faithful to the novel. According to the *New York Times*, "Those who were interested in the book will probably find much to praise in this film."

Orson Welles was familiar with the Tarkington novel long before he came to film it. In October of 1939, he presented an hour-long version on the "Mercury Theater of the Air." The film version of *The Magnificent Ambersons* (RKO, 1942) opens with a voice-over narration by Welles, a long nostalgic passage lifted and condensed from the first chapter of the novel. "The magnificence of the Ambersons began in 1873," intones Welles. "Their splendor lasted throughout all the years that saw their midland town spread and darken into a

Peggy Ross and Will Rogers as Olivia and Earl Tinker in *Business and Pleasure* (1932).

Two of the twelve "Edgar" stories which Booth Tarkington wrote especially for the screen in 1920–21, starring Johnny Jones.

Roscoe Karns as Clarence Smith and Eleanor Whitney as his boss's daughter, Cora, in Tarkington's *Clarence* (1937).

city. In those days, all the women who wore silk or velvet knew all the other women who wore silk or velvet. And everybody knew everybody else's family horse and carriage." The entire passage evokes a beautiful way of life long past and introduces us to the Ambersons, a family that was as close to royalty as America has produced and whose magnificence was "as conspicuous as a brass band at a funeral."

As Welles speaks, soft-focus images, like a haze around a memory, also convey this sense of the past—the front of the Amberson house where a horse-drawn streetcar waits for Isabel Amberson (Dolores Costello); hatted men in a saloon as the narrator turns his remarks to hats; Eugene Morgan (Joseph Cotten) standing in front of a mirror trying on hats and successively more ridiculous coats and trousers; the Amberson house bathed in snows. Welles says, "In those days they had time for everything."

Eugene is rejected as a suitor, and Isabel, the love of his life, marries Wilber Minafer (Don Dillaway), and as one townswoman has predicted, "they'll have the worst-spoiled lot of children this town will ever see." As she utters these words, George Amberson (Tim Holt), Isabel's son, sporting a wide-brimmed hat, his hair in

Jackie Cooper as Billy Baxter and Betty Field as his girlfriend, Lola Pratt, in Tarkington's *Seventeen* (1940).

ringlets of curls, rides down the street in his tiny carriage upsetting a gardener while the people of the town mutter how they live in expectation of the boy's comeuppance.

Wilber Minafer subsequently dies, and Eugene Morgan, now a widower and a successful automobile manufacturer, returns to town with his attractive daughter, Lucy (Anne Baxter), hoping to rekindle his relationship with Isabel. George is attracted to Lucy but is rebuffed by her, and at this point he refuses to allow Eugene access to his mother. George and his mother go to Europe on an extended trip, but return when she has a heart attack. By now the Amberson fortune has all but disappeared, and the house, no longer the center of dances and light, has become a dark mausoleum. George blames the invention of the automobile for the downfall of his family.

His mother dies, and George must close up the old house and find a job to support himself and his Aunt Fanny (Agnes Moorehead). Injured in an accident, he is taken to the hospital. Eugene comes to visit him there and makes it clear that he will take care of George as he would his own son, an act that Eugene says makes him feel that he is finally being "true to my own true love."

While the last scene, directed by Robert Wise while

Tim Holt as spoiled George Minifer enjoying the company of Anne Baxter as Lucy Morgan and watching with consternation as Dolores Costello as his mother talks with Joseph Cotten as her old flame and Lucy's father, Eugene, in Orson Welles's version of Tarkington's *The Magnificent Ambersons* (1942).

Welles was in South America, has often been criticized for subverting the intention of Welles, it was, however, in the spirit of Tarkington. In the last lines of the novel, Eugene, lying in his hospital bed, contemplates his fate: "For Eugene another radiance filled the room. He knew that he had been true at last to his true love, and that through him she had brought her boy under shelter again. Her eyes would look wistful no more."

Welles, as both director and writer, mirrors the surface of the novel to perfection, capturing all the details and nuances of a way of life that had vanished. However, he failed to be faithful to Tarkington on another level. To Tarkington, the Ambersons were slightly absurd, and their grandeur, because it was really materialistic, an ironic social commentary. Welles saw it differently. His camera roams the house like a secret visitor in love with the place, and when the Ambersons fall, it is more tragic than Tarkington's vision.

The original running time was 148 minutes, and the studio bosses, upset over bad audience reaction at previews, had the film recut to 88 minutes without the permission of Welles. First, all the documentary sequences of the growth of the city were deleted. Also cut was a four-and-a-half minute single take as the camera explores the deserted Amberson mansion. However, like von Stroheim's *Greed,* Welles's *Magnificent Ambersons* became a classic despite the truncated and censored print that survives today, which is a testament to its filmmaker. Welles handled his source material with so much sensitivity and so much intelligence that, in one of those rare

George Arliss as kindly James Alden in *The Millionaire* (1931), for which Booth Tarkington wrote the dialogue from Earl Derr Bigger's "Idle Hands," and the remake, called *The Trouble With Women* (1947), with Sidney Greenstreet surrounded by (from left) Charles Arnt, Dane Clark, Martha Vickers, Barbara Brown, and Howard Freeman.

instances, the film emerges as a greater work of art than the novel on which it is based.

Following *The Magnificent Ambersons*, the adaptations of Tarkington went back to his romantic works and turned out a series of unimpressive musicals. *Presenting Lily Mars* (MGM, 1943) was the story of a young Indiana girl (Judy Garland) who gets her chance on Broadway. *On Moonlight Bay* (Warner Bros., 1951), supposedly based on *Penrod* and *Alice Adams*, was a musical vehicle for Doris Day and Gordon MacRae. The reviewer for the *New York Times* said, "Booth Tarkington may be stirring fitfully in Paradise. . . . Although it strives to develop a genuine nostalgic mood, all that *On Moonlight Bay* seems to create, sadly enough, is the feeling that this film format is old hat." However, the film proved a hit, and a sequel, *By the Light of the Silvery Moon* (Warner Bros., 1953), was released two years later with the same stars, but the story, which allowed room for seven songs, had even less to do with Tarkington than its predecessor.

Booth Tarkington knew and understood films, and shortly after World War One, he was writing scenarios for the Goldwyn company, a series of two-reel comedies (under the overall title, *The Adventures and Emotions of Edgar Pomeroy*) about a precocious boy. There were titles like *Edgar's Hamlet* (1920), *Edgar and the Teacher's Pet* (1920), *Edgar's Little Saw* (1920), *Edgar the Explorer* (1921), and *Get Rich Quick, Edgar* (1921). In an article praising the best films of 1920, the reviewer for the *New York Times* pointed out that the Edgar comedies were among "the most significant works of the year." Ten years after the last Edgar film, Tarkington again worked in Hollywood, collaborating with two other screenwriters on *The Millionaire* (Warner Bros., 1931), an adaptation of "Idle Hands," a short story by Earl Derr Biggers. If the greatest films drawn from his work, *Alice Adams* (1935) and *The Magnificent Ambersons*, include certain changes, Tarkington would have understood.

The vast majority of the films adapted from Tarkington were second-rate romantic flops, and some of the blame must go to the inadequacies of the original source material. While today most of these adaptations are largely forgotten, so is most of Tarkington's fiction. Only *Alice Adams* and *The Magnificent Ambersons* are remembered, and they mostly because of the films.

Marie Prevost and Kenneth Harlan as the fast living couple in *The Beautiful and the Damned* (1922).

FIVE

THE TWENTIES

Sinclair Lewis, F. Scott Fitzgerald, Ernest Hemingway,
William Faulkner, Katherine Anne Porter, Thornton Wilder

Mainstream writers of the 1920s pushed at the limits of acceptable literature. Sex was the subject these authors often chose to explore, but they also examined and criticized politics, religion, racism, and even the family structure, often challenging the very foundations of American culture and society, and in doing so, they opened up new territory that allowed later authors to push the limits even further.

The writing career of Sinclair Lewis (1885–1951) began in 1912 when, under the pseudonym of Tom Graham, he published *Hike and His Aeroplane*, but his period of greatest achievement began with *Main Street* (1920), an attack on small-town America. A play made from the novel and produced in 1921 softened much of the social criticism of Lewis, and the film, *Main Street* (Warner Bros., 1923), also deleted most of the biting social commentary. What remained relied heavily on comedy to set the tone.

The first three reels moved along nicely, establishing the heroine (Florence Vidor) in Gopher Prairie. However, the film slows to a crawl when she sets out to change the town, an act that the local inhabitants see as disturbing their comfort more than a challenge to their intellectual abilities. This film (adapted by Julien Josephson) missed the novel by a wide margin.

The studio remade *Main Street* as *I Married a Doctor* (Warner Bros., 1936), which relied more heavily on drama than comedy in the script by Casey Robinson, Harriett Ford, and Harvey O'Higgins. Will Kennicott (Pat O'Brien), a doctor, and his wife, Carol (Josephine Hutchinson), move to a small town—Williamsburg, not Gopher Prairie—where he sets up a practice and she finds it difficult to adapt to rural life. The local gossips turn the residents against her, and when she informs her husband that she is returning to Chicago, he tells her that every town has a gossip center, its "Main Street." Once she discovers this to be true, she returns for a happy reunion, not only with her husband but also with the town, which has admitted its errors and welcomes her back.

Lewis followed the success of *Main Street* with *Babbitt* (1922) in which he created an enduring perception of an American type. The story reached the screen twice. In the first *Babbitt* (Warner Bros., 1924), adapter Dorothy Farnum turned the story into that of a middle-aged man (Willard Lewis) who is seduced by a golddigger but is rescued by his son. The *New York Times* called it a "hapless effort." A decade later when *Babbitt* (Warner Bros., 1934) returned, it was no closer to the novel than its predecessor. Like the novel, the film (adapted by Mary McCall Jr. and Ben Markson) opens with a long sequence detailing the life of George Babbitt (Guy Kibbee) at home and at work, the loyal friend, the gruff parent, the businessman, but rather than the acid treatment dished out by Lewis, the script displays a great affection for Babbitt. He becomes involved unwittingly with two local Zenith citizens who plan to loot the city treasury via a crooked land deal. Too thick-witted to understand what is happening, he falls in with a woman who tries to blackmail him. In the end, his wife (Aline MacMahon) comes to his rescue by persuading the city fathers that George's participation was only an effort on his part to save Zenith from the crooks. While it garnered some good reviews, most critics were quick to point out that the film had little to do with the novel.

After *Babbitt*, Sinclair Lewis produced what many critics feel is his most important work, *Arrowsmith* (1925). Samuel Goldwyn purchased the rights to the Pulitzer Prize-winning novel and put playwright Sidney Howard to work on the script, which, although it took liberties with the novel, Lewis himself praised for its maturity. Of necessity, the plot of the film (Goldwyn, 1931) had to be condensed, and some of the subplots omitted for the sake of clarity and time. Martin Arrowsmith (Ronald Colman) is an idealistic young doctor who marries Leora (Helen Hayes) and then hangs out his shingle in a small country town. When a plague breaks out among cattle, he develops a vaccine that attracts the attention of Washington, D.C. Eventually Martin winds up in New York, where he finds little time for Leora. Undaunted, she accompanies him to the West Indies where he intends to fight an outbreak of the bubonic plague. At the suggestion of a local official, he goes to another island but this time he insists that she stay where she is safe. A spot of the virus spills on a cigarette, and when Leora smokes it, she catches the disease and subsequently dies. Overcome with guilt, Arrowsmith breaks the rules of his experiment and gives the vaccine to everyone. In doing so he renounces the dictates of pure science and is reunited spiritually with his dead wife.

In the novel, Lewis inserted bits of occasional humor, but it was never directed toward his hero; however, Sidney Howard and director John Ford often made Arrowsmith's dedication look like a selfish act. Excluded from her husband's world, Leora becomes increasingly dissipated the longer the marriage lasts until she dies of the disease that Arrowsmith seeks to eradicate. In combatting the plague, Arrowsmith must use inhuman methods, giving one group the lifesaving drug but keeping it from others. Only under such laboratory conditions can the test be scientifically validated. Thus, the film chose to show the dark side of Arrowsmith, the destructive nature of his dedication. In addition, the whole last section of the novel which includes his second marriage has simply been omitted.

Arrowsmith first came to television in 1950, with Van Heflin starring in the *Robert Montgomery Presents* production. Ten years later, it was produced again on *DuPont Show of the Month,* with an adaptation by Philip Reisman, Jr., and Farley Granger in the lead.

After *Arrowsmith*, Lewis turned out a potboiler, *Mantrap* (1926), which was serialized in the *Saturday Evening Post*. In the first film adaptation, *Mantrap* (Paramount, 1926), screenwriter Adelaide Heilbron took a minor character from the novel, Alverna (Clara Bow), and made her the central one of the film. She is a backwoods girl who runs away with a big city lawyer (Percy Marmont), but by fadeout she has returned to her husband, although her roving eye has landed upon a handsome forest ranger.

When Lewis himself caught the film at a local theater, the manager found out he was in attendance and asked him to say a few words to the audience. In his short speech, he said that it was a good thing he had read the novel for he would not have recognized it from the film.

The remake, *Untamed* (Paramount, 1940), strayed even further afield, thanks to screenwriters Frederick Hazlitt Brennan and Frank Butler. A doctor (Ray Milland), while visiting the north country, steals a woman (Patricia Morison) away from her husband (Akim Tamiroff). When an epidemic strikes the area, the doctor takes the wife off to fight it, and the two are snowbound. The husband makes it through the blizzard with much-needed medicine and promptly freezes to death, allowing the doctor and his lover to be together.

Lewis's next work, *Elmer Gantry* (1927), caused a greater stir than any of his previous novels mainly because his hero is an evangelist more interested in money, power, and sex than in God. The novel sold over 200,000 copies within the first ten weeks, but it also stirred up the religious community, and Lewis was attacked from pulpits all across the country.

In 1946, Lewis was called to the defense of writer and future director Richard Brooks, under attack by the Marine Corps for his novel, *The Brick Foxhole*. The furor over the book died, but during this time, Lewis and Brooks discussed *Elmer Gantry*. Brooks was an admirer of the novel, believing it would make a splendid motion picture, but Lewis thought the work unsuitable for

Ronald Colman as Martin Arrowsmith with Myrna Loy as Joyce Lanyon, the woman he spurns, and Helen Hayes as Leora Toser, the woman he marries, in *Arrowsmith* (1931).

filming. "It was a helluva good pamphlet but not such a good novel," Lewis told Brooks.

Brooks ultimately made *Elmer Gantry* (United Artists, 1960), tightening the plot by interweaving various episodes of the novel into a unified whole. We first see a roaring drunk Elmer Gantry (Burt Lancaster) weaseling drinks from a barroom crowd by spouting his own brand of religious rhetoric. When he tries to latch on to Sister Sharon Falconer (Jean Simmons) and her traveling ministry, she sees him for the charlatan that he is, but he worms his way into her organization and becomes a big hit with the local yokels on the evangelical circuit. Despite herself, Sharon falls in love with Gantry, and he finally seduces her under the brightly lit cross above her seaside temple. While she is conducting a revival meeting later, the temple catches fire and Sharon is killed, trampled by her flock. Elmer delivers her eulogy before packing up his bags and moving on.

As a character, Elmer has undergone a major change from novel to film. He is no longer a defrocked minister but a snake oil salesman who uses Jesus in his sales pitch. In a conversation with an atheistic newsman (Arthur Kennedy), Gantry confesses that he believes in God and that he sees some goodness in his questionable preaching tactics. His seduction of Lulu (Shirley Jones) is excused by implying that her fall to prostitution was

Guy Kibbee as George Babbitt offers advice to Maxine Doyle as his daughter, Verona, in *Babbitt* (1934).

Josephine Hutchinson as Carol Kennicott and Pat O'Brien as her doctor husband, William, in *I Married a Doctor* (1936), a remake of Sinclair Lewis's *Main Street*.

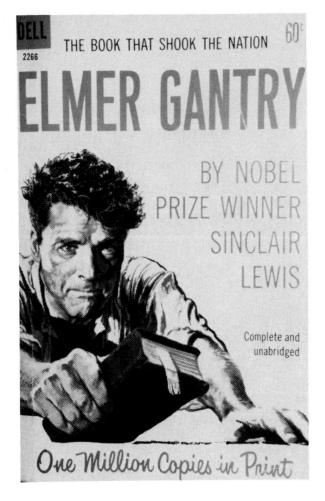

DELL
2266
THE BOOK THAT SHOOK THE NATION   60¢

ELMER GANTRY

BY NOBEL
PRIZE WINNER
SINCLAIR
LEWIS

Complete and
unabridged

One Million Copies in Print

not the seduction itself but because she was the daughter of a hard-line minister. At the end, Elmer is partially redeemed because his love for Sharon was genuine. By inventing a good side to Elmer, who in the novel was an unrelenting hypocrite, and providing an upbeat ending, Brooks undercut the satire inherent in the story.

The changes that Brooks made failed to hurt the film either at the box office or with critics. The *New York Times* said that *Elmer Gantry* had "been lifted from the pages of the justly controversial novel and impressively transformed into an exciting film." If anything, Brooks's screenplay, while missing the biting satire of the novel, tightened the plot considerably, and his frank approach to religion and sex complemented Lewis's own views. Although the moral and social climate had considerably changed since Lewis had written the novel, the studio still feared possible repercussions from the public and thought it prudent for exhibitors to advertise that no one under sixteen would be admitted because some of the scenes and dialogue were of such an adult nature.

Although Lewis continued to churn out books until his death in 1951, *Dodsworth* (1929) was his last important novel. Here he explored the possibility of whether a man could be a builder and also remain artistic and humane. It may well have been the publication of this novel and its critical reception that helped Lewis become the first American to win the Nobel Prize for Literature, awarded in 1930.

It wasn't until 1936, after a successful run on Broadway of Sidney Howard's stage adaptation of Lewis's novel, that Samuel Goldwyn paid $165,000 and turned the directing chores over to William Wyler. Walter Huston was brought in to repeat his stage role as Sam Dodsworth.

Dodsworth (Goldwyn, 1936) followed the structure of the Howard play rather than the book, although both contain the major scenes of the novel. Dodsworth is a reserved and kindly manufacturer who is forced, through the machinations of his scheming social-climbing wife, Fran (Ruth Chatterton), to sell his business and embark on an extended tour of Europe. Where Fran seeks excitement, Dodsworth wants only peace. "You're rushing at old age," she screams at him. Constantly in the company of gigolos and opportunists, she meets a European baron and tells Dodsworth that she wants a divorce. In Italy, Dodsworth again meets Edith Cortright (Mary Astor), an attractive widow, whom he had previously encountered on the ship coming over. Although he falls in love with her, he leaves, but once parted, understands that his life is meaningless without her.

The film omitted some of Lewis's philosophy, especially about life and art, but it remained faithful in its portrayal of Dodsworth. Walter Huston invested Dods-

Paperback movie tie-in for Sinclair Lewis's *Elmer Gantry* (1960), showing Burt Lancaster in the title role for which he would win the Academy Award.

worth with sympathy, humor, irony, and crudity, making him a complex individual in whom the audience could readily believe, prompting the *New York Times* to observe, "Mr. Huston so snugly fits the part we cannot tell where the garment ends and he begins."

In 1933, Lewis published *Ann Vickers*, a story in which the heroine is far more unconventional than Carol Kennicott of *Main Street*. Ann grows up in a small midwestern town, attends an eastern college, and becomes an exponent for women's suffrage. The film *Ann Vickers* (RKO, 1933) picks up the story with Ann (Irene Dunne) already a social worker. She has a brief romantic interlude with Captain Resnick (Bruce Cabot) before his affections toward her cool, and he goes off to war. Once she becomes head of Copperhead Gap Prison, she discovers that the female inhabitants are treated inhumanely and sets out to change things. She meets Judge Barney Dolphin (Walter Huston), who she discovers was responsible for her appointment as superintendent. A romantic relationship develops but ends when the judge is accused and then convicted of various crimes. The film toned down much of the sex and made the relationship between Ann and Barney far more conventional. The reviewer of the *New York Times* commented that although the movie (written by Jane Murfin) was very short—only seventy-five minutes—"little more than a digest of the original work," it "captured more than a mere suggestion of the spirit of the author."

After *Ann Vickers*, Sinclair Lewis produced a string of second-rate novels, among which was *Cass Timberlane* (1945). The film of it (MGM, 1947) is all too predictable. Cass (Spencer Tracy), an idealistic middle-aged Minnesota judge, marries the much younger Jinny Marshland (Lana Turner), a sexpot whom he meets beside a swimming pool. Shunned by her husband's snobbish friends, she turns to rakehell Brad Criley (Zachary Scott) for comfort. After giving birth to a stillborn child, she persuades the judge to accept a position in New York. The judge soon wants to return to his hometown, but she takes up with Criley, who has followed them to the city. Jinny is injured, but her wise and loving husband takes her back.

Since the novel itself had received bad press, the changes made by screenwriter Donald Ogden Stewart were accepted by most film critics. "Mr. Lewis's story of the billing and phooeying of a middle-aged judge with his young and provokingly restless helpmate was so obviously designed for motion picture translation that it couldn't be very much abused," said *Times* critic Bosley Crowther.

A few other works of Lewis also reached the screen. In 1930, *Let's Play King* appeared as a three-part installment in *Cosmopolitan*. It was a minor effort that

Ruth Chatterton and Walter Huston as Fran and Sam Dodsworth take a hard look at their marriage in *Dodsworth* (1936).

Walter Huston as Barney Dolphin in *Ann Vickers* (1933).

81

Irene Dunne (right) in the title role speaks to some concerned citizens (including Jane Darwell, second left, and Arthur Hoyt) about the woman's prison of which she is in charge in *Ann Vickers* (1933).

Clara Bow as Alverna Easter, the married flapper, and Percy Marmont as Ralph Prescott, the woman-hating divorce lawyer, in Sinclair Lewis's *Mantrap* (1926).

turned up the following year as a slight film comedy called *Newly Rich* (aka *Forbidden Adventure*, Paramount, 1931), about two child actors who, while in Europe with their feuding moms, rescue a boy king. In 1938, Lewis collaborated on a play with Fay Wray, *Angela Is 22*, which became *This Is the Life* (Universal, 1944), a romance about a young girl (Susanna Foster) who has a crush on an older man (Patric Knowles) and follows him to New York. The man turns out still to be in love with his ex-wife, to whom he is ultimately reunited, and the girl is paired with the teenage performer (Donald O'Connor) who has loved her throughout and whose scheming has set things right.

The same year that Sinclair Lewis published *Main Street*, 1920, F. Scott Fitzgerald, age twenty-three, published his first novel, *This Side of Paradise*. In a career that seemed to mirror the times, booming in the twenties and skidding during the thirties, Fitzgerald would become the spokesman for the Jazz Age, a man immersed in his times yet able to view them objectively.

While the structure of *This Side of Paradise*, embedded with poems, plays, and short stories, made it unsuitable for adaptation, his second novel, *The Beautiful and the Damned* (1922), his bleakest and most cynical work, was constructed along more traditional lines. The film of it (Warner Bros., 1922) was produced before the story even reached the stores as a novel—it had first been published in an abridged form in *Mademoiselle* in 1921.

Patricia Morison as Alverna Easter has her arm around Akim Tamiroff as her husband, Joe, while Ray Milland as Dr. William Crawford is being hauled away in *Untamed* (1940), an adaptation of Lewis's *Mantrap*.

Adapted by Olga Printzlau, it opens on a light note, documenting the wild life of the generation of Anthony and Gloria Patch (Kenneth Harlan and Marie Prevost). There is a great deal of drinking and dancing and a little bit of slapstick, all without sermonizing. The sermons, however, delivered in heavy-handed titles, arrive in the second half. The hero goes broke, he drinks even more—and this time not just for the fun of it—and his wife waxes sentimental about their third wedding anniversary. Then they inherit several million dollars and sail for Europe. On board ship, Anthony says, "Gloria, darling, I'll try to be worthy of our good fortune and you."

The *New York Times* found that the story "fails to satisfy as entertainment and means nothing." Fitzgerald himself told one friend that if he wanted a good laugh, he should go see it, and to another he wrote that it was "by far the worst movie I've ever seen in my life—cheap, vulgar, ill-constructed, and shoddy."

After several false starts, Fitzgerald wrote *The Great Gatsby* (1925), arguably his finest work and one of America's great novels. Nick Carraway narrates the story of Jay Gatsby, who believes that riches are the way to capture the girl of his dreams, socialite Tom Buchanan's wife, Daisy. At first, Nick disapproves of Gatsby, who gives lavish parties in his garish mansion, but he finally comes to learn that Gatsby was "worth the whole

Jonathan Hale as Doctor Plum with the help of Sarah Padden as the housekeeper tries giving advice to Donald O'Connor as his son, Jimmy, in *This Is the Life* (1944), based on the play *Angela Is 22*, which Sinclair Lewis cowrote with actress Fay Wray.

damned bunch put together." Gatsby's greatness lies in his capacity for illusion, his singleminded, fanatical desire to see Daisy as he wants her to be rather than as she really is, a self-centered, materialistic, shallow woman. Gatsby's inability to separate the ideal from reality leads to his death.

The first dramatization of the novel was written by Owen Davis and directed for Broadway by George Cukor. Opening in February of 1926, the play ran for 112 performances, and its success encouraged Famous Players to offer $50,000 for the screen rights, which Fitzgerald promptly accepted. The result was *The Great Gatsby* (Paramount, 1926).

Showing more care than inspiration, the script by Becky Gardiner from an adaptation by Elizabeth Meehan retained much of the plot of the novel. Gatsby (Warner Baxter) gives parties where most people who attend do not know him or care to. Daisy (Lois Wilson), who had been in love with Gatsby before he went to war, has married Tom Buchanan (Hale Hamilton). When she learns that Gatsby has returned, she uses Nick Carraway (Neil Hamilton) to meet him again. As Daisy drives herself and Gatsby home after confronting Tom, she runs over Myrtle (Georgia Hale), Tom's mistress, killing her. Taking the blame for the accident, Gatsby is shot by Wilson (William Powell), Myrtle's husband.

Certain incidents undercut the characters. For one, Wilson in the film is a chauffeur instead of a mechanic, and as played by William Powell, he projected a far more sophisticated demeanor than the Wilson of the novel. It is much harder to believe that the film's Wilson could be tricked into killing Gatsby as in the novel. Some of the actions of the other characters also are difficult to accept. Daisy, upset and disappointed, seeks solace by drinking absinthe, consuming enough to knock out three ordinary people, yet she appears only mildly intoxicated and quickly recovers. At one of his parties, Gatsby tosses gold $20 pieces in the swimming pool where a number of girls dive for the money. While the scene is not in the novel, it might have worked had Gatsby been allowed to appear a little bored, but instead he watches with a good deal of interest, even excitement.

Each change by itself might not have hurt the film, but taken together they caused considerable damage. Added to these problems was another, even greater one: the film lacked subtlety. So much depended upon the observances of Nick—the "I" of the novel—and these are not to be found in this film.

The first sound version of *The Great Gatsby* (Paramount, 1949) encountered a harsh critical reception, especially in its choice of Alan Ladd for the lead. Bosley Crowther felt that "most of the tragic implications and bitter ironies of Mr. Fitzgerald's work have gone by the board." As for Ladd, Crowther said that the actor was "quite in accordance with that stock character he usually plays." Manny Farber in *The Nation* said of Ladd: "An electric, gaudily graceful figure in action movies, here he has to stand still and project turbulent feeling, succeeding chiefly in giving the impression of an isinglass baby-face in the process of melting." In retrospect, Ladd seems perfectly fit to play Jay Gatsby, a man full of youthful disillusionment yet exuding a quiet gentility, a man who is tough yet vulnerable, a man who is melancholy yet hopeful. Ladd captured these qualities far better than Warner Baxter who preceded him and Robert Redford who followed him.

As the film opens, Gatsby and his two henchmen, Myron Lupus (Ed Begley) and Kilpspringer (Elisha Cook Jr.), drive into West Egg where he selects a mansion. Inspecting the place, he walks through the cavernous rooms that dwarf him. Standing with Lupus on the balcony, Gatsby tells him of an affair he had years before with Daisy (Betty Field), who now lives across the bay. Gatsby throws one of his parties and invites Nick Carraway (Macdonald Carey) to whom he tells various lies about his background. "Now that you've met me, what do you think of me?" he asks Nick. Then occurs a flashback, not found in either of the other two film versions. Jimmy Gatz (later to become Jay Gatsby) befriends Dan Cody (Henry Hull), who then takes the young man on a cruise around the world during which Cody's wife makes a pass at Jimmy. This amuses the older man. He tells Jimmy that his wife will never leave him because he has money and Gatz has none. "Money is the only thing that counts," says Cody. Armed with this philosophy, Gatsby begins his pursuit of Daisy.

In the meantime, Nick discovers from Jordan Baker (Ruth Hussey) that during the war before being shipped overseas Gatsby had an affair with Daisy. Daisy later married wealthy Tom Buchanan (Barry Sullivan), who has recently begun an affair with Myrtle Wilson (Shelley Winters). Eager to receive help from any quarter, Gatsby buys Jordan a roadster the same size and color as Daisy's, hoping she will set up a clandestine meeting between him and Daisy. When Gatsby finally goes to take Daisy away, Tom confronts him by saying, "Look here, old sport, Daisy doesn't love you. She has loved me since eleven years ago."

On the trip back to Long Island, Myrtle sees the roadster, and believing it is her lover, rushes out to flag it down. Daisy, who is behind the wheel, accidentally runs her over but keeps on going. Gatsby is determined to accept the responsibility for the accident. Only when he hears Daisy agree with Tom that she will let Gatsby take the blame are his illusions destroyed. When he nobly still insists on taking responsibility, Nick asks why. "Daisy can't help being Daisy," says Gatsby. Nick then tells Gatsby, "You are a gentleman, the only one I know."

Betty Field as Daisy, Alan Ladd as Gatsby, and Barry Sullivan as Tom Buchanan in *The Great Gatsby* (1949), the initial sound version of Fitzgerald's classic.

Thinking Gatsby is responsible for the death of his wife, Wilson (Howard Da Silva) arrives on the scene and shoots Gatsby, who stumbles forward and falls into the swimming pool. Only Nick and Jordan attend the funeral, and afterward she agrees to accompany Nick back to his midwest home.

Much of this film, including some of the dialogue, is lifted straight from the novel, but two points of departure weaken this adaptation by Cyril Hume and Richard Maibaum. The first is the lack of Nick's narration. In the novel he offered many insights into characters and events; here there are none. The second is the relationship between Nick and Jordan. In the book it ends badly because Nick, unlike Gatsby, is able to see a woman for who she actually is rather than who he wants her to be. The studio demanded a happy ending of sorts, and if it couldn't have one with Gatsby and Daisy, it would have one with Nick and Jordan. These deficiencies, however, fail to keep this from being a taut ninety-two minute adaptation.

The most recent *Great Gatsby* (Paramount, 1974), directed by Jack Clayton, was universally castigated by critics. "The language is right, even the chunks of exposition that have sometimes been turned into dialogue," said *New York Times* critic Vincent Canby. "The sets and costumes and most of the performances are exceptionally good, but the movie itself is as lifeless as a body that's been too long at the bottom of a swimming pool." Rich colors, superb photography, and a truly believable 1920s atmosphere were undercut by a script

that poured on romantic nostalgia and missed all the subtleties of Fitzgerald's novel.

Originally, Paramount hired Truman Capote to write the screenplay, but his final draft portrayed Nick as a swishy homosexual and Jordan as a repulsive lesbian, which, had the studio used it, would certainly abort the romantic relationship that developed between the pair in the 1949 film version. The final script by Francis Ford Coppola showed a fidelity to Fitzgerald. In this version Nick (Sam Waterston) once again becomes the narrator of Gatsby's (Robert Redford) attempts to win Daisy (Mia Farrow), allowing the film to incorporate great chunks of the text through voice-over narration.

Fitzgerald once told fellow writer Edmund Wilson that he had no feeling or knowledge of the relationship between Gatsby and Daisy from the time of their reunion to the death of Myrtle. In the novel, this gap is used to cover Gatsby's early years, including his brief love affair with Daisy and his relationship with Dan Cody. The 1974 film contains one flashback to Louisville during the war, but the whole section with Dan Cody has been dropped, replaced by scenes of Gatsby and Daisy having a picnic, holding hands, kissing—all in romantic soft focus like a television commercial for tampons. Yet the film fails to communicate any passion between the lovers.

The first television *Gatsby* was in 1955, adapted by Alvin Sapinsley and starring Robert Montgomery, Phyllis Kirk (as Daisy), Lee Bowman (as Nick), and Gena Rowlands (as Jordan). The next was three years later on

Mia Farrow and Robert Redford as Daisy and Jay in a romantically
soft-focused shot from the second remake of *The Great Gatsby*
(1974).

Playhouse 90. David Shaw did the adaptation, and Robert Ryan, Jeanne Crain, and Rod Taylor starred.

Much of Fitzgerald's work was autobiographical in nature, including one of his best short stories, "Babylon Revisited" (1931), which became the big Technicolor production, *The Last Time I Saw Paris* (MGM, 1954), directed by Richard Brooks and starring Elizabeth Taylor and Van Johnson. In a few phrases, Fitzgerald evoked a feeling of the end of the twenties, but the glossy film extends his story far beyond what is prudent, turning the whole thing into a romantic soap opera. The sound track is constantly filled with syrupy renditions of the Jerome Kern melody that supplied the title of the film. MGM claimed that Fitzgerald's story "inspired" the film, which seems a polite way to say that the studio threw out most of Fitzgerald and substituted its patented brand of suds.

Fitzgerald's last important work, a long, introspective novel, *Tender Is the Night* (1934), told of a psychiatrist who marries one of his schizophrenic patients. The film (20th Century-Fox, 1961), directed by Henry King from a screenplay by Ivan Moffat, and starring Jennifer Jones and Jason Robards, proved to be fitfully faithful, but too much of the interior action was missing. A six-hour television adaptation of *Tender Is the Night* (teleplay by Dennis Potter, Showtime Entertainment, BBC-TV, Seven Network Australia, 1985), while superior to the theatrical film, was burdened by excessive length, which included an entire early section that was not part of the novel. Peter Strauss and Mary Steenburgen starred.

During the last year of his life, Fitzgerald managed to steal enough time between working on screenplays to begin a novel, *The Last Tycoon* (1941). Unfinished at the time of his death, it was published posthumously in fragmentary form. Its protagonist, Monroe Stahr, based on MGM's Irving Thalberg, is a poor boy from New York who has risen to become the head of a Hollywood studio, which he tries to run single-handedly by his talent and personal magnetism.

In the 1950s, both *Robert Montgomery Presents* and *Playhouse 90* presented live productions of *The Last Tycoon* (with Montgomery himself and Jack Palance, respectively, in the leads), but there was simply not enough story to carry a feature film (Paramount, 1976), especially one that ran over two hours. The novel was narrated by a woman character, Cecilia Brady (Theresa Russell), but the film relegates her to a supporting role as she romantically pursues Stahr (Robert De Niro).

Stahr himself is the real force in the film. In his final notes on the novel, Fitzgerald wrote, "Action is Character," but the character of Stahr (né Thalberg) is far from the flamboyant movie czar usually envisioned by the public. Rather he is a quiet, polite businessman. The Harold Pinter screenplay followed Stahr through his dealings with a neurotic matinee idol (Tony Curtis), a

Jason Robards as the psychiatrist and Jennifer Jones as his mentally unstable wife in *Tender Is the Night* (1962).

Robert De Niro as studio production chief Monroe Stahr gets an earful from Tony Curtis as egotistical actor Rodriguez in *The Last Tycoon* (1976).

Robert Mitchum as studio head Pat Brady in *The Last Tycoon* (1976).

rival studio boss (Robert Mitchum) who happens to be Cecilia's father, and a union organizer (Jack Nicholson). Along the way he becomes enamored of an English actress (Ingrid Boulting) to whom he attempts unsuccessfully to make love. But, without an end, the film, directed by Elia Kazan, drifts to an ambiguous conclusion in which little is resolved.

Three separate entries attempted to explore Fitzgerald's own life, which often sounded like one of his own novels. *Beloved Infidel* (20th Century-Fox, 1959) was Sheilah Graham's wildly popular account of her time spent with Fitzgerald (Gregory Peck), a film written by Sy Bartlett that critic Penelope Houston called "catastrophically misguided."

F. Scott Fitzgerald and "The Last of the Belles" (teleplay by James Costigan, ABC, Titus Productions, 1974) successfully integrated a part of the life of Fitzgerald (Richard Chamberlain) with one of his stories, "The Last of the Belles," a semifictional account of his first meeting with his wife, Zelda (Blythe Danner). Portions of Fitzgerald's story were enacted by Susan Sarandon and David Huffman. A sequel, *F. Scott Fitzgerald in Hollywood* (teleplay by James Costigan, ABC, Titus Productions, 1976), this time starring Jason Miller and Tuesday Weld as Scott and Zelda, was a biopic without the advantage of a story adaptation to add a needed spark of originality.

As Sinclair Lewis became the spokesman for the middle class, and F. Scott Fitzgerald for the Jazz Age, so Ernest Hemingway (1899–1961) spoke for the Lost Generation, those expatriates who were set adrift by World War One and struggled to find a meaning to their lives. A six-hour television production called *Hemingway* (teleplay by Arthur Hopcraft, Daniel Wilson Productions, 1988) attempted to tell the life of the author (played by Stacy Keach) from 1925 through 1961. While his adventurous life and stormy relationships were at its core, the script also emphasized that many of the stories and novels of Hemingway's were frankly autobiographical.

On the very first adaptation of *A Farewell to Arms* (Paramount, 1932), Ernest Hemingway discovered an inalienable truth about the movie industry: the purpose of a motion picture is to earn the greatest possible profit. The experience was a bitter one for the author. The studio advertised the film as "Ernest Hemingway's world famous story of two who began in passion's reckless abandon with a love that grew until it heeded neither shame, nor danger, nor death." Another studio brochure claimed it was "the most tumultuous, passionate romance yet written or screened! The mad mating of two souls lost for love's sake to the thunder of a world gone mad." A recurrent slogan for the ad campaign ran, "As you read it in the novel, you'll see it on the screen," but the mere fact that the advertisements stressed the romantic aspects of the novel said otherwise. *A Farewell to Arms* might loosely be based on the 1929 novel (as adapted by Benjamin Glazer and Oliver H. P. Garrett), but it was going to be, according to the Hollywood definition, "a woman's picture."

The studio and director Frank Borzage's intentions are best seen in a comparison of the conclusions of the novel and the film. The book ends with Catherine's (Helen Hayes) death. Avoiding any hint at sentimentality, Frederic (Gary Cooper) relates the incident unemotionally, telling the nurses to get out so that he can be alone with her. However, Borzage, utilizing a Wagnerian score and romantic artiness, wanted his audience to weep. In fact, he and the studio were so concerned that Hemingway's ending would keep people away that they gave the story an ambivalent, happy ending. As Cather-

Gary Cooper as Frederic and Helen Hayes as Catherine, the lovers
in *A Farewell to Arms* (1932).

Akim Tamiroff as Pablo, the partisan fighter, offers up a piece of bread, but Ingrid Bergman as Maria and Gary Cooper as Robert Jordan are more interested in each other in *For Whom the Bell Tolls* (1943).

ine lies in the bed, Frederic sits beside her, leaning close, and they vow that they will never part. Catherine almost expires, but suddenly outside church bells chime, doves flutter by the window, crowds cheer. With the sudden infusion of new hope, Catherine revives and is able to smile. "Armistice," says Frederic. "Peace," she answers. The happy lovers move in so their faces touch, and they hold it so while the scene dissolves and "The End" appears on the screen.

Frank Borzage had some doubts about this happy ending, and he filmed a second one, different only in the final moments. Catherine dies just as the bells toll. Frederic lifts her from the bed, the bedsheets caught around her in lavish folds, and he carries her to the window where bright light streams through. "Peace . . . Peace," Frederic utters. Despite having Catherine die, this ending is still far removed from Hemingway's intention. It is played for sentimentality and for tears.

Hemingway was seriously worried that people, after seeing the film, would not want to read his novel, but it was rereleased twice and continued to make money until

Lauren Bacall and Humphrey Bogart clinch in the most famous version of Hemingway's *To Have and Have Not* (1944).

Lobby card for *The Breaking Point* (1950), the first remake and much more faithful version of *To Have and Have Not*.

World War Two dated the material. On the other hand, the novel did not date, and Hemingway was constantly amazed that people continued to read it long after the film had run its course.

In November of 1955, Hemingway learned by telegram from David O. Selznick that he had purchased the rights to *A Farewell to Arms*. Other than the fact that Selznick would recall all the television prints of the Borzage version, Hemingway benefited very little; he wasn't even going to get paid any more.

Selznick hired Ben Hecht to do the script, and the first draft was very close to Hemingway's novel. Selznick didn't like it, and demanded a revision. Successive revisions followed, each one drifting further from Hemingway. Selznick had no compunctions about emasculating the book, claiming that while Hemingway was a great writer, he was no movie producer, and gave John Huston the job of directing his (Selznick's) version (20th Century-Fox, 1957). Like Borzage before him, Huston saw his job as taking a very sophisticated novel and turning it into a vehicle for mass consumption. Although styles had changed and Hollywood no longer made "a woman's picture"—at least the studios did not admit to the practice—Selznick zeroed in on the love story and added spectacle.

The scene where Catherine gives the St. Anthony

Ava Gardner (in the first of her three Hemingway movies) and Burt Lancaster (in his screen debut) in a flashback sequence in *The Killers* (1946), a scene not in Hemingway's original short story.

91

medal to Frederic is an excellent example of how the screenplay introduced spectacle. In the novel, the scene takes place on the steps of the hospital. In the Selznick film, it occurs in a large village square jammed with townspeople who are sending off the troops for the great offensive. Whole regiments of troops and military vehicles lumber past. Frederic (Rock Hudson) keeps searching the crowd for a glimpse of Catherine (Jennifer Jones). At last he sees her white nurse's headdress amid the throng. They embrace and kiss. Quickly Frederic hurries back to his ambulance with Catherine calling after him: "I'll be waiting! I'll be waiting!"

In one of a myriad of memos to John Huston (who claimed to be "memoed" to distraction and left the project, which Charles Vidor took over), Selznick wrote that the film had to have, "Love, Love, Love." The novel didn't have enough, so he instructed screenwriter Hecht to construct new scenes for Frederic and Catherine. In this way, Selznick's version was no different in intent than Borzage's version; it was only bigger.

Of all of Hemingway's works, the most cinematic in terms of style is *For Whom the Bell Tolls* (1940). First, the point of view often shifts rapidly and cleanly just as a film cuts from one scene to the next. Within the same scene, the viewpoint often shifts from the objective to the subjective, just as a camera might do. In addition, the chapters are intercut with one another. The novel opens with Jordan and Anselmo on a mountain slope looking down at the bridge to be blown. Three pages later, Jordan recalls the night before when he met with General Golz to discuss the mission. Jordan sends a messenger to the general to call it off because the Fascists have learned of their plans. Chapters thirty-three through forty-two cut back and forth between the guerrilla band and scenes of Andres trying to get through the Republican lines.

In September of 1940, Hemingway met and became friends with Gary Cooper. Although still with bitter feelings toward *A Farewell to Arms*, Hemingway nevertheless suggested that he would like to see Cooper as the lead in a film version of *For Whom The Bell Tolls*. Soon afterward, Cooper was instrumental in Paramount purchasing the book for $150,000 and assigning Dudley Nichols to write the screenplay. Cecil B. DeMille was set to direct, but he pulled out, and Sam Wood (who had just directed Cooper in *The Pride of the Yankees*) took over. Filming began in late 1942 with Vera Zorina as Maria and with the Sierra Nevada standing in for Spain. Zorina ultimately was replaced by Ingrid Bergman.

Perhaps because Hemingway's novel is so cinematic, *For Whom the Bell Tolls* (Paramount, 1943) is one of the more faithful adaptations of the author's work, including the ending where Jordan (Cooper) dies. In fact, much of the dialogue is lifted straight from the novel. The film did make compromises. The more intimate love scenes were deleted because they would never have passed the Hays Office. Also, various references to the Catholic Church and to Spain were excised because of studio fears of political repercussions.

Despite the faithfulness of the film, which originally ran 170 minutes (current versions are only 130 minutes), many reviewers of the day found fault with it. James Agee, in *The Nation,* said, "The rhythm of this film is the most defective I have ever seen in a super production . . . color is very nice for costume pieces and musical comedies, and has a great aesthetic future in films, but it still gets fatally in the way of any serious imitation of reality." Bosley Crowther wrote in the *New York Times*, "Gary Cooper as Robert Jordan and Ingrid Bergman as Maria are fine, though limited in their opportunities."

In retrospect, the film has aged particularly well, especially in light of other wartime propaganda movies. If the characters don't always go the full distance that Hemingway intended, they go far enough to make us believe in them.

In the fifties, a two-part adaptation of *For Whom the Bell Tolls* was produced for television's *Playhouse 90*, directed by John Frankenheimer from a script by frequent Hemingway adapter A. E. Hotchner. Jason Robards and Maria Schell played Jordan and Maria, in a cast that also included Eli Wallach and Maureen Stapleton.

While *For Whom the Bell Tolls* is among Hemingway's finest works, *To Have and Have Not* (1937) ranks with his worst. Director Howard Hawks once told the story of how he came to film *To Have and Have Not* (Warner Bros., 1944). He and Hemingway were hunting together when he told the author that he (Hawks) could take his worst story and make a movie out of it. Hemingway then asked Hawks what was his worst book. "*To Have and Have Not*," Hawks replied. Hemingway stated that he didn't believe that Hawks could make a film out of it, but if he wanted to try, go ahead . . .

Hawks disliked the novel so much that he threw it out and replaced it with a script by William Faulkner and Jules Furthman. Only a few scenes and incidents remain from the book, the most notable being the opening where Johnson (Walter Sande) tries to cheat Morgan (Humphrey Bogart) out of the money he owes for chartering Morgan's boat.

After the opening sequence, the film plays like another version of *Casablanca*. Even the setting was changed from Florida to Martinique. No matter. Whether the decision was Hawks and Hemingway's or Faulkner and Furthman's, it proved to be the right one. The script was far better than the novel, and while the finished product may have contained little Hemingway, it proved to be classic Hawks, but is best remembered for bringing Bogart and Lauren Bacall together.

Soon after finishing *To Have and Have Not*, Bogart was approached by Ranald MacDougall, one of the studio's writers, and asked if he would be interested in playing Harry Morgan in another film using material left untouched by Hawks. Although Bogart expressed interest, the studio didn't, and the project lapsed for a number of years before being revived as *The Breaking Point* (Warner Bros., 1950), one of the most intelligent adaptations of a Hemingway work.

MacDougall's script changed the location to Newport Beach, California, and a small, unnamed town on the Mexican coast. There is a crime, but nothing the law cannot handle. Essentially the story is about a charter boat captain who falls in with crooks but turns against them when they kill his friend. The script also changed the character of Harry Morgan (John Garfield) to make him more sympathetic. Unlike the novel where the hero cares very little for his children, Morgan is a loving, devoted family man whose head is turned by a vixen. At one point in the book, Morgan is wounded and his left arm amputated, but the film forgoes such an antiromantic incident. The end of the novel has Morgan on the way to the hospital where he dies. The film's ending is more ambiguous. Morgan kills a man in self-defense but is wounded himself. As he is taken away to the hospital, his wife tells the children that their father will be fine.

Despite tampering with the original story, the script remained as faithful as possible. If the characters are not quite the ones that Hemingway created, they are as close as any film would come. Hemingway himself said he thought the movie was pretty good.

To Have and Have Not reappeared once more as *The Gun Runners* (United Artists, 1958), a moderately effective action melodrama directed by Don Siegel. In an effort to keep somewhat true to the Hemingway novel, Siegel wanted the hero (this time played by Audie Murphy) to die in the end, but producer Clarence Greene, who had the final say on the script, was a believer in the old school of screenwriting that preferred invincible heroes who survived. Siegel did the best he could considering the warmed-over material.

Ernest Hemingway claimed that of all the movies based on his works, he liked *The Killers* (Universal, 1946) best. In later years, Hemingway would haul out a projector and show the film to friends, but he always fell asleep after the first reel. That was because ten minutes into it, his short story had run its course and a studio script carried the plot forward. But those ten minutes may well be the finest Hemingway ever to reach the screen, a black and white *film noir* with dialogue lifted straight from the story. (It also had newcomer Burt

Lee Marvin as one of the hit men carrying out his assignment in the remake of *The Killers* (1964).

Lancaster in his film debut.) "There is nothing unique or even valuable about the picture," wrote James Agee in *Time*, "but energy combined with attention to form and detail doesn't turn up every day; neither does good entertainment."

There wasn't enough material in the Hemingway short story to make a complete feature film, but director Robert Siodmak and screenwriter Mark Hellinger fashioned a taut, dark thriller that owed more to Cornell Woolrich than Ernest Hemingway. Still, the initial ten minutes are pure Hemingway—and, even if the rest of the film had been a disaster, which it wasn't, those ten minutes were worth the price of admission.

Anyone who saw the remake of *The Killers* (Universal, 1964) would wonder where the Hemingway went. There is a scene at the beginning in which two killers (Lee Marvin and Clu Gulager) enter a home for the blind and shoot one of the teachers. The victim is very calm about his death. Otherwise, any resemblance to the short story disappears, and the plot, concocted by Gene L. Coon, follows a similar line to the 1946 version. As an adaptation of a Hemingway short story, the film (with Ronald Reagan in his last movie—as a vicious crime kingpin) was a complete misfire.

Among Hemingway's most noted short stories is also "The Short, Happy Life of Francis Macomber" (1938), the story of Macomber, his wife Margot, and the white hunter Wilson who are thrown together on a safari. Wilson and Margot have a quick, dispassionate, and

Gregory Peck as Robert Wilson, the white hunter, and Joan Bennett and Robert Preston as Margaret and Francis Macomber in *The Macomber Affair* (1946), an adaptation of "The Short, Happy Life of Francis Macomber."

One-sheet for *Under My Skin* (1950), adapted from Hemingway's "My Old Man."

mechanical affair, and in the end, the wife kills Macomber just as he discovers his courage.

In the movie, *The Macomber Affair* (United Artists, 1947), Wilson (Gregory Peck) and Margot (Joan Bennett) fall in love, although it is late in the film before Wilson admits this, even to himself. He has gone off with Macomber (Robert Preston) to kill the wounded buffalo. Up to this point, the film has followed the story closely, even using Hemingway's dialogue. But now, as a sop to Hollywood formula, love rears its ugly head. The two men pause. "You've fallen in love with her, haven't you?" asks Macomber. "Yes, I have," answers Wilson. "All I want is an even break," replies Macomber. They shake hands and plunge into the brush after their quarry.

The film returns to Hemingway's story for the shooting. As the buffalo charges Macomber, Margot fires her rifle, killing her husband. Then the scene shifts to Nairobi where Wilson must write his report. Even he is not sure whether Margot shot her husband by accident or murdered him.

The short story concludes minutes after the shooting. While Hemingway's ending is perfectly suited to the printed page, it would not have worked on the screen; it was too sudden, too abrupt, which was often the problem of Hemingway's fiction as far as the movies were concerned. However, the ending of the film, while fulfilling Hollywood's needs, was properly ambiguous and in keeping with Hemingway's intent. Minutes before the inquest begins, Wilson tries to assure Margot that she will get through the ordeal, but she walks into the courtroom alone. Fade out. Credits.

The critics were generally favorable. In *Time*, James Agee wrote, "The best movie job on Hemingway to date." London's *Daily Mail* said, "It has survived the hazardous crossing from brilliant short story to film with practically no casualties." Over the years, the story of the white hunter and his women has become something of a cliché, but good writing, solid acting, and competent direction lifted this film above the ordinary. As a film and as an adaptation (by Casey Robinson) of a Hemingway short story, *The Macomber Affair* has aged well.

Hollywood must have thought that Hemingway missed obvious opportunities to heighten the melodramatic elements of his plots, opportunities Hollywood would not miss. A perfect example is "My Old Man" (1923). A boy's jockey father is killed in a steeplechase, and after the accident, the youngster overhears a conversation between two men who imply that his father was a crook who "had it coming to him."

The Jean Negulesco movie, *Under My Skin* (20th Century-Fox, 1950), elaborated on the father's involvement with underworld gamblers, and in stretching the story to a feature film, screenwriter Casey Robinson also included a love affair for the jockey (John Garfield). The jockey's reformation, the sentimental love affair, and the trite ending make this a hokey drama at best, and Hemingway all but disappears.

In a television production of *My Old Man* (teleplay by Jerome Kass, CBS, Robert Halmi Productions, 1979), the boy becomes a girl (Kristy McNichol) and the father (Warren Oates) a horse trainer rather than a jockey. Other changes contributed to undermining the Hemingway short story until little of the original is recognizable.

While most of Hemingway's stories and novels failed as adaptations, *The Snows of Kilimanjaro* (20th Century-Fox, 1952), advertised by the studio as "Hemingway's greatest love story," works well under Henry King's sure direction. The strong script by Casey Robinson moved beyond the bounds of the original 1938 short story and extended the action to include various tales from the Hemingway persona. King said of the story and script, "You couldn't tell where Hemingway's quit and Robinson's began. He developed a Hemingway style, drew a little bit on everything Hemingway had written."

The film, with Gregory Peck starring with two leading ladies—Susan Hayward and Ava Gardner—came in for its share of negative reviews. *Newsweek* wrote, "The succinct and vivid qualities associated with Hemingway are rarely evoked, and what has been substituted is for the most part meandering, pretentious and more or less maudlin romance." Hemingway himself complained that the film should have been entitled "The Snows of Zanuck." In retrospect, during its best moments *The*

Gregory Peck as Harry with his two leading ladies, Ava Gardner as Cynthia and Susan Hayward as Helen, in *The Snows of Kilimanjaro* (1952).

The stellar cast of *The Sun Also Rises* (1957): Eddie Albert, Errol Flynn, Mel Ferrer, Tyrone Power, and Ava Gardner.

Spencer Tracy prepares to fight the elements in *The Old Man and the Sea* (1958).

Snows of Kilimanjaro, despite much tampering that includes the addition of a happy ending, evokes a feeling of Hemingway.

On the surface, the film *The Sun Also Rises* (20th Century-Fox, 1957), with a screenplay by Peter Viertel, tells the same story as the 1926 novel, and on this level, it is one of the better Hemingway adaptations. On other levels, it misses completely. The film received favorable reviews, but it has not aged well. The young Bohemians of the novel became middle-age businessmen who wear nice clothes and have plenty of money. Lady Brett (Ava Gardner, in her third Hemingway movie) continually looks as if she has dressed for a 1950s fashion show rather than for 1920s Paris. Also, the film ignored the themes of the novel. To Hemingway, the fishing trip is important in defining the character of Jake (Tyrone Power), but it is only a minor episode in the film. The whole bullfighting sequence, which is the moral center of the book, is truncated; the Hays Office wouldn't allow bloodletting to be shown on-screen. Thus the film, like the novel, has both fishing and bullfighting, but unlike the book, it misses the emotional and thematic content of these scenes. This is especially true of the ending. Brett asks, "Darling, there must be an answer for us somewhere," and Jake, the impotent hero, replies, "I'm sure there is." In the book, far more pessimistic, Jake merely says, "Isn't it pretty to think so."

Hemingway was dissatisfied with most films made from his works, and *The Sun Also Rises* was no exception. "It's all pretty disappointing, and that's being gracious," he said. The majority of critics tended to agree with the author. Stanley Kauffmann, writing in *The New Republic*, said, "[The film] is a remarkably faithful transcription of its source. Yet Hemingway has been lost." The most biting review came from Robert Hatch in *The Nation*,

96

who said: "They should have done Ernest Hemingway the courtesy of putting another title on *The Sun Also Rises*—something like *The Nymph and the Masochists* would get the idea across better. . . . The picture is not only not Hemingway's novel, it is not much of a story on its own terms."

A four-hour, two-part television "expansion" of *The Sun Also Rises* (teleplay by Robert L. Joseph, NBC, 20th Century-Fox Television, 1984) created additional characters and events, but the story of Jake (Hart Bochner) and Lady Brett (Jane Seymour) sank under a barrage of extraneous plot complications. Producer-writer Robert Joseph excused his teleplay by saying, "This is the way Papa Hemingway would have written it for TV, I'm sure."

Peter Viertel's screenplay for *The Old Man and the Sea* (Warner Bros., 1958) also stuck closely to the 1952 Hemingway novel, focusing on the quest of the aging Cuban fisherman (Spencer Tracy) who has gone eighty-four days without a catch. Because he has lost his luck, the old man becomes the butt of jokes among the younger fisherman. Only a young boy (Felipe Pazos) gives the old man any support and encouragement. Undaunted by his failure, the old man continues to go out on his boat alone each morning. Finally, he hooks a big marlin, which drags him far out to sea.

The bulk of *The Old Man and the Sea* is the pursuit of the marlin and the old man's attempt to bring it back home; therefore, Spencer Tracy is the only one on-screen for most of the time. His voice-over narration fills in the thoughts and feelings of the old man, yet it proved difficult to sustain suspense and interest with only one character on-screen for such a long period. In addition, the old man's single-minded struggle soon becomes monotonous, and long stretches of the film are simply boring. Finally, far too much footage was shot on a sound stage, and the scenes so poorly executed that occasionally the audience can see the microphone suspended over the old man and his boat. Even director John Sturges admitted that it was technically the sloppiest picture he ever made. The film died at the box office, and Hemingway had an explanation for its failure. "No picture with a fucking rubber fish ever made a dime," he said. This was before *Jaws*.

A television remake of *The Old Man and the Sea* (teleplay by Roger O. Hirson, NBC, Storke Entertainment, Yorkshire Television, 1990) drifted much further afield than the film, inventing all sorts of extraneous characters and situations. In this version, the old man (Anthony Quinn) has a daughter (Valentina Quinn) who argues that her father is too old and should give up fishing. Also, a writer (Gary Cole) and his wife (Patricia Clarkson), only mentioned in the novel, consume much larger roles.

Hemingway's Adventures of a Young Man (20th Century-Fox, 1962) cannibalized various Hemingway works, specifically parts of *A Farewell to Arms* and various short stories—"Indian Camp," "A Pursuit Race," "The Battler"—in order to make a film about Nick Adams (Richard Beymer). A curious assortment of material, it had no shape, and the material was so badly truncated that it lost all connection with Hemingway. For instance, in the section based on "Indian Camp," Nick is nineteen rather than the ten or eleven as he is in the story; thus, his introduction to the pain of birth and death makes little sense.

In the late 1940s Hemingway began working on a long narrative that appeared posthumously as *Islands in the Stream* (1970). When Denne Bart Petitclerc wrote the screenplay for the film version (Paramount, 1976), he reshaped a large portion of the material until the latter third of the film resembled *To Have and Have Not*. In her review, Pauline Kael said, "In general, the liberties

Anthony Quinn, somewhat more ideally cast, in his television interpretation of *The Old Man and the Sea* (1990).

Richard Beymer as Hemingway's alter ego, Nick Adams, covers the body of a fallen World War I comrade in *Hemingway's Adventures of a Young Man* (1962).

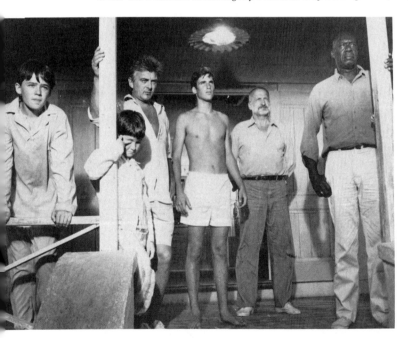

(From left) Michael-James Wixted, Brad Savage, David Hemmings, Hart Bochner, George C. Scott, and Julius Harris have just been awakened by the explosion of an enemy ship in Scott's production of Hemingway's *Islands in the Stream* (1976).

Petitclerc takes with the novel make good sense." Still, she disliked the film and concluded, "*Islands* brings out the worst in Hemingway."

Another Hemingway African story, "Hills Like White Elephants," appeared as part of a trilogy in *Women and Men: Stories of Seduction* (teleplay by Joan Didion and John Gregory Dunne, HBO, David S. Brown Productions, 1990). The twenty-three-minute script remained faithful to Hemingway, which relied heavily on interior action, and emerged as the best of the three stories.

Too often the films based on Hemingway's fiction relied on romance rather than his hard-edge realism. *For Whom the Bell Tolls* came closest to welding the romantic Hemingway with the realistic Hemingway, but too much of the brutality and sexual fire was omitted due to censorship restrictions. Often the parts of a film were better then the whole. *The Killers, The Snows of Kilimanjaro*, and *The Sun Also Rises* each had moments. *To Have and Have Not* may indeed be a classic, but Hemingway has been gutted and thrown away, his title and name the only connections with the novel. *The Macomber Affair* comes closest to capturing Hemingway from beginning to end, and even here, scriptwriter Casey Robinson softened the ending to appease Hollywood tastes.

With *The Sound and the Fury* (1929), William Faulkner (1897–1962) began his radical experimentation with stream of consciousness and subject matter. The tragedy is a family tragedy, the Compson family, told through the perspective of three brothers: Quentin, the oldest, who dreams of incest with his sister Caddy; Jason, who is haunted by self-doubt and guilt; and Benjy, who is mentally retarded and has been castrated after showing signs of sexuality. The action revolves around the sister, Caddy, but the reader never shares her viewpoint, only those of her brothers. Through this self-centered family, Faulkner examined the decline of the traditional South and the rise of the commercial South.

Despite its difficult accessibility, *The Sound and the Fury* remains one of Faulkner's most praised works, but the Martin Ritt film (20th Century-Fox, 1959), although occasionally displaying a Faulkner-like atmosphere, has little connection with the novel. Decadence becomes the order of the day, and characters not only change their personas but also their sex. Caddy (Margaret Leighton)

is a nymphomaniac; Quentin (Joanne Woodward) is her illegitimate daughter; Jason (Yul Brynner) is the stepson who desperately tries to keep the family together. Caddy returns home because she is washed up and needs a place to live, and love-starved Quentin has an affair with a carnival man (Stuart Whitman). After Jason breaks up the affair, Quentin comes to realize that she loves him and refuses to let a little thing like an uncle-niece relationship stand in the way of true happiness.

Little of the novel remains, and what does is certainly not Faulkner. (Irving Ravetch and Harriet Frank Jr. wrote the screenplay.) "Make every allowance for the legitimate needs of screen adaptation," said critic Stanley Kauffmann in *The New Republic*. "Even then, if words mean anything at all, how can this . . . movie of a declining family's regeneration be called a film of Faulkner's work?"

By 1931, Faulkner had already published five novels, none of which had proven very profitable, but with the publication of *Sanctuary* (1931), he had a best-seller, one that caused an uproar throughout the South where

Lobby card for Faulkner's *The Sound and the Fury* (1959).

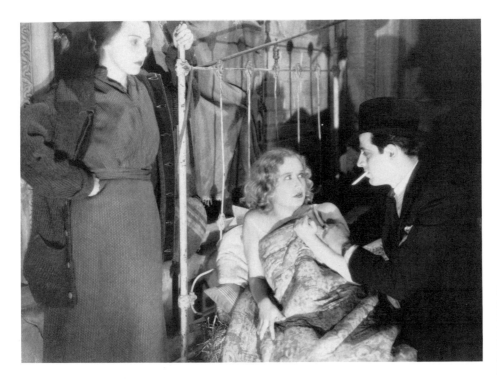

Florence Eldridge as Ruby Lemar stands over the bed as Miriam Hopkins as Temple is threatened by Jack LaRue as Trigger, whom she later shoots in *The Story of Temple Drake* (1933), based on William Faulkner's *Sanctuary*.

outraged literary critics castigated it. Certainly the story is sensational, and Faulkner readily admitted he had written it for money.

His shocking novel was a bombshell in its day, and Hollywood's self-censorship Hays Office warned the studios against attempting it. When Paramount elected to do it anyway, the Hays Office ordered the studio to refrain from using Faulkner's name or the novel's title in the credits. *The Story of Temple Drake* (Paramount, 1933) also holds the dubious distinction of being the main reason that the Roman Catholic Church formed the Legion of Decency a year later.

Seldom seen today, *The Story of Temple Drake* is a surprisingly compelling adaptation by Oliver H. P. Garrett of Faulkner's novel. The wildly hedonistic and virginal Temple Drake (Miriam Hopkins) is kidnapped, raped, and turned into a prostitute by the evil gangster, Trigger (Jack LaRue). Temple soon finds herself enjoying her role in the bordello, but after a falling-out with Trigger, she shoots him. Since his demise is mourned by no one, the killing goes unpunished. Retaining a spark of decency, she then testifies at the trial of a man framed for murder by Trigger.

The remake of this Mississippi-bred Greek tragedy restored Faulkner's title, although *Sanctuary* (20th Century-Fox, 1961), directed by the British Tony Richardson and starring Lee Remick and Yves Montand, drew its story from both the original 1931 novel and its 1950 sequel, *Requiem for a Nun*. Framed around a flashback, the story (adapted by James Poe) was full of degradation and corruption but missed the feeling of Faulkner. The problem was not that the film violated the novels but that the novels were not really very good to begin with. The fact that Faulkner wrote them for a quick buck was evident on the screen where the producers were also after a quick buck.

Pylon, like *Sanctuary,* was lesser Faulkner. Set in New Orleans, *Pylon* tells the story of three barnstorming pilots who defy conventional rules. It became *The Tarnished Angels* (Universal, 1957), written by George Zuckerman and set at Mardi Gras during the early Depression days. Flier Roger Shumann (Robert Stack), his wife LaVerne (Dorothy Malone), and their young son come to participate in an air show, along with their mechanic, Jiggs (Jack Carson). Reporter Burke Devlin (Rock Hudson) is assigned to write some stories about the family, and at first he is cynical about their lifestyle. As he becomes intertwined in their lives, the reporter comes to suspect that Jiggs rather than Roger Shumann is the boy's real father. When Roger's plane is grounded, he sends his wife to bed Matt Ord (Robert Middleton), an obese old man who owns an experimental plane, which he will allow Roger to fly if Ord's sexual desires are met. At the race, Roger dies in a fiery crash. Burke,

who in the novel is revealed as the most pathetic of all the characters, loans LaVerne enough money to get her and her son back to their farm.

In the late thirties, Faulkner mapped out a trilogy of novels about the Snopes family which began with *The Hamlet* (1940), chronicling the rise of Flem Snopes, whose single-minded purpose is to get land. Although sexually impotent, he marries Eula Varner, pregnant by another man, to acquire property offered by her father. By the end of the novel, Flem has pulled off several financial coups and is preparing to take on the city of Jefferson.

When Martin Ritt came to film *The Hamlet,* which became *The Long Hot Summer* (20th Century-Fox, 1958), he and screenwriters Irving Ravetch and Harriet Frank Jr. decided to use parts of the novel, part of "Barn Burning," and part of "The Spotted Horse." Ben Quick (Paul Newman), a hot-tempered drifter from Mississippi whose father settled disputes by burning down his enemies' barns, arrives in a town dominated by Will Varner (Orson Welles), a big landowner. In Quick, Varner sees a man who might be able to take over the empire he has created, since he believes his son, Jody (Anthony Franciosa) to be an ineffectual weakling. Varner immediately sets about trying to match Quick with his daughter, Clara (Joanne Woodward). At first

Lee Remick as Temple Drake and Yves Montand as Candy Man in *Sanctuary* (1961), a melding of Faulkner's *Sanctuary* and *Requiem for a Nun*.

101

(From left) Joanne Woodward, Paul Newman, Anthony Franciosa, Lee Remick, Orson Welles, and Richard Anderson in *The Long, Hot Summer* (1957), adapted from *The Hamlet* and two of Faulkner's short stories.

she resists, but finally she comes to see that she indeed loves Quick.

The story was soap opera, but good soap opera. The script was superior, containing tension, some humor, and excellent characterizations, although the dialogue sounded more like a romantic Tennessee Williams than Faulkner. Little of Faulkner's South and almost none of the novel show up on the screen.

A television production of *The Long Hot Summer* (teleplay by Rita Mae Brown and Dennis Turner, NBC, Leonard Hill Films, 1985) expanded the story to four hours. While it was often atmospheric, having been filmed on location in Louisiana and Texas, the ludicrous ending in which middle-class blacks and middle-class whites band together to punish Ben Quick (Don Johnson), who they think is responsible for barn burning, is totally foreign to Faulkner's fictional world.

On several occasions, Faulkner tried selling his short stories to the *Saturday Evening Post*, but its editors found his work unsuitable until he submitted "Tomorrow" in 1940. The short story was first dramatized on TV by

Horton Foote in 1960* on *Playhouse 90* with Richard Boone, and came to the big screen twelve years later as *Tomorrow* (Filmgroup, 1972). Fentry (Robert Duvall), a quiet Mississippi farmer who shelters an abandoned pregnant girl (Olga Bellin), falls in love with her, and helps her through her pregnancy. He marries her, but only minutes after the ceremony, she dies in childbirth. For a few years, Fentry raises the child, only to have his wife's relatives take it away. Although an obviously low- budget effort, this is a beautifully scripted film that creates a realistic atmosphere and captures much of the Faulkner short story despite the radical altering of the plot.

In 1948, Faulkner published *Intruder in the Dust*, which received almost universal critical acclaim, and a year later it reached the screen (MGM, 1949). More than five hundred people appeared in the film, yet only a

*Foote also adapted Faulkner's 1951 novelette *Old Man* for *Playhouse 90* in 1958, but the work has gone unfilmed. Sterling Hayden and Geraldine Page starred in the television version.

102

Claude Jarman Jr. as Chick Mallison (left) watches Juano Hernandez as Lucas Beauchamp (center) make a purchase under hostile eyes in Faulkner's *Intruder in the Dust* (1949).

dozen or so were professional actors. Most were residents of Oxford, Mississippi, where director Clarence Brown, himself a Southerner, shot ninety percent of the film. During production, he followed the strict segregationist policies of the city—the white actors were free to go wherever they wanted, but the black actors had to stay in the homes of the blacks and eat with black families. The production received the enthusiastic endorsement of the town, including the Chamber of Commerce and the *Oxford Eagle*, the local paper, which ran a full page ad announcing: "We Are Proud to Be the Stage for Mr. William Faulkner's Great Story, Intruder in the Dust." Photographs accompanying the ad showed various scenes around town—the square, the jail, and one of Faulkner at the quicksand scene location. Given the novel's political stand, one wonders how many townspeople had read the novel.

Although he received no screen credit, Faulkner read the Ben Maddow script and found it acceptable, making only a few suggestions about the final scene. The story remains much the same as the novel. Lucas Beauchamp

(Juano Hernandez), a black man, is falsely accused of murder, and Chick Mallison (Claude Jarman, Jr.), a young white boy, sets out to clear him with the help of his uncle, Gavin Stevens (David Brian). In the novel, Gavin Stevens was the spokesman for Faulkner, but in the film his various posturings and observations, considerably pared down, make him look like an ineffectual liberal. On the other hand, the film increases the stature of Lucas, who becomes, as Stevens says at the end, "the keeper of the conscience." One of the most chilling scenes in the film occurs as the townsfolk create a circus atmosphere while waiting for a lynching.

The one weak spot of the film lies in its portrayal of Aleck (Elzie Emanuel), the black friend of Chick. In the novel, Aleck is a defiant boy who often echoes the sentiments of Lucas, but the film chose to portray him as stereotypical and far less articulate. When he and Chick are in the graveyard digging up the body of the murdered man, Aleck's eyes roll and bulge in fear. The scene does Faulkner a great disservice and weakens a film that, in all other respects, should be applauded for its honesty and courage.

So goes a Hollywood axiom: When a movie makes no sense, add a narration. This axiom was applied to *The Reivers* (National General, 1969), based on the novel published in 1962 just a month before Faulkner died. With a screenplay by Irving Ravetch and Harriet Frank Jr., the film needed a narration by Burgess Meredith to tie up all the loose ends. In turn-of-the-century Mississippi, Boon Hogganbeck (Steve McQueen), a hired hand, borrows the new family auto for a trip into Memphis with Lucius (Mitch Vogel), the grandson of the family, and Ned, a black stablehand (Rupert Crosse). The trio visits a bordello, gets involved in a brawl, and wins a horse race before returning home. The story is a pleasant but insubstantial yarn, "a Faulkner tall-tale comedy celebrating the fun of storytelling," said critic Pauline Kael. It was attractive to look at but without much substance and without ever reaching a point.

Because of his sometimes convoluted style, his handling of subject matter and his complex, often baffling characters, Faulkner has failed to translate easily to the screen. *The Story of Temple Drake* and *Sanctuary* included some of the sensational aspects of the novel, but neither film gained much of a reputation. *The Long*

Rupert Crosse as Ned McCaslin has a philosophical discussion with Steve McQueen as Boon Hogganbeck about skin pigmentation after the two have taken a mud bath in *The Reivers* (1969).

Robert Duvall as Jackson Fentry with Johnny Mask as the boy in *Tomorrow* (1972), based on the Faulkner short story.

Hot Summer proved popular at the box office because of the stellar cast, but the story had little to do with Faulkner. Only two films, *Intruder in the Dust* and *Tomorrow*, remained somewhat faithful to his work, and even in these, the script writers overhauled the original stories to make them more accessible to the paying public.

Katherine Anne Porter (1890–1980) began her writing career in 1922, but her only real novel was *Ship of Fools* (1962), which follows a boatload of passengers who embark from Vera Cruz bound for Germany. The novel became an instant best-seller and was immediately swept up by Columbia, which paid $400,000 for the rights. Abby Mann, whom the author described as "the dullest man I ever met in my life," was assigned to write the screenplay.

Mann began by moving the date from 1931 to 1933, an insignificant change, until one remembers what happened in 1933. In addition, Glocken (Michael Dunn), in the film a dwarf, narrates the proceedings, opening with, "This is a ship of fools. I'm a fool. You'll meet more fools as you go along." In the end, he announces, "I told you they were fools, didn't I? Fools, pimps, whores, cowards, potential murderers. Is there any hope for such people? I'll tell you. I have a feeling that lives don't have to be wasted this way. They can have meaning, that there is some beauty in people. But you'd be crazy to take my word for it. Who am I? I'm just a fellow who's three-foot-six and wants to be six-foot-three." The dwarf then walks off, and as he does, he reminds us that life may be a little misshapen, a little tawrdy, but it still possesses some beauty of the soul.

This Hollywood attempt at an upbeat ending, given all that has come before, is more than a bit unconvincing. Denny (Lee Marvin) has been bloodied by the shoe of a Mrs. Treadwell (Vivien Leigh); La Condesa (Simone Signoret) has discovered the only man she ever respected, the doctor (Oskar Werner), dead of heart failure; and the Germans continue to spout their philosophy of the New Order and the unfitness of the Jews. The character of David (George Segal), puritanical and possessive in the novel, has become an artist with a social conscience who is being kept by Jenny (Elizabeth Ashley), a rich-bitch who hates her lover's art because he cherishes it more

The cast of *Ship of Fools* (1965): Vivien Leigh, Simone Signoret, José Ferrer, Lee Marvin, Oskar Werner, Elizabeth Ashley, George Segal, José Greco, Michael Dunn, Charles Korvin, and Heinz Ruhmann.

Francis Lederer and Louis Calhern prepare to duel in *The Bridge of San Luis Rey* (1943).

Martha Scott and William Holden as the young lovers in Thornton Wilder's *Our Town* (1940).

(From left) Wallace Ford, Robert Morse, Shirley MacLaine, Anthony Perkins, Paul Ford, and Shirley Booth in The *Matchmaker* (1958).

than her. Although some critics, impressed at the gravity of the subject, gave admiring reviews, most agreed with the author, who claimed that the film had put aside the whole point of her book.

One of the last in the long line of New England Puritan writers, Thornton Wilder (1897–1975), worked in various media. Best known as a novelist and playwright, he also toiled in films, not only adapting Tolstoy's *Resurrection* into *We Live Again* for Samuel Goldwyn in 1936, but also adapting his own Pulitzer Prize-winning play,

Our Town, to the screen. However, it was his second novel, *The Bridge of San Luis Rey* (1927), that first reached the screen.

The initial version of *The Bridge of San Luis Rey* (MGM, 1929) was basically a silent production with dialogue added at the beginning and end. The story concentrated too heavily on Camila (Lily Damita), she of loose morals and easy virtue. When the bridge collapses, the townspeople fear that St. Louis, patron saint of bridges, has deserted them because of their sins. Camila heads the list of sinners. While much of Wilder's novel made it to the screen, several scenes were added, the most obnoxious being a romance between two characters who in the book held little interest for one another. The young Brother Juniper who investigates the deaths has aged considerably—he is an old man—and it is he (Henry B. Walthall) who delivers the opening and closing sermons to a throng of parishioners looking for answers to their questions.

The remake of *The Bridge of San Luis Rey* (United Artists, 1944) was so far removed from its source that the *New York Times* began its review, "You had better forget that Thornton Wilder ever wrote a book called *The Bridge of San Luis Rey* when (and if) you see the film." The core of the story involving the deaths of five people on the rickety bridge remains, but much is missing. Invented for this version by Howard Estabrook and Herman Weissman is the character of Michaela (Lynn Bari), a dancer representing the old Spanish ways who has become the courtesan of a viceroy. The story gets lost under the weight of a distorted script that spends too much of its time on melodrama rather than Wilder's story.

The 1958 television adaptation by Ludi Clare of Wilder's tale was overshadowed by its stellar cast headed by Judith Anderson, Hume Cronyn, Eva Le Gallienne, and Viveca Lindfors.

In 1938, Wilder wrote *Our Town*, a play that seemed to capture the living spirit of ordinary people in an ordinary American town. It not only had a very successful Broadway run but also won the Pulitzer Prize. Its popularity prompted Hollywood to give it a try, and Wilder himself adapted it for the screen. The result was an *Our Town* (United Artists, 1940), full of vigor and style, directed with sensitivity and honesty by Sam Wood, who used a variety of techniques—dissolves, moody lighting, and montages—to capture the flavor of life in simpler days. Just as in the play, Grovers Corners becomes a microcosm of small-town America. The story is divided into three parts—1901, 1904, and 1913—with events seen principally through the eyes of two families, the Gibbs and the Webbs. One of the most impressive scenes in the film is an extended excursion through the local graveyard where Emily (Martha Scott) meets her

relatives, friends, and acquaintances who have died before her. But one very important concession was made to Hollywood demands; rather than have Emily really dead as she was in the play, the script has her awaken to discover that she is still alive, and she is happily reunited with her husband, George (William Holden). What might have been a genuine American classic is thus compromised because of a studio's reluctance to treat a play with the reverence and dignity it deserved.

The same year that Wilder wrote *Our Town*, he also turned out one of his true theatrical flops, *The Merchant of Yonkers*. He revised the material in 1954, and the play became *The Matchmaker*, the story of Dolly Levi. Three

Walter Matthau as blustering Horace Vandergelder is beset by the womanly wiles of Barbra Streisand as matchmaker Dolly Levi in *Hello, Dolly!* (1969), the musical version of *The Matchmaker*.

years later it turned up as a film (Paramount, 1958), with an adaptation by John Michael Hayes. Dolly Levi (Shirley Booth) is a matchmaker hired by curmudgeonly Yonkers shopkeeper Horace Vandergelder (Paul Ford) to arrange a match between him and a quite-a-bit-younger Irene Molloy (Shirley MacLaine), who much prefers his shy clerk, Cornelius Hackl (Anthony Perkins). Dolly wants Horace for herself, but she must first appear to make an effort to do the job for which Horace engaged her.

The Matchmaker ran into some censorship problems in language, but overall the film remained faithful to its source. It did have one very annoying trait: the characters would often stare directly into the camera and speak to the audience. While this technique might work very well on the stage, it was disconcerting in the film.

The story returned as a Broadway musical *Hello Dolly!* which also made the transition to the screen (20th Century-Fox, 1969), with a script by producer Ernest Lehman and directed by Gene Kelly. The musical numbers increased the running time by only thirty minutes, and all the characters made it intact, but much of Wilder's story had been changed and rearranged to make room for the songs. Because of these changes and omissions, the transformation of Horace (Walter Matthau) is even less convincing than in the original play. The biggest drawback, however, was that Barbra Streisand was only twenty-six at the time and, except for her singing, totally miscast as Dolly.

Wilder's last novel was *Theophilus North* (1973), which became *Mr. North* (Goldwyn Company, 1988). North (Anthony Edwards) is a genial young doctor who rides into Newport, Rhode Island, where he makes an impact on local society. Some of the community, jealous of North, accuses him of practicing medicine without a license, and at his trial, his only defense is that he cures people with optimism and positive thinking. The case is dismissed, and North becomes a local hero. Despite some differences, the film (adapted by Janet Roach, John Huston, and James Costigan) remained fairly close to its source. Unfortunately, it never brought the book to life.

Sinclair Lewis, F. Scott Fitzgerald, Ernest Hemingway, William Faulkner, Katherine Ann Porter, and Thornton Wilder—all were modernists, writers whose works carried a certain amount of ambivalence and ambiguity. In adapting their fiction to films, Hollywood has often emasculated the novels and short stories, turning them into romantic pulp. Despite an impressive number of classics produced by these authors, only a few titles can be considered faithful adaptations in spirit if not in actual fact: Lewis's *Dodsworth* and *Elmer Gantry*; Hemingway's *The Macomber Affair* and the first ten minutes of *The Killers*; Faulkner's *Intruder in the Dust* and *Tomorrow*; and except for its conclusion, Wilder's *Our Town*.

Angelica Huston as Persis Bosworth-Thompson dances with Anthony Edwards in the title role in *Mr. North* (1988), an adaptation of Wilder's *Theophilus North*.

Jack Oakie as baseball star Elmer Kane and Evelyn Brent as Corey, his actress girlfriend in *Fast Company* (1929), based on the Ring Lardner–George M. Cohan play, *Elmer the Great*.

SIX

MASTERS OF THE SHORT STORY

*O. Henry, Ring Lardner, Damon Runyon,
James Thurber*

In 1902, William Sidney Porter (1862–1910) moved to New York City and began to publish short stories under the pseudonym O. Henry; during the first decade of the twentieth century, he commanded a readership in the millions, prompting some critics to call him "the Yankee Maupassant." After his death, however, his reputation declined as his works were often attacked for their overt sentimentality and lack of a moral stance, but nevertheless he has remained along with Edgar Allan Poe and Mark Twain one of the most widely read American authors.

O. Henry was dead seven years before the first of his works reached the screen under the title of *The Green Door* (Vitagraph, 1917), based on his short story. While much of the film was created by the scenarists, the basic plot was strong enough for the *New York Times* reviewer to comment that "the picture is so far superior to the majority of its kind that the suspicion arises that what the movies need is ideas."

Other silent films included *Everybody's Girl* (Vitagraph, 1918), based on "Brickdust Row"; *An American Live Wire* (Vitagraph, 1918), based on "The Lotus and

the Bottle"; and *You're Fired* (Famous Players–Lasky, 1919), based on "The Halberdier of the Little Rheinschloss." At best, these films retained shreds of O. Henry's plots.

In 1903, O. Henry published "A Retrieved Reformation" in *Cosmopolitan*, and it quickly became one of his most famous tales. Six years later, the story was adapted for Broadway as *Alias Jimmy Valentine*, and turned into one of the biggest hits of the early 1900s. It was only natural that the movies would latch on to the success of the play, and ultimately *Alias Jimmy Valentine* (Metro, 1920) reached the screen with Bert Lytell. It was remade as the studio's first talkie (MGM, 1928). The story remained basically the same as Jimmy (William Haines) is a reformed safecracker who has landed a position as an assistant cashier in a bank and fallen in love with a beautiful woman (Leila Hyams). A detective (Lionel Barrymore) suspects the truth, but when Jimmy saves a little girl trapped in a safe, he is allowed to go free.

The Return of Jimmy Valentine (Republic, 1936) had ex-safecracker Jimmy (Roger Pryor) much further afield than simply saving a little girl's life as he carries a gun and gets involved with crooks who he must ultimately put away. The subsequent *Affairs of Jimmy Valentine* (Republic, 1942) has an intrepid reporter (Dennis O'Keefe) discovering that Jimmy is a newspaper editor in a small town. A series of brutal murders is also part of the plot, but the film had even less to do with O. Henry's short story than its predecessor.

In *Heart of the West* (1907) appears "The Caballero's Way," a brilliantly cynical tale in which O. Henry avoided his usual sticky sentimentality. The Cisco Kid is an American gunman who "killed for the love of it—because he was quick-tempered—to avoid arrest—for his own amusement—any reason that came to mind would suffice." As the story opens, the Kid's mistress, Tonia Perez, betrays the Kid to her new lover, Texas Ranger Sandridge. The Kid discovers the truth and repays Tonia for her unfaithfulness in the "caballero's way" by tricking the ranger into shooting Tonia by mistake.

The Cisco Kid (Warner Baxter) arrived on the screen in *In Old Arizona* (Fox, 1929), the first major sound Western, which set the pattern for all those to follow. It turned the Cisco Kid into a Hispanic Robin Hood of the border. When Sergeant Mickey Dunn (Edmund Lowe) shows up on the scene, the film turns into a Western *What Price Glory?* with the Kid and Dunn substituting for Flagg and Quirt. Tonia (Dorothy Burgess) betrays the Kid, almost costing him his life, and he exacts his revenge, but no one gets killed. Twenty-two sequels of varying quality followed with a number of different actors playing the Kid, although only *In Old Arizona* claimed to be based on "The Caballero's Way." All the others claimed to be based on a character created by O. Henry; even this was not true. The one O. Henry created has never been put on film.

Another Western, "The Double-Dyed Deceiver," became *The Texan* (Paramount, 1930). In a Texas town of 1885, run by scripture-quoting Sheriff John Brown (John Marcus), the Llano Kid (Gary Cooper) shoots a young man during a poker game and flees town on a stolen horse. On board a steamer headed for South America, he meets Thacker (Oscar Apfel), hired by Señora Ibarra (Emma Dunn) to find her son, who ran away at the age of ten. Thacker persuades the Kid to assume the identity of the now-grown son, and the Kid easily fools the old woman. But Señora Ibarra is kind and generous, and this tugs at the Kid's conscience. Then he learns that he was responsible for the death of her real son. Complicating things even further, the Kid falls in love with his lovely "cousin," Consuelo (Fay Wray). He calls off his deal with Thacker, who hires some thugs to take care of the welcher. When this fails, Thacker and his henchmen attack the Ibarra ranch just as Sheriff Brown shows up to

Roger Pryor and Charlotte Henry in *The Return of Jimmy Valentine* (1937).

Gary Cooper as the Llano Kid receives some advice on hats from Oscar Apfel as Thacker in *The Texan* (1930), an adaptation of O. Henry's "The Double-Dyed Deceiver."

William Haines as the reformed safecracker and Lionel Barrymore as the detective in O. Henry's *Alias Jimmy Valentine* (1928).

take the Kid back. In the ensuing battle, Thacker is killed. The sheriff realizes that the Kid has reformed and agrees to let the dead Thacker assume the identity of the Llano Kid.

Lighter in tone, "The Badge of Policeman O'Roon" showed up on the screen as *Dr. Rhythm* (Paramount, 1938). Ramsen (Bing Crosby) is an easy-going doctor whose policeman friend (Andy Devine) asks him to cover for him. Ramsen becomes a bodyguard to Judy Marlowe (Mary Carlisle), and the two fall in love. A number of unmemorable songs punctuate what little action there is.

Irony was at the center of O. Henry's "The Passing of Black Eagle," a tale of a drifter who gets mixed up with an outlaw gang, takes control, and becomes known as "Black Eagle." But he is a man who wants to escape commitment, and in the end, he boards another freight and rides away, leaving his successful career as bandit chief behind. The film *Black Eagle* (Columbia, 1948) padded the story to a seventy-six-minute running time. Jason Bond (William Bishop) is a drifter who wants to avoid contact with people but comes into conflict with a crooked contract agent. It was nothing more than a "B" film which used the O. Henry name but little of his story.

To this point, each film had attempted to build an entire feature around one of O. Henry's short stories, and none had proven particularly successful. However, *O. Henry's Full House* (20th Century-Fox, 1952) rectified this problem by bringing five of his stories together in

Warner Baxter as the first Cisco Kid, taking a refreshing and much needed bath in *In Old Arizona* (1929).

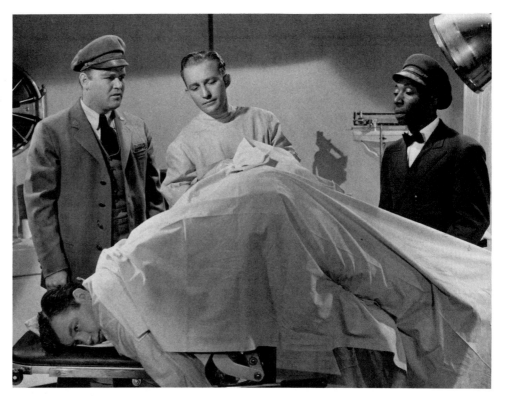

Andy Devine in a prone position, being ministered to by Rufe Davis, Bing Crosby, and Charles Moore in *Doctor Rhythm* (1938), adapted from "The Badge of Policeman O'Roon."

William Bishop gets a whip lash from Virginia Patton in *Black Eagle* (1948), based on O. Henry's "The Passing of Black Eagle."

one film with each separate tale sporting a different cast and a different director.

The first of the stories, "The Cop and the Anthem," has Soapy (Charles Laughton), a haughty tramp who befriends a streetwalker (Marilyn Monroe), trying to get arrested so that he can spend the winter in jail. In "The Clarion Call," a decent cop (Dale Robertson) must arrest his old friend (Richard Widmark), now turned crook but to whom he owes a debt. In "The Last Leaf," a young woman (Anne Baxter) watches the leaves wither and fall from the tree outside her window as she is dying. She believes that when the last left drops from the tree, she will die. Perhaps the most famous of all O. Henry's stories, "The Ransom of Red Chief," tells of a pair of bunglers (Fred Allen and Oscar Levant) who kidnap a child from hell and have to pay the family to get them to take the youngster back. "The Gift of the Magi" is the familiar story of the young couple (Jeanne Crain and Farley Granger) who exchange gifts only to discover the truth in the old proverb: it is better to give than to receive.

Fox hired John Steinbeck to appear as on-screen narrator. We see him first as he tells the audience about O. Henry. Then he takes a book from the shelf and begins to read. Steinbeck fades from the screen, and the first story begins. Most reviewers found his narrative linking the stories superfluous and irritating, and *The Nation* reported that Steinbeck's voice had been dubbed by Ward Bond. Otherwise, most critics found *O. Henry's Full House* to be an entertaining film anthology that captured both the spirit and flavor of the author's stories. The writing was first rate, and each episode remained faithful to the original story.* Of all the adaptations of O. Henry, this remains the most truly representative of the author.

*Lamar Trotti wrote the screenplay to "The Cop and the Anthem"; Richard Breen, "The Clarion Call"; Ivan Goff and Ben Roberts, "The Last Leaf"; Nunnally Johnson, "The Ransom of Red Chief"; and Walter Bulloch, "The Gift of the Magi."

The stellar anthology, *O. Henry's Full House* (1952): Marilyn
Monroe and Charles Laughton in "The Cop and the Anthem," Dale
Robertson and Richard Widmark in "The Clarion Call," Jean Peters
and Anne Baxter in "The Last Leaf," and Jeanne Crain and Farley
Granger in "The Gift of the Magi."

By 1920, O. Henry's reputation as a serious writer had deteriorated, and other writers were finding favor with the public. Among these was Ring Lardner (1885–1933). In recent years Lardner himself has been largely neglected, and today his reputation exists on the strength of a half dozen sports stories, classics of the genre.

Lardner first reached the screen in *The New Klondike* (Paramount, 1926), for which he contributed an original story and the titles, all of which he wrote in a fast four-day period. After seeing the film in a theater, an unimpressed Lardner wrote to his close friend, F. Scott Fitzgerald, "The picture, I believe, will be the worst ever seen on land or sea, and the titles are excruciatingly terrible." Lardner wrote a couple of other scenarios, and later he appeared as himself in *Glorifying the American Girl* (Paramount, 1929).

In 1927, Lardner wrote "Hurry Kane" for *Cosmopolitan*, the story of a hick baseball player who is called up to the White Sox. In order to keep him happy, members of the team hatch an imaginary romance between Kane and a showgirl by faking letters from her to him. Lardner's story attracted the attention of George M. Cohan, and the two men joined in a collaboration. The result was *Elmer the Great*, a disaster that ran on Broadway for only forty performances.

Lardner and Cohan recouped part of their losses by selling the property to Hollywood, where it first became *Fast Company* (Paramount, 1929), about a yokel baseball player (Jack Oakie) who turns pro, defies crooks, and wins not only the big game but also the girl who loves him. The *New York Times* called it "a thoroughly entertaining screen adaptation."

It was remade four years later as *Elmer the Great* (Warner Bros., 1933), with Joe E. Brown in the title role, a natural because at one time he had been a professional baseball player. The plot (by Tom Geraghty) remained the same with Elmer showing up just in time to win the big game for the Cubs as they defeat the Yankees.

A third version was called *Cowboy Quarterback* (Warner Bros., 1939), changing the sport from baseball to football. A scout (William Demarest) discovers a country yokel (Bert Wheeler) heaving sacks of potatoes around a general store and offers to make him the quarterback of his pro team. The hick gets involved with crooks but manages to show up at the last minute to save the big game and win the girl. All of these screen variations, while entertaining to a degree, reflected the weakness of the play rather than the short story.

Somewhat atypical of Lardner's output was "Some Like It Cold" (*Saturday Evening Post*, 1921), an exchange of letters between Charles and Mabelle after they have met briefly on a train platform going in opposite directions. A relationship develops through their correspondence, but in his last letter, Charles announces that he is about to marry a woman who is obviously a golddigger, and Mabelle replies in barely controlled fury that she doesn't want to hear from him anymore.

The story provided the nucleus for a 1929 play, *June Moon*, by Lardner and George S. Kaufman, which in turn became a film of the same title (Paramount, 1931). A team of screenwriters, including Joseph L. Mankiewicz, transferred much of the dialogue straight from the play, but shifted the emphasis from satire to romance. Frederick Stevens (Jack Oakie) is a somewhat dense electrician who wants to be a songwriter. He is helped through various pitfalls by his sweetheart (Frances Dee) before writing his masterpiece "June Moon." A remake six years later entitled *Blonde Trouble* (Paramount, 1937) changed the plot to that of a small-town boy, Fred Stevens (Johnny Downs), tackling the Big Apple, falling in love, selling a hit song, and becoming a Hollywood success. This version, written by Lily Hayward, stressed the music, but neither it nor the previous version contained the cynicism of Lardner's story.

Far more typical of Lardner was "Alibi Ike" (1915), the story of a man driven to make excuses for his every failure and every success. Although less substantial than some of his other stories, its light tone and the comical leading character found popularity with the public, who adapted the phrase "Alibi Ike" in reference to anyone who makes excuses. For the film *Alibi Ike* (Warner Bros., 1935), screenwriter William Wister Hayes added slapstick comedy, threw in some crooked gamblers, and provided a snappy ending where Ike (Joe E. Brown) arrives just in time to save the big game for his team, all of which sounds suspiciously like *Elmer the Great* made two years earlier.

In October of 1921, Lardner had five previously published stories appear as *The Big Town*, which became *So This Is New York* (United Artists, 1948). In fashioning a screenplay out of Lardner's loosely structured novel, writers Carl Foreman and Herbert Baker changed much of the dialogue to suit the personality of radio comedian Henry Morgan. They also restructured the plot. The best scenes are those involving the city dwellers, especially the cabbies, whose dialogue is subtitled.

Lardner's best known story may well be "Champion," which appeared in the *Saturday Evening Post* (June 18, 1921), a study of a brutal boxer, Midge Kelly, a man totally without moral principles who is guided only by an overriding self-interest. As the story opens, Midge beats up his crippled brother and knocks down his mother when she complains. Running away, he becomes a boxer. He soon gets a girl pregnant and is forced to marry her, and on their wedding night, "the gift of the

Jack Oakie as Frederick Martin Stevens with his first check as a songwriter in *June Moon* (1931), the first of several film adaptations of the play by Ring Lardner and George S. Kaufman. Looking on are Wynne Gibson (left), Ernest Wood, and June MacCloy.

bridegroom, when once they were alone, was a crushing blow on the bride's pale cheek." He becomes champion, and the press promotes him as a Frank Merriwell of the ring who loves his wife and adores his mother.

The film *Champion* (United Artists, 1949) departed significantly from Lardner's story, erasing almost every trace of humor and irony. To be sure, Midge (Kirk Douglas) remains ruthless and manipulative, but he is a product of poverty. He seduces his cafe-owner boss's daughter, Emma Bryce (Ruth Roman), and when pressured to marry her, he flees to Los Angeles. There he becomes a boxer and finally champion under the guidance of Tommy Haley (Paul Stewart). Later, he loses the title and dumps Haley to take a better deal from crime kingpin Jerome Harris (Luis Van Rooten). When Midge seduces Harris's wife (Lola Albright), the mobster pays off the boxer to dump her, and with the bills wadded in his hand, Midge tells her, "You're his wife." He then takes up with Grace Diamond (Marilyn Maxwell), girlfriend of a fellow prizefighter. Eventually Midge gets another shot at the champion, and just before the big fight, asks Emma and his crippled brother Connie (Arthur Kennedy) to join him, but he rapes Emma and then knocks down his brother when he confronts Midge over the deed.

The end opts for sentimentality. Midge dies in the locker room after taking the championship, and Connie makes a speech to the press extolling his virtues. Despite its variances from the short story, the film is a compelling and powerful drama, and in its own way, a deeply felt character study, helped by a literate script by Carl Foreman. Another strength lies in the interpretation of the character of Midge by actor Kirk Douglas, whose performance prompted the reviewer for *The Hollywood Reporter* to say, "Kirk Douglas is Lardner's immortal character." Of the adaptations of the author's work, only *Champion* stands as a true classic.*

Ring Lardner himself was portrayed by writer/director John Sayles in the latter's 1988 baseball film, *Eight Men Out*, about the 1919 Black Sox Scandal.

In the best of Lardner's fiction such as "Champion" and "Haircut," a bitter, cold irony was a mainstay. Irony was also a mainstay in many of the stories of Damon Runyon (1880–1946), but it was of a softer kind. Although his stories were often filled with murder and mayhem, his colorful characters and plots were usually saturated with humor often spoken in a jargon that has

*The following year (1950), *Champion* was produced on television for *Robert Montgomery Presents*, with Richard Kiley in the lead.

come to be termed "Runyonese." Throughout the 1930s he was America's most popular short-story writer, and magazines like the *Saturday Evening Post* and *Collier's* paid exorbitant fees for his stories during a time of economic depression. His stories of Broadway and his particular language caused Hollywood producers to besiege him with film offers.

Runyon's first taste of the movies was *The Great White Way* (1924) in which the journalist appeared as

Kirk Douglas as boxer Midge Kelly in Ring Lardner's *Champion* (1940) with his three leading ladies: Ruth Roman, Marilyn Maxwell, and Lola Albright.

himself, and he repeated the lark in *Madison Square Garden* (Paramount, 1932). From these experiences came a lifelong association with films that included a stab at producing *The Big Street* (RKO, 1942) and *Irish Eyes Are Smiling* (20th Century-Fox, 1944).

The first of his own works to reach the screen was "Madame La Gimp," published initially in *Cosmopolitan* (October 1929), a screwball comedy about the efforts of Dave the Dude to convince a visiting aristocratic Spanish family that Madame La Gimp and her daughter are rich and respectable.

Adapted to the screen by Robet Riskin and directed by Frank Capra, who acquired the rights from Runyon for $1,500, the film became *Lady for a Day* (Columbia, 1933). Madame La Gimp became Apple Annie (May Robson) minus the limp, a streetcorner apple seller. When her daughter, Louise (Jean Parker), is about to arrive in New York from Spain along with her wealthy fiancé and his family, Annie turns for help to Dave the Dude (Warren William), a gambler who believes that the apple he buys from Annie every morning brings him luck. He arranges a luxurious suite, dressmakers, and servants to help impress Louise's intended. And for Annie he even provides a husband, "Judge" Blake (Guy Kibbee), a pool shark who possesses sophisticated mannerisms and language. Dave and his boys sweep the daughter and aristocratic family off to the hotel where they successfully carry out the ruse. Once her daughter is safely married, Apple Annie blissfully returns to the street.

Lady for a Day, a variation on *Pygmalion*, was a lighthearted, sentimental tale that was calculated to make people laugh and cry, and did a good job of both. It proved to be Capra's first big success and was nominated for an Academy Award. The *New York Times* pointed out that the film was based on a Runyon story and said, "Its plausibility may be open to argument, but its entertainment value is not to be denied"—an accurate description of most of Runyon's stories.

Capra remade his own film almost thirty years later as *Pocketful of Miracles* (United Artists, 1961), with screenwriters Hal Kanter and Harry Tugend adapting the earlier Robert Riskin screenplay. Bette Davis, Glenn Ford, Ann-Margret, and Thomas Mitchell had the roles previously played by May Robson, Warren William, Jean Parker, and Guy Kibbee.

Lady for a Day had been a swift ninety-five minutes, but *Pocketful of Miracles* ran sixteen minutes over two hours, far too long for such a delicate comedy. The film was castigated by the critics, who claimed that the Runyon story had not worn well; "The bloom is off Mr. Runyon's gilded lily," said *New York Times* reviewer A. H. Weiler.

One of Lardner's most enduring stories, "Little Miss Marker" (*Collier's*, March 26, 1932), was a fusion of Dickensian sentimentality and biting social satire and has often been compared to Bret Harte's "The Luck of Roaring Camp" because, like Luck, little Marky becomes a redemptive character, changing the lives of racetrack tout Sorrowful and his friends, and when she dies, they return to their former ways.

Four times the story reached the screen. The first was *Little Miss Marker* (aka *Girl in Pawn*, Paramount, 1934). As in each of its versions, the basic tale remained the same. The little tyke (Shirley Temple) is left with Sorrowful (Adolphe Menjou), an inveterate bookie who takes her home. He soon learns that the father has committed suicide, and Marky is his. There are several touching scenes, including one where Marky climbs into bed with Sorrowful and asks him for a story. He reads her the tout sheets with the names of the horses and the various odds on each race. One night, he teaches her a prayer, and she adds a last request that God give

Warren William (seated left) as Dave the Dude awaits the approval of May Robson (seated right) as Apple Annie with the assembled throng gathered together by Glenda Farrell (standing right) as Missouri Martin in Frank Capra's *Lady for a Day* (1933), based on Runyon's "Madame La Gimp."

Thomas Mitchell as Judge Harry Blake practices his manners on Hope Lange as Queenie Martin while Glenn Ford as Dave the Dude offers advice in *Pocketful of Miracles* (1961), Frank Capra's remake of his *Lady for a Day*.

117

Adolphe Menjou as bookie Sorrowful Jones and Shirley Temple in the title role in *Little Miss Marker* (aka *Girl in Pawn*, 1934).

Mary Jane Saunders as Miss Marker prays with Bob Hope as Sorrowful in *Sorrowful Jones* (1949), the second version of Runyon's "Little Miss Marker."

Sorrowful new clothes. The next day, he goes out and buys a new suit, surprising all his friends who are well aware of his parsimonious nature. There is also a hilarious scene at a nightclub where Sorrowful's cronies dress up in medieval costumes and bring in a doped horse in full regalia.

In this and each succeeding adaptation, Sorrowful is given a sweetheart, here Bangles Carson (Dorothy Dell), a torch singer, whom the bookie eventually marries. In addition, problems with a rival gangster (Charles Bickford) surface. Finally, little Marky winds up in the hospital, but in true Hollywood fashion, she survives to be reunited with Sorrowful and Bangles. Of all the adaptations of "Little Miss Marker," this is the best, in no small part because of Shirley Temple, who brought her particular touch of freshness and sentimentality to the role.

Next came *Sorrowful Jones* (Paramount, 1949), tailor-(re)made for Bob Hope, with Lucille Ball as his girlfriend, and it strayed further from the story, not so much in plot as in atmosphere. The film opened with Walter Winchell paying homage to his old friend, the late Damon Runyon, and the characters he created, but as the *New York Times* pointed out, "A serious student of the late Damon Runyon's works, in which the story of 'Little Miss Marker' is somewhere near the top, might even find it difficult to recognize a Runyon character in this film." *Forty Pounds of Trouble* (Universal, 1962) moved even further from its source (Tony Curtis starred) and the climax occurs with a slapstick chase through Disneyland. The final version returned the title to *Little Miss Marker* (Universal, 1980) but despite starring Walter Matthau and Julie Andrews, failed to impress either critics or the public, especially those familiar with the 1934 version, which remains the best and closest in spirit to Runyon's story.

"The Old Doll's House" (*Collier's*, May 13, 1933) included an O. Henry twist which made it into the film adaptation by Warren Duff. In *Midnight Alibi* (Warner Bros., 1934), Lance (Richard Barthelmess) is in love with the sister (Ann Dvorak) of gangster Angie the Ox McGowan (Robert Barrat), who is trying to have Lance rubbed out. Lance escapes into the house of Abigail (Helen Lowell), and from the start it is obvious that they speak in different languages. He uses words like "sweetheart" and "kid" in addressing the old lady, and she speaks softly and acts like the stereotypical little old grandmother. When Angie is bumped off and Lance accused of the crime, Abigail provides his alibi. The film was a minor effort from a major studio, and the running time of only sixty minutes still seemed to stretch the material beyond its limits.

Runyon returned to form with "The Lemon Drop

Helen Lowell (center) as Abigail Ardsley, Purnell Pratt (standing with dotted tie), and Richard Barthelmess (standing right) as Lance McGowan in *Midnight Alibi* (1934), adapted from Damon Runyon's "Old Doll's House."

Kid," a tale that combined sentimental humor and social satire. The Kid, who is invariably sucking on lemon drops, is a racetrack bum who makes his money selling tips to bettors. The first version of *The Lemon Drop Kid* (Paramount, 1934) followed the short story with surprising fidelity. Wally Brooks (Lee Tracy) is the fast-talking tout who swindles an old man out of $100 and then must flee the track. He meets the small-town beauty (Helen Mack), they marry, and she gets pregnant, contracting a fatal illness in the process. To pay the medical expenses, the Kid robs a bank to get money but is caught and sent to prison, and while he is serving his time, his wife dies. When the Kid is released from jail he discovers that his child has been raised by friends he knew at the track. The old man the Kid swindled, it turns out, has never pressed charges because he believes that the lemon drops given him cured his arthritis, and he settles upon the Kid a large reward.

The first part of the film, with Lee Tracy giving one of his patented staccato-paced, comic performances, is especially effective. It is only when he leaves the track that the story dips into melodrama. However, for the finale, it returns to its comic roots and to the Professor (William Frawley), who, reflecting upon the Kid's marriage, says of his own: "I remember saying 'Suppose we get married' and immediately everything went dark. When I woke up, my ears were full of rice and I had a two-year-old baby." Inspired lines like these from an intelligent script that did not stray far from its source made this an excellent adaptation by Howard Green and J. P. McEvoy.

The Lemon Drop Kid (Paramount, 1951) returned as a vehicle for Bob Hope. Here, the Kid gives bad advice to a gangster's moll (Marilyn Maxwell) and must pay back $10,000 by Christmas Day or face some very unpleasant consequences. Hope works very well as the fast-talking bookie, but any hint of Runyon disappears soon after the credits, which listed Edmund Hartmann and Robert O'Brien as screenwriters.

The same problem affected both versions of "Princess O'Hara," the story of a female hansom cabbie whose father dies and the Broadway gang who help her out by stealing a racehorse to attach to the carriage that she drives around Central Park. It was an entertaining story, although not Runyon's best, but *Princess O'Hara* (Universal, 1935), with Jean Parker and Chester Morris, threw in all sorts of extraneous situations that turned the tale into a mawkish exercise and not at all representative of Runyon. *It Ain't Hay* (Universal, 1943) was an Abbott and Costello rehash that was even further removed from Runyon than its predecessor.

The 1930s saw a number of other adaptations of Runyon stories. *Million Dollar Ransom* (Universal, 1934), based on "Ransom, One Million Dollars," involved a gangster (Edward Arnold), just released from prison, who sacrifices himself to save his daughter (Mary Carlisle), a film that the *New York Times* called "definitely below the standard of *Lady for a Day* and *Little Miss Marker*." *A Very Honorable Guy* (Warner Bros., 1934) was a Joe E. Brown vehicle that contained little of the Runyon flavor even though it stuck fairly close to the story of a gambler who sells his body to a mad doctor to get money to pay a gambling debt. *No Ransom* (Liberty, 1935), based on "The Big Mitten," has a family man paying to have himself murdered because he believes that his family doesn't love him anymore. *Hold 'Em Yale* (Paramount, 1935) had little to do with the short story of the same title, although the dialogue sounded Runyonesque. *Professional Soldier* (20th Century-Fox, 1936), based on "Gentlemen, the King," contained recognizable parts of Runyon, especially the scene in which the kidnapper (Victor McLaglen) teaches the boy king (Freddie Bartholomew) how to play baseball and shoot craps. *The Three Wise Guys* (MGM, 1936) was a Runyonese parable of three crooks whose hearts are softened by a baby.

Also during the thirties, Runyon wrote two plays, and although neither proved successful, both were adapted for the screen. *A Slight Case of Murder* (Warner Bros., 1938) was a comedy about a former bootlegger, Marco Remy (Edward G. Robinson), who goes legit after Prohibition but gets drawn back into underworld shenanigans when gangsters shoot it out on his property. The *New York Times* called the effort "just about the funniest show the new year has produced." The remake, *Stop, You're Killing Me!* (Warner Bros., 1952), with Broderick Crawford, was an inferior effort that turned satire to overdone farce.

Runyon also sold to Hollywood an unproduced play, *Saratoga Chips*, which became *Straight, Place and Show* (20th Century-Fox, 1938), a Ritz Brothers vehicle about three owners of a ten-cents-a-ride pony who come across a racehorse that can jump. It was weak farce that prompted the *New York Times* to comment, "Mr. Runyon should stick to his muggs and keep away from muggers."

During the 1930s, Runyon also created a series of fictional letters from a character named Joe Turp, who tells about the daffy doings of his wife, Ethel. One of these pieces, "A Call to the President" (*Saturday Evening Post*, August 13, 1937), became the basis for a movie, *Joe and Ethel Turp Call on the President* (MGM, 1939).

When a Brooklyn mailman (Walter Brennan) destroys a registered letter intended for his former sweetheart because he knows it will cause her pain, he is fired. Upset over the treatment of their friend, Joe and Ethel

Turp (William Gargan and Ann Sothern) drive to Washington to see the President (Lewis Stone). The couple is unaware of the importance of world affairs. "Things are going okay," Joe tells the President, "but the Dodgers need more pitching." The benevolent President ultimately gets the mailman reinstated and all ends happily. The script by Melville Baker worked well on the screen and maintained the spirit of Joe Turp's letters that had been so carefully constructed by Runyon.

While excellent pieces, the Joe and Ethel Turp stories were not the kind for which Runyon had become famous. More in line was "Tight Shoes," once again told by the author's anonymous narrator in his typical Runyonese. Shoe salesman Rupert Salsinger sells a gambler a pair of shoes that are too small and is fired by his boss. When Rupert gets drunk in a saloon with millionaire Calvin Colby, the two inadvertently start a melee that leads to Rupert being hailed as a new leader of social reform. He devotes too much time to his politics, and millionaire Calvin falls in love with and wins Rupert's girlfriend. For the film *Tight Shoes* (Universal, 1941), screenwriters Leonard Spigelgass and Art Arthur threw out most of Runyon's story. Gangster Speedy Miller (Broderick Crawford) buys a shoe store as a front and ends up firing salesman Jimmy Rupert (John Howard), who, with the help of his girlfriend, Ruth (Anne Gwynne), begins a campaign to curb corruption in the city. Speedy and his gang try to entice Jimmy to stop his harmful activities, but Ruth intercedes, setting Jimmy back on the right track. This was a short sixty-eight-minute "B" film that, with the exception of a few pieces of dialogue and a character or two, missed the flavor of Runyon.

Although Runyon's anonymous narrator rarely makes jugdments on the characters, he does so in "Butch Minds the Baby" (*Collier's*, September 13, 1930), one of the author's most popular stories. When the narrator encounters Harry the Horse, Little Isadoe, and Spanish John, he characterizes them as "three parties from Brooklyn" who were "always doing something that is considered a knock to the community, such as robbing people, or maybe shooting or stabbing them." The three hoods want Butch to help them crack a safe, but Butch is minding his baby while his wife is out. However, when Harry and the others agreee that Butch can bring along the kid and get fifty percent of the fifty G's plus five percent for the baby, Butch agrees. From the beginning, problems arise. First, the kid wakes up and Butch has to bottle feed him. Then Butch uses too much explosives to blow the safe. The hoods get the money, but as they are making their escape, the cops arrive. A shoot-out follows, but Butch and the narrator get away because the cops believe that a guy walking with his kid wouldn't be involved in a robbery.

The film *Butch Minds the Baby* (Universal, 1942), another of the studio's "B" productions, was not as successful as the story. Butch Grogan (Broderick Crawford) is an ex-safecracker who lands a job as a janitor in a New York brownstone, and one of his first tasks includes saving Susie O'Neill (Virginia Bruce) from committing suicide. Susie has a baby, whom Butch comes to adore, but Dennis Devlin (Dick Foran), the cop on the beat, has his eye on Butch, sure the con man is up to no good. Complications arise, and Butch has to blow a safe and take the rap to secure the baby's future. In many ways an ordinary comedy, *Butch Minds the Baby*, adapted by Leonard Spigelgass, did manage to create a few laughs along the way, especially with Squinty Sweeny (Shemp Howard), a nearsighted thug who peers out at the world through incredibly thick glasses.

In his later fiction written during the 1940s and after, Runyon often forsook happy endings. "Little Pinks" (*Collier's*, January 27, 1940) is an excellent representation of this turn in the author's work. The story became *The Big Street* (RKO, 1942) and was produced by Damon Runyon himself, although script chores were turned over to Runyon regular, Leonard Spigelgass. Little Pinks (Henry Fonda) is a mild-mannered busboy at Mindy's on Broadway who has a crush on Gloria (Lucille Ball), the brassy moll of small-time gangster Case Ables (Barton MacLane). Gloria, however, treats Little Pinks terribly until he saves her dog from being run over. When she is crippled after being knocked down by Ables, Little Pinks arranges a party for her where the old Broadway gang shows up. With her last bit of strength, she dances with Little Pinks, expiring in his arms. Incidentally, one of the Runyon characters introduced here, Nicely Nicely Johnson (Eugene Pallette), would turn up again in *Guys and Dolls*.

It was a love story of no great weight—but with a hard edge, just the kind that Runyon actually wrote, and since Runyon had such a close hand in the production, one might assume that the results were to his liking.

Far less successful was the adaptation by Richard Landau of "Johnny One Eye," a dark but entertaining tale of a wounded gangster hiding out in a deserted building who comes upon an injured cat with one eye. Gangster and feline become fast friends, and in the end, the cat inadvertently helps the gangster kill the man who betrayed him. The film *Johnny One Eye* (United Artists, 1950) substituted a dog for the cat and changed the story to a feud between a good gangster (Pat O'Brien) and a bad gangster (Wayne Morris). The latter hates little girls and kicks little dogs. The film concludes with a shootout during which both gangsters die. There is little evidence of Runyon throughout, and only the mere suggestion of his plot survives. Runyon's oddball characters and rich dialogue are noticeably absent.

Joe E. Brown as the gambler willing to sell his body to pay off his debts in *A Very Honorable Guy* (1934). With him is James Donlan.

Jean Parker in the title role, Chester Morris as Vic Toledo, and Tom Dugan as Deadpan in *Princess O'Hara* (1935).

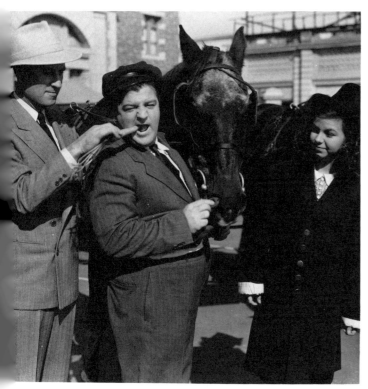

Bud Abbott and Lou Costello with horse and Patsy O'Connor in *It Ain't Hay* (1943), the comedy team's version of Runyon's "Princess O'Hara."

Freddie Bartholomew as the young king hears tales of baseball and valor from Victor McLaglen as the paid mercenary in *Professional Soldier* (1935), based on *Gentlemen, the King.*"

121

Betty Furness as Clarabelle, the shill for con men Bruce Cabot as Blackie Swanson and Raymond Walburn as Doc Brown, is reformed by Robert Young as wealthy and charming Joe Hatcher in *The Three Wise Guys* (1936).

The Ritz Brothers do their thing in *Straight, Place and Show* (1938), based on Runyon's unproduced play, *Saratoga Chips*.

In several of Runyon's stories, including "Little Miss Marker," the character of Regret, a rather heavy-set, talkative man, is a minor character, but in "Bloodhounds of Broadway" (*Collier's*, August 5, 1933), one of the author's best stories, he becomes the protagonist. The first film version of *Bloodhounds of Broadway* (20th Century-Fox, 1952) dropped most of the plot, and although its amiable story—and Mitzi Gaynor—looked good in Technicolor, the racy style associated with Runyon was barely in evidence. (Screenwriter Sy Gomberg did the adaptation.)

The thirty-seven-year-later remake, *Bloodhounds of Broadway* (Vestron, 1989), confined all its action to one New Year's Eve during Prohibition, interweaving four separate Runyon stories, with many of the author's original characters, at least in name, finding their way in. The least interesting of the segments, based on "The Brain Goes Home," opens the film and keeps reappearing throughout. The Brain (Rutger Hauer) is stabbed and then dragged all over town as his cronies try to find at least one person to take him off their hands. Another segment is based on the short story, "Bloodhounds of Broadway." Regret (Matt Dillon) is accused of a murder he didn't commit, but his involvement with Lovey Lou (Jennifer Grey) is pure invention on the part of the screenwriters. In "Social Error," Harriet MacKyle (Julie Hagerty) is a socialite whose party is ruined when a thug shoots her pet parrot. Only one segment, "A Very Honorable Guy," crackles with some energy, mainly because the leads (Randy Quaid and Madonna) show some appreciation for the cadence of Runyon's language. The adaptation was by producer-director Howard Brookner and Colman deKay.

With 1943's *It Ain't Hay*, Abbott and Costello attempted to merge Damon Runyon with their own particular style of comedy. Ten years later, Dean Martin and Jerry Lewis tried the same thing with their version of "Money From Home" (*Cosmopolitan*, October 1935), a story admirably suited to a slapstick approach. The final sequence has klutzy Eddie Yokum riding in a steeplechase in order to save his lady love from marrying an insensitive millionaire. The race itself is a series of pratfalls, and the film *Money From Home* (Paramount, 1953) also made it the climax of the story. Although characters such as Seldom Seen Kid (Robert Strauss) and Bertie Searles (Richard Haydn) are holdovers from the Runyon, all the fun of his story has disappeared.

Critics have compared Runyon to such great American authors as Sherwood Anderson and Ernest Hemingway, yet today he might well be forgotten by the general public if not for the enduring success of the Broadway musical, *Guys and Dolls* (1950), adapted by Abe Burrows from two Runyon stories, "The Idyll of Miss Sarah Brown" and "Pick the Winner." Producer Samuel

Broderick Crawford (in jacket and hat) as Remy Marco with Claire Trevor as his wife in *Stop, You're Killing Me* (1952), a semi-musical remake of *A Slight Case of Murder*. Virginia Gibson and Howard Freeman are on the left; Sheldon Leonard right.

Shemp Howard as Squinty Sweeny, Richard Lane as Harry the Horse, and Broderick Crawford as Butch Grogan in *Butch Minds the Baby* (1942), a Damon Runyon production.

Wayne Morris, Lawrence Cregar, and Dolores Moran in Damon Runyon's *Johnny One-Eye* (1950).

Ray Collins as the Professor, Agnes Moorehead as Violette, and Henry Fonda as Little Pinks in *The Big Street* (1942), adapted from Damon Runyon's "Little Pinks."

Goldwyn brought *Guys and Dolls* (MGM, 1955) to the screen, and director Joseph L. Mankiewicz adapted the stage play himself, keeping the plot intact, but the real fun came from the breezy Runyonesque dialogue.

Shiftless Nathan Detroit (Frank Sinatra) is the operator of the oldest permanent floating crap game in New York, but he needs one grand up front to keep it going. In fact, he does not even have enough to buy an anniversary gift for Hot-Box chanteuse Adelaide (Vivian Blaine, repeating her Broadway role), to whom he has been engaged for fourteen years. In order to get the needed cash, Nathan bets high-roller Sky Masterson (Marlon Brando) that he cannot get Sister Sarah Brown (Jean Simmons) to go along on his upcoming trip to Havana. Aware that Sarah is having problems keeping open her Save-a-Soul Mission, Sky offers to produce a dozen sinners for her meeting if she will have dinner with him. The dinner turns out to be in Havana, and after a few drinks, Sarah loses her inhibitions, dances, sings, and makes a pass at Sky. She even takes part in a brawl. Making good on his promise, an admiring Sky wins a dozen sinners for Sarah's mission in a crap game. In the end, Sky and Sarah and Nathan and Adelaide are married in a double wedding ceremony with all the Runyonesque denizens of Broadway looking on.

Bob Hope as the Kid
surrounded by his cronies in *The
Lemon Drop Kid* (1951).

Hillbilly Mitzi Gaynor and city slicker Scott Brady with inept
Timothy Carey and Wally Vernon in Damon Runyon's *Bloodhounds
of Broadway* (1952).

Randy Quaid and Madonna in the remake of *Bloodhounds of
Broadway* (1989).

124

Jean Simmons as prim and proper Sister Sarah Brown who succumbs to charm of Marlon Brando as gambler Sky Masterson and decides to fly off to Havana with him for a night of romance in *Guys and Dolls* (1955).

Of the two stories that formed the basis of the original play, "The Idyll of Miss Sarah Brown" remains almost intact. On the other hand, except for the long-standing relationship between Nathan and Adelaide, "Pick a Winner" is little in evidence. Actually, Nathan Detroit was a minor character in the first story and not to be found at all in "Pick a Winner." Despite these changes and despite failing to provide some of Runyon's hard-edged irony, the film, as did the play, remained amazingly faithful to the Runyon characters.

Like Ring Lardner and Damon Runyon, James Thurber (1894–1961) was a satirist who produced a series of books full of his unique brand of humor and graced with his wonderful line drawings. The movies ultimately got around to using his material but seldom did justice to his stories.

The first screen adaptation was a comedy supposedly based on *My Life and Hard Times*, a book of hilarious autobiographical vignettes. The film was *Rise and Shine* (20th Century-Fox, 1941), but other than using Thurber's name in the credits, it had little to do with him. Actually it sounded more like *Elmer the Great*. The story concerned a football player (Jack Oakie) who gets mixed up with gangsters, is kidnapped, but escapes in time to save the big game. Milton Berle, George Murphy, and Linda Darnell were those involved.

The following year, *The Male Animal* (Warner Bros.,

Gene Nelson, Virginia Mayo, Ronald Reagan, and Phyllis Thaxter in *She's Working Her Way Through College* (1952), a loose musical adaptation of *The Male Animal*.

Linda Darnell, George Murphy, and Milton Berle in *Rise and Shine* (1941), supposedly based on Thurber's *My Life and Times*.

Henry Fonda as slightly absent-minded Professor Tommy Turner, Olivia de Havilland as his wife, Ellen, and Jack Carson as former football champ Joe Ferguson, her old flame, in *The Male Animal* (1942), based on the play by Thurber and Elliot Nugent.

1942) reached the screen directed by Elliot Nugent, who had coauthored the 1940 Broadway play with Thurber. There were only a few minor changes. In it, Tommy Turner (Henry Fonda), a professor at a stuffy midwestern college, announces that he is going to read to his students a letter written by Vanzetti of Sacco and Vanzetti fame. Afraid of the inflammatory nature of the missive, the college trustees threaten to fire him if he does so. Tensions grow between Tommy and his wife Ellen (Olivia de Havilland) as the campus divides in its support of the teacher. Despite the college threats and the family trouble, Tommy reads the letter, which turns out to be a moving plea for understanding and contains no political message whatsoever. The campus returns to order, and Tommy and his wife patch things up.

A quick summation of the plot makes it sound far more serious than it was. The film actually contains some very funny sequences, especially the one in which a drunk Tommy believes his friend, ex-football hero Joe Ferguson (Jack Carson), is trying to steal his wife. He challenges the much larger man to a fight, but inadvertently knocks himself out. The real charm of this film is that it has something to say and says it in a funny way. It's a comedy with heart and head, which prompted the *New York Times* to call it an "exceptional screen translation [by Julius and Philip Epstein and Stephen Morehouse Avery] of the James Thurber–Elliot Nugent play."

The play found its way to the screen again a decade later disguised as *She's Working Her Way Through College* (Warner Bros., 1952), a silly musical farce about a burlesque queen (Virginia Mayo) who wants a college education. This time, the professor is played by Ronald Reagan. The story's relationship to *The Male Animal* was flimsy at best.

Elliott Nugent did the 1950 television adaptation of *The Male Animal* for *Robert Montgomery Presents*, playing the lead role himself. In the later adaptation for *Playhouse 90* by Don M. Mankiewicz, Andy Griffith starred in the 1958 production of *The Male Animal* in this country and Anthony Perkins starred in the 1960 one in Great Britain.

Thurber's most famous short story is certainly "The Secret Life of Walter Mitty." Mitty is a henpecked husband who daydreams his life away in a series of adventures that are right out of a Saturday matinee serial. After selling the rights to Samuel Goldwyn, Thurber was so despondent that he offered the producer $10,000 to return the story. Goldwyn refused, and the result was *The Secret Life of Walter Mitty* (Goldwyn/RKO, 1947). Mitty (Danny Kaye) is dominated by his mother (Fay Bainter), his fiancée, Gertrude (Ann Rutherford), and his boss, Mr. Pierce (Thurston Hall). To escape his milquetoast life, Mitty daydreams, becoming everything from a heroic RAF pilot to a brilliant surgeon. In each of his dreams appears the same beautiful blond (Virginia

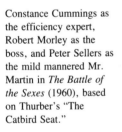

Constance Cummings as the efficiency expert, Robert Morley as the boss, and Peter Sellers as the mild mannered Mr. Martin in *The Battle of the Sexes* (1960), based on Thurber's "The Catbird Seat."

Mayo), who suddenly turns up in real life pursued by villains after her jewels.

The Thurber story provided a peg on which the story hung its hat. Screenwriters Ken Englund and Everett Freeman added most of the plot, and only a few of Mitty's daydreams plus his character made the transition to the screen. However, Danny Kaye's inspired madness, which Thurber despised, kept the pace at a frantic level with only a few asides for a musical number or two. Thurber was so upset with Goldwyn and Kaye that he wrote a letter to *Life* in which he apologized to his fictional hero. "Sorry, Walter, sorry for everything."

Thurber reached the screen once more with an adaptation of "The Catbird Seat," and the result, *The Battle of the Sexes* (Bryantston/Continental, 1960), again had less to do with Thurber and more to do with screenwriter Monja Danischewsky, who not only expanded on a thin

little story but also changed the locale from the United States to Edinburgh, Scotland. Mr. Martin (Peter Sellers) is a mild-mannered clerk who tries to save his boss's (Robert Morley) textile manufacturing concern from an American efficiency expert (Constance Cummings). The result is a mixture of sophisticated humor and slapstick that, while not the story Thurber had written, nevertheless made for an entertaining little film.

Despite the great number of short stories adapted for the screen, very few work well, and certainly not without a great deal of addition and changes. Short stories are, by design, short enough to be read in one sitting, and their content is usually too skimpy to fill a feature-length movie. As a result, most adaptations of short stories are largely studio concoctions; the best are those that maintain some semblance of the author's style and tone.

John Garfield as Frank and Lana Turner as Cora in *The Postman Always Rings Twice* (1946).

SEVEN

TROUBLEMAKERS OF THE THIRTIES

James M. Cain, John Steinbeck

At first glance, James M. Cain and John Steinbeck would seem an oddly matched pair. Cain wrote of a world full of hard men and hard women; Steinbeck was a regional writer who loved the land and the people. Cain made crime part of the American mainstream; Steinbeck stirred the political waters. Yet these two men exemplify the 1930s when each did some of his best writing. Both authors developed lean, hard styles; both wrote of the little guy struggling against society and fate; both explored forbidden subjects, and both became immensely popular, and as a result, were swept up and embraced by Hollywood.

Although James Cain had been a screenwriter himself, he seldom saw the films adapted from his work, but one day he turned on the television and seated himself beside his wife, Florence. Years before, *Serenade* had been made into a film, and at the time, he had suggested possible changes to Warner Bros. that he believed would make the story acceptable to the Hays Office, but he had never seen the end result. Fifteen minutes into the film, Cain asked his wife if she minded if he turned it off. He had had enough.

Not all of the screen adaptations of Cain's fiction were as bad as *Serenade*. Of the fourteen American films thus far based on his work, a few were even worse, most were merely adequate, and two became cornerstones of *film noir*, excellent adaptations that captured the spirit and substance of Cain.

Of all the American writers who are labeled hard-boiled, James Cain may well be the most influential. His supercharged style became the model for a whole generation of writers, his frank sexual scenes helped break down puritanical barriers, and his dialogue, which he once described as the way he heard American spoken, helped make the American novel more dramatic. Often classified as a crime writer, Cain showed little concern with private detectives or mobsters. His novels and short stories were usually filled with little people driven by lust and greed, and the reader's sympathy was often hard to place, but because of the way the characters talked, it was easy to believe in them.

The first of Cain's works adapted for films was "The Baby in the Icebox," written in 1933 for H. L. Mencken's *American Mercury*. By the time the story reached the screen as *She Made Her Bed* (Paramount, 1934), an ironic tale of relationships had become a silly little romance. One of the central characters, the narrator, had been dropped, and the sexual content, although not as overt as in Cain's later fiction, had been toned down to such an extent that passion disappeared from the Casey Robinson–Frank R. Adams script. The *New York Times* found, "Though the story is fastened upon a story by James M. Cain, the blame for this picture is too large, too richly complicated, to be attached to any one person however a source of imbecilities."

The film failed to hurt the reputation either of Cain's short story or of Cain himself. Alfred Knopf had just published *The Postman Always Rings Twice*, and its impact was already being felt. In 1936, Cain's *Double Indemnity* appeared as a magazine serial. (Knopf published it as a novel in 1943.) Although the steamy sex and the amoral characters of what would be his two most popular works prevented American film studios from touching either right away, their popularity caught Hollywood's notice, resulting in the adaptations of three of Cain's lesser works first.

The novelette *Two Can Sing* (aka *Career in C Major*) had been serialized in *American Mercury* in 1938. Although enjoyable, it was pretty weak stuff. Basically the lighthearted story concerns a self-centered woman who wants to become a diva but is really without talent. Unexpectedly, her husband, who owns a construction company, discovers that it is he who has the voice, and he becomes an opera star. The short novel was adapted by Nunnally Johnson and became *Wife, Husband and Friend* (20th Century-Fox, 1939), starring Loretta Young and Warner Baxter. Like the book, it was a piece of fluff, although enjoyable fluff. *Two Can Sing* included an affair between the husband and another opera singer, but the film dropped all reference to it. Since the story was rather slim, additional characters were added, but the entire thing took only eighty minutes.

The Nunnally Johnson story was remade as *Everybody Does It* (20th Century-Fox, 1949), and although it ran eighteen minutes longer, the affair was again deleted. Also, several scenes relied heavily on slapstick, including a hilarious opera sequence where the husband (Paul Douglas) is given "the bird," that is, booed off the stage. Douglas gave a fine comic performance, but it was not the character Cain created, and the original tone and mood of the story disappeared.

The second Cain film of 1939, *When Tomorrow Comes* (Universal, 1939), was based on an unsold magazine serial "A Modern Cinderella," which wasn't published until 1952, and then as an original paperback under the title *The Root of His Evil*. It is told by the heroine who is more involved with labor problems and a

strike than romance. As it appeared on the screen, the story (with a screenplay by Dwight Taylor) was almost unrecognizable, except for one scene in a church on Long Island during a hurricane. Thinking they will not survive, the romantic leads, played by Irene Dunne and Charles Boyer, make love. The scene did not appear in "A Modern Cinderella," but a similar one did appear in *Serenade*, published in 1937. Cain unsuccessfully sued the studio for plagiarism. Despite the suds, *When Tomorrow Comes* was remade as *Interlude* (Universal, 1957) and again, unofficially, under the same title (Columbia, 1968).

Up to this point, the films based on Cain's works had been weak entries, but at least they had been "A" productions. Not so with *Money and the Woman* (Warner Bros., 1940). It was economy all the way. The studio hired Cain to work on the script, and his first outline stuck closely to the original story. One Warner "B" unit director tried to veto it, believing that the Hays office would never approve, but in the end, studio heads decided to do it Cain's way, and the script (credited to Robert Presnell) somehow passed the Hays censors. It didn't matter. It remained a "B" that couldn't make heads or tails of its plot. At one point, a character cries, "I won't sleep a wink until this mess is cleared up," and one reviewer advised his readers that they might take this as fair warning.

In the forties, Hollywood decided to try its luck with *Double Indemnity* (Paramount, 1944). The war had created a demand for more realistic films, and some of the puritanical zeal of the Hays Office had waned. Billy Wilder was chosen to direct, and he brought in Raymond Chandler to collaborate on the script when his (Wilder's) regular partner, Charles Brackett, turned down the project as "too dirty." Attempting to do the story as Cain had written it, Wilder auditioned actors to read scenes straight out of the book, but it just didn't work. Chandler pointed out the problem: Cain's dialogue, which looked good on paper, sounded like a high school play. It was dialogue for the eye, not the ear.

The plot remained basically the same in both book and film. Walter Neff (Fred MacMurray) meets Phyllis Dietrichson (Barbara Stanwyck) while on a routine call to sell auto insurance to her husband, who is not at home. Walter and Phyllis are immediately drawn to each other. His is a purely physical attraction, hers a more calculating one. On a subsequent visit, she outlines a plan to buy insurance without her husband's knowledge, but Walter understands that it is a prologue to murder. At first, he rejects the idea, but the attraction is too strong. Together, he and Phyllis plot and carry out her husband's killing. Once the murder has taken place, Burton Keyes (Edward G. Robinson), a crafty insurance investigator who is

Lobby card picturing for *She Made Her Bed* (1934), based on James Cain's "The Baby in the Ice Box."

Charles Boyer, Irene Dunne, Barbara O'Neil, and Nella Walker in *When Tomorrow Comes* (1939), based on Cain's "A Modern Cinderella," which was unpublished at the time of the film's release.

Jeffrey Lynn (center), John Litel, and Brenda Marshall in *Money and the Woman* (aka *The Embezzler*, 1940).

Walter's boss and mentor, becomes suspicious. Walter knows just how dangerous Keyes is, and decides he can meet Phyllis only in inconspicuous places, and then for just a few moments at a time. There comes a point when Walter wants out (he has learned that she's two-timing him), but Phyllis tells him that they both chose to ride the trolley and must stay on it together "all the way down the line."

At this point, the book and the film go their separate ways. In the novel, after Keyes discovers the truth, the insurance company figures out that it can save money by not prosecuting Walter and Phyllis, and gives them both a chance to leave the country. The final scene has the couple on board ship somewhere at sea where they are set to jump overboard and join the sharks. The screen needed an ending with more visual impact. Hence, Walter confronts Phyllis in her home. They struggle for a gun. He shoots and kills her, but in the process is seriously wounded. Keyes discovers Walter, dying from the gunshot wound, as he is recounting the events into a dictating machine back in his office.

Fred MacMurray became the screen embodiment of Walter, and in praising the actor's performance, James Cain wrote, "The way you found tragedy in his shallow, commonplace, smart-cracking skull will remain with me a long time." Barbara Stanwyck also proved to be the ideal choice to play Phyllis. When Wilder put the blond wig on her, one Paramount production head said, "We hire Barbara Stanwyck and here we get George Washington." But Wilder wanted her to look as sleazy as possible. Never a great beauty, Stanwyck was a fine actress, and turning her blond added a slutty sensuality to her character. Later, James Cain would say, "It is a very creepy sensation to see a character imagined by yourself step in front of your eyes exactly as you imagined her."

Billy Wilder was proud of the film, too, believing that it was *Double Indemnity* and not *The Maltese Falcon* which taught Hollywood a whole new approach to the gangster film. Despite changes he and Chandler made, the film emerged as pure Cain, including the staccato style of his writing, which seemed to find its way into the dialogue and editing. When *Double Indemnity* opened, critics fell over themselves praising it. Bosley Crowther wrote that "the fans of James Cain's tough fiction might gloat over it with gleaming joy."

A television production of *Double Indemnity* (teleplay by Steven Bochco, ABC, Universal Television, 1973) followed the film rather than the novel, including the ending where Keyes (Lee J. Cobb) discovers Neff (Richard Crenna) dying after being shot by Phyllis (Samantha Eggar). It contained little excitement and none of the originality of the Wilder film.

After *Double Indemnity* became big box office, producer Jerry Wald immediately approached James Cain about doing a film of *Mildred Pierce*, which had been published four years earlier in 1941. He asked the author to write a memorandum to send to Jack Warner, but after several attempts, Cain told Wald, "I wrote *Mildred Pierce* as a novel, and it is hard for me to rethink it as a picture." As written, the book would never have worked on the screen. There was no murder, and the studio wanted a murder; plus the novel was both overlong and far too shapeless to accommodate a tight 110-minute script.

Except in some of the early flashback sequences, the *Mildred Pierce* (Warner Bros., 1945) of director Michael Curtiz is not the *Mildred Pierce* of author James Cain, and Cain didn't like it. For one thing, the film (adapted by Ranald MacDougall) dropped all reference to Mildred's daughter, Veda, becoming an opera star. For another, Cain believed that the film missed the point of the book—that is, the struggle of one woman against social injustice—and he resented it being turned into a whodunit.

As the film opens, wealthy Monty Beragon (Zachary Scott) is shot. Gripping his chest, he falls to the floor and mutters, "Mildred." The unseen killer runs out the door. In the next scene, a woman in a fur coat walks onto a pier, apparently intent on throwing herself into the sea. A policeman tells her to move on. The woman is Mildred Pierce (Joan Crawford), who is soon picked up for questioning. Trying to convince the police that she murdered Monty, she tells her story in a flashback, beginning on the day she and her first husband separated and ending when, as Mrs. Monty Beragon, she caught her husband and her daughter, Veda (Ann Blyth), in a passionate embrace. Interrupting her story, the police tell Mildred that they know who killed Monty. It was Veda, not Mildred. When Monty refused to marry Veda and called her a "rotten little tramp," Veda shot him. Veda is arrested, and in the final scene, Mildred is left to piece together her life, reunited with her first husband, Bert (Bruce Bennett).

Overall, *Mildred Pierce* is a superior example of *film noir*, improving the novel on several counts. For one, it tightened the story. Many of the extraneous incidents were omitted and some of the characters were dropped. Also, time was constricted. The novel took place over a seven-year span, and while time is ambiguous in the film—it may well have been seven years—the pace is quickened. In addition, the mood of the film was far more intense than the mood of the novel. In the beach house where Monty is killed, on the pier where Mildred contemplates suicide, and in the police station where she is interrogated, the scenes are dark and shadowy, adding a sense of foreboding and gloom.

Now that James Cain was hot property, MGM began to think seriously of filming *The Postman Always Rings Twice*, which the studio had owned since 1934. The book had already been brought to the Broadway stage in 1936 and had been filmed twice, first as *Le Dernier Tournant* (France, 1939) and then as *Ossessione* (Italy, 1942), the latter directed by Luchino Visconti and regarded as one of the precursors of Italian neorealism. *Ossessione* was first banned by the Fascist government in Italy, then after the war, blocked entrance into the United States by MGM.

The film *The Postman Always Rings Twice* (MGM, 1946) is told in flashback. It opens with Frank Chambers (John Garfield) sitting on death row and pouring out his

Lobby card for *Wife, Husband and Friend* (1939), an adaptation of Cain's *Career in C Major*.

Fred MacMurray as insurance agent Walter Neff admires the slipper of Barbara Stanwyck as seductive but deadly Phyllis Dietrichson when stopping by to talk to her husband about his policy. and then receiving friendly advice from Edward G. Robinson as Barton Keyes, Neff's boss and mentor, in *Double Indemnity* (1944).

Ann Blyth as the evil Veda, Zachary Scott as Monty, and Joan Crawford in the title role in *Mildred Pierce* (1945).

story to a priest and the local district attorney. As in the novel, Frank's viewpoint colors the entire narrative. The audience sees Cora Smith (Lana Turner) as Frank sees her, dressed always in immaculate white. She first appears as the camera follows her lipstick rolling across the floor, then it pans up her bare legs, revealing her white shorts and halter top. Her head is wrapped in a white turban; she is a plaster Madonna with a heart of ice.

Just as in the novel, the goals of love and success turn out to be traps. Cora wants respectability and security, and so she has entered into a loveless marriage with a much older man (Cecil Kellaway). Frank has constantly drifted as a way to escape responsibility, but once he accepts responsibility with Cora, it leads to murder, Cora's death, and then his own. Like most of Cain's heroes, Frank and Cora are doomed from the start.

The film, adapted by Harry Ruskin and Niven Busch, made some changes in the characters. Nick Papadakis became Nick Smith, no longer a Greek, because MGM was afraid that Greece, if offended, wouldn't grant an export license. In the novel, Cora was dark—dark hair, dark eyes—so much so that she says to Frank, "You

think I'm a Mex." Then she adds, "You're not the first one. Well, get this. I'm just as white as you are, see?"

Despite the changes, James Cain liked the performance of Lana Turner as Cora, but he was not very complimentary toward the movie itself. When asked what he thought of it, he said, "Well, I don't think it stunk any worse than most of them do."

Jack Nicholson conceived the idea of filming *The Postman Always Rings Twice* (Paramount, 1981) again without the constraints of censorship, but it took almost ten years for his idea to be realized. When he and director Bob Rafelson finally got around to doing it, from an adaptation by playwright David Mamet, they included parts of the novel that had been omitted in the MGM version, but left out others included in that film. The remake dropped the first person narrative, and the omniscient viewpoint put distance between the audience and Frank, which was the opposite of Cain's intention. The sympathy the audience felt for Frank in the novel and in the 1946 film never materialized for Nicholson. Cain wanted the reader not only to sympathize but also to pull for the lovers to get away with it. Also in the novel and the MGM version, Frank is much younger than

Nick. Thus, it is easy for the audience to understand Cora's decision to take up with the drifter. But in the remake, the Nicholson character, seedy and disreputable, is almost the same age as Nick (John Colicos). Therefore, the passion that Cora (Jessica Lange) develops for him is less believable.

In the conclusion of the 1981 version, there is the accident, and Cora is killed. The last image shows Frank's hand holding hers. When he takes his hand away, only the image of her bloody one remains. Certainly, this is an ironic ending, but both the novel and the 1946 version contained a double irony when Frank is also accused and convicted of Cora's murder. Thus the meaning of "the postman always rings twice."

After the release of the first *Postman* in 1946, no new Cain reached the screen for a decade until *Slightly Scarlet* (RKO, 1956) was made from *Love's Lovely Counterfeit,* a novel published in 1942. Cain readily admitted that it was his only work he wrote directly with the movies in mind, but because it dealt with corrupt politics in a midwestern city, no studio would touch it during the war years.

The film (adapted by Robert Blees) was generally panned by the critics. Bosley Crowther wrote, "Two red-headed women and one fat-headed man [Arlene Dahl, Rhonda Fleming, and John Payne] are the principal characters. In the end, all their faces are red. So, we say, should be the faces of the people responsible for this film, which is said to be taken from a novel (unrecognizable) of James M. Cain."

Within a week of the release of *Slightly Scarlet, Serenade* (Warner Bros., 1956) also reached movie houses. In 1937, when Cain had written *Serenade,* he believed it to be unfilmable because of the homosexual content, but after the success of *Double Indemnity,* Warners bought the rights anyway. The studio avoided the homosexual theme by making the man in the narrator's life Kendall Hale (Joan Fontaine), a wanton blueblood. She sponsors Damon Vincenti (Mario Lanza), a California vineyard worker who becomes an opera singer, but then loses interest and turns to other men, leaving him somewhere in Mexico with a bottle and his Mexican girlfriend. A complex and touchy subject emerged as a basically simple, albeit lengthy tale (rewritten by Ivan Goff, Ben Roberts, and John Twist) of an opera singer who is deeply hurt by one woman but redeemed by another. It certainly was not Cain's *Serenade.*

To date, the last James Cain novel to reach the screen is *Butterfly* (1947), a story set in West Virginia that deals with incest, murder, and retribution. By the time Hollywood got around to using it, the once-shunned material was no longer taboo, but the new freedom failed to help

Jessica Lange and Jack Nicholson as the ill-fated lovers in the more explicit remake of *The Postman Always Rings Twice* (1981).

Paul Douglas as the failed opera singer and Celeste Holm as his understanding wife in *Everybody Does It* (1949), based on James Cain's "Two Can Sing."

a muddled script by John Goff and Matt Cimber. The novel was told in the first person, constructed much along the lines of *Postman* and *Double Indemnity*, but *Butterfly* (New Realm, 1981), starring Stacy Keach and Pia Zadora, chose an omniscient viewpoint, distancing itself from the audience. Where the novel concentrated on characters, the film played up the sensational elements at their expense.

Cain seldom liked a film based on his work, finding complete satisfaction only in Billy Wilder's *Double Indemnity*. It may have bothered him that Hollywood emasculated and mutilated his fiction, but he held a realistic view of the relationship between literature and the movies. "They're entitled to do whatever they want," Cain said, "because they paid me the money."

While Hollywood mistreated James Cain, it revered John Steinbeck (1902–68), who proved phenomenally successful with such novels as *Of Mice and Men*, *The Grapes of Wrath*, and *East of Eden*. Steinbeck may well have the distinction of having had more film classics adapted from his work than any other major American author.

With *Of Mice and Men* (1937), Steinbeck began the practice of writing the novel and play simultaneously, and it won the New York Drama Critics Circle award. It was only natural that Hollywood would want to take advantage of the successes of the book and play, but the major studios feared that the language and subject matter

Mario Lanza and Norma Zimmer in the "La Tosca" sequence from *Serenade* (1956).

Arlene Dahl and John Payne in *Slightly Scarlet* (1956), based on
James Cain's *Love's Lovely Counterfeit*.

were too shocking for the screen. Director Lewis Milestone, who in 1930 had helmed *All Quiet on the Western
Front*, and screenwriter Eugene Solow acquired the
rights and then gained the backing of independent
producer Hal Roach, who gambled that they could make
a low-budget version. They brought it in for less than
$300,000, a minimal sum for an "A" production even in
1939, prompting *Life* to call it "the most economical
Grade A movie to come out of Hollywood in a decade."

Steinbeck himself not only approved the screenplay
but also added some dialogue that Solow thought the
most beautiful he had ever read. Solow deleted some of
the author's more censurable language—though "hell"
and "son-of-a-bitch" were really the only profanity
Steinbeck used in the book—but retained the feel and
cadence of the characters' speech. Using the play as the
basis for his screenplay, Solow supplemented it with
details from the novel and opened up the action, giving
the story additional fluidity and movement.

With the Solow script as his guide, director Milestone
zeroed in on life on the farm and the migrants' love of the
land with far more effect than was done on a stage
burdened with static sets. His camera moved lovingly
among the fields of grain, farm hands, and machinery,
creating a rural lyricism seldom found in American
movies, including John Ford's more highly praised
Grapes of Wrath.

Paperback tie-in for the 1981 film of *Butterfly* with Pia Zadora. The
film dropped the "The" in Cain's title.

Of Mice and Men (Roach–United Artists, 1940) opens with a pre-credits sequence as George (Burgess Meredith) and Lenny (Lon Chaney Jr.) flee the wrath of a posse from the California farming community of Weed. This opening establishes the theme of fear and flight; it also establishes the characters so well that once the credits have ended, George and Lenny jump right into a key dialogue sequence without confusing the audience.

However, several early scenes are weakened by subtle but important script changes. In the novel and play, George discovers Lenny petting a dead mouse, but Solow and Milestone must have thought that a mouse would frighten too many women in the audience because they substituted a dead bird, a substitution that substantially weakens the symbolic meaning of the title. Once at the farm, George has Lenny prove how strong he is by lifting a wagon with Slim (Charles Bickford) sitting on it and George hanging on to the wheel, the only scene invented for the film.

Milestone made use of a fluid camera to bring added movement to the story. In the novel, Steinbeck used only a couple of lines to describe Curley (Bob Steele) beating up the stable hand, Whit (Noah Beery Jr.), who he believes has been paying too much attention to his—Curley's—wife, Mae (Betty Field); but in the film, Milestone begins with a long shot of the two of them walking toward each other, and like a participant, the camera slowly moves closer and closer until they meet. Another scene involves Candy (Roman Bohnen) and his dog. In the play, when his dog is shot, the audience is forced to concentrate upon Candy's torment. But Milestone cuts to the faces and the dialogue of the other men as they wait for the fatal shot to be fired. After what seems an eternity, the sound of a single shot is heard off camera, and Candy, lying on the bunk, stiffens. In despair, he turns toward the wall, and the screen fades to black.

Hollywood's Production Code also forced a few mild compromises. In the novel, Curley wears a glove filled with Vaseline on his left hand to keep it soft for his wife. However, in the film he wears gloves on both hands like some on-the-prowl prizefighter, thus depriving the scene where Lenny crushes Curley's hand of its added significance. The film also made the killing of Mae less brutal

The Joad Family at dinner: Jane Darwell as Ma, Dorris Bowdon as Rosasharon, Henry Fonda as Tom, Shirley Mills as Ruth, Darryl Hickman as Winfield, Frank Sully as Noah, Frank Darien as Uncle John, and Russell Simpson as Pa in *The Grapes of Wrath* (1940).

than the novel and play. Because the Code said that crime had to be punished, Solow was forced to devise a slightly different ending. As in the book, George shoots Lenny to save him from being torn apart by Curley and the posse. However, Solow added a scene where George hands over his gun to the sheriff and then is led off by the law. Although superfluous, this minor change does not compromise the film in the least, mainly because screenwriter Solow made it so ambiguous. George's fate is still the same. He has killed Lenny, and in doing so, has killed his own dream.

The film proved to be a critical success. The reviewer for *The Nation* echoed the sentiment of the majority of movie critics when he wrote, "Hollywood for once displays deep respect for a serious writer." Despite its compromises, at every crucial juncture the film evokes the same mood and same compassion as the novel, a rare accomplishment in the history of film adaptations.

Using many of the creative talents from his *Baretta* TV series, Robert Blake produced an extremely faithful adaptation of Steinbeck's *Of Mice and Men* (teleplay by E. Nick Alexander, NBC, Of Mice and Men Productions, 1981) and starred as George. Much of the material cut from the film was brought back, including the reference to Curley's gloved hand, and as a whole, the production projected an authentic and timeless appearance. If the film based more on Eugene Solow's 1940 screenplay than on the original novel has a fault, it lies in the script's two-and-a-half-hour running time, which stretches the limits of Steinbeck's slim story.

A new production by Chicago's esteemed Steppenwolf Company of *Of Mice and Men* premiered at the 1992 Cannes Film Festival. The new adaptation by Horton Foote stars John Malkovich as George and Gary Sinese as Lenny. Sinese also directed.

Whatever controversy *Of Mice and Men* generated was minuscule compared to that created by *The Grapes of Wrath* (1939). Although that novel won the Pulitzer Prize, it seemed to many a call to revolution, and more than one critic compared its impact to Harriet Beecher Stowe's *Uncle Tom's Cabin*.

When Darryl Zanuck acquired the rights for $75,000, he received thousands of letters telling him that he didn't have the courage to film the story that Steinbeck had written. Communists accused him of buying the novel to keep it off the screen, and liberals said he would either shelve the project or turn it into sentimental tripe in order to protect business and agricultural interests. Zanuck himself was afraid of the negative press in Oklahoma and Texas, and when he came to film certain sequences there, he disguised the script by using a working title, *Highway 66*, in order to avoid trouble from local chambers of commerce.

Betty Field as Mae fights off the advances of Lon Chaney Jr. as Lenny in *Of Mice and Men* (1939).

Hollywood has seldom displayed courage in its choice and handling of controversial subjects, and in light of this record, Steinbeck himself was suspicious of the project. However, Zanuck told Steinbeck that he intended to follow the book exactly. Then he added, "But there are certain things we can't show. We can't show the baby sucking the woman's breast. These things can never be passed by the Hays Office." Apparently Zanuck had in mind the final scene where Rosasharon breast-feeds the old man. Zanuck also told Steinbeck that he was dissatisfied with the last scene because he wanted to hear from Ma and Pa Joad again. Although Steinbeck felt uneasy about Zanuck's comments, he gave his approval.

When Nunnally Johnson came to the actual writing of the screenplay, he deleted almost all the action after the episode at the government camp, shuffled other sequences around, and altered the context of others; yet, in the end, Zanuck got what he wanted. While the finished screenplay was vastly different from the novel, it departed little from Steinbeck's intention.

Zanuck chose John Ford to direct. "I'd read the book—it was a good story," Ford said. "Darryl Zanuck had a good script on it. The whole thing appealed to me—being about simple people." It was Ford's interest in the family, a recurring theme in many of his films, that shifted the emphasis away from Steinbeck's angry politi-

Akim Tamiroff as Pablo, Frank Morgan as The Pirate, John Qualen as José Maria Corcoran, and Spencer Tracy as Pilon in Steinbeck's *Tortilla Flat* (1942).

Henry Travers as the defiant mayor faces Sir Cedric Hardwicke as the Nazi commandant in *The Moon Is Down* (1943), while Lee J. Cobb (left) as the town doctor and Margaret Wycherly as the Mayor's wife look on.

Peter Miles as Jody admires his pony while Robert Mitchum as Billy Buck offers advice in *The Red Pony* (1949), an uncharacteristic prestige release from Republic Pictures boasting a musical score by Aaron Copland.

cal and social ideology. To Ford, the people came first; politics followed. Given this disparity of visions, it is remarkable that the film captured so much of the spirit of the novel.

The Grapes of Wrath (20th Century-Fox, 1940) opens with Tom Joad (Henry Fonda) returning home after serving four years in prison only to discover that the Depression and the Dust Bowl have taken their toll. The Joads along with hundreds of their tenant farmer neighbors are being forced off their land. Hearing that there is plenty of work for fruit pickers in California, and with all their belongings stacked high on a truck that tips precariously from side to side, the Joads set off for the promised land. On board are Tom, Ma Joad (Jane Darwell), Pa Joad (Russell Simpson), Grandma (Zeffie Tilbury), Grandpa (Charley Grapewin), Rosasharon (Dorris Bowden), her husband Connie (Eddie Quillan), Uncle John (Frank Darien), and other brothers and sisters, together with their friend, defrocked minister Jim Casy (John Carradine).

Tragedy rides with them. First Grandpa dies, and just as they are about to cross into California, Grandma dies. Soon thereafter, Rosasharon is deserted by Connie. However, the worst occurs when the Joads reach California only to find that the handbills telling of jobs have been a pack of lies. Work is scarce, and living conditions in the squalid camps are horrendous.

When the family finally lands a job at starvation wages, it is on a ranch where the workers are on strike and are attempting to organize a union. When Casy becomes involved on the side of the strikers, he is killed by deputies hired by the landlords. In retaliation, Tom kills one of the attackers but is himself severely injured. The family flees, ending up in a sanitized government camp that, compared to the Hoovervilles, is a paradise. But Tom can no longer stay with the family because he has broken parole and is a fugitive. Promising to fight for social justice, he says goodbye to Ma and sets out on his own. The film ends as the family continues its search for work. When Pa mentions that they have taken a beating, Ma replies with the famous "We're the people!" speech:

> Rich fellas come up an' they die, an' their kids ain't
> no good, an' they die out. But we keep a-comin'.
> We're the people that live. Can't nobody wipe us
> out. Can't nobody lick us. We'll go on forever, Pa.
> We're the people.

Much of the novel never made it to the screen. The most glaring omissions were the interposed chapters in which Steinbeck postulated his own political concerns and generalizes the narrative beyond the experiences of the Joads—the car salesman who cheats the migrants, the dumping of the food surpluses, the growth of the revolutionary spirit among the migrants. The film also dropped most of Steinbeck's animal imagery and symbolism in favor of a more direct and concentrated narrative. Johnson and Ford also pruned most of the bawdy scenes and the religious satire, probably because the Hays Office would never have approved.

The film did retain some watered-down political statements. One Hooverville man is almost arrested for explaining the law of labor contracting. In a raid on a Hooverville, a deputy sheriff fires his pistol wildly, shooting an innocent woman bystander. Later, Jim Casy and Tom Joad discuss the ranch owners' tactics in wage pricing and strike breaking, which seems to be a strong statement for unionism, but only in the most general terms. In his role of labor leader, Casy is murdered by vigilantes. However, in all of these incidents, it was not the fault of the law, which seemed above reproach, but of the irregular "deputies" hired by the ranch owners. Also, by setting the sanitized government camp episode near the end and by having Ma deliver her "We're the people!" speech, the film concluded on a far more upbeat note than Steinbeck intended. The angry political message of the novel had been subtly waylaid.

Steinbeck was impressed. In a letter to his friend, Elizabeth Otis, he wrote, "Zanuck has more than kept his word. He has a hard, straight picture in which the actors are submerged so completely that it looks like a documentary film and certainly it has a hard, truthful ring. No punches were pulled—in fact, with descriptive matter removed, it is a harsher thing than the book, by far. It seems unbelievable, but it is true."

The Ford movie also opened to terrific reviews. "A great film has come out of Hollywood called *The Grapes of Wrath*," wrote Howard Barnes in the *New York Herald Tribune*, ". . . it is an eloquent and challenging screen masterpiece." Barnes even praised Nunnally Johnson for lopping off "the embarrassing and lurid ending of the Steinbeck novel." While the ending may be too simplistic, *The Grapes of Wrath* remains a powerful and compelling drama whose message of humanity is as important today as it was when Steinbeck wrote the novel and Ford directed the film.

The next Hollywood adaptation of a Steinbeck work was *Tortilla Flat*, written in 1935 before *Of Mice and Men* and *The Grapes of Wrath*. On the surface, the novel would seem to be unsuitable for filming since it was virtually plotless, consisting of rambling episodes connected only by the characters. In addition, the morality of the powerful Hays Office would be unlikely to pass on any script that followed the events and philosophy of the novel.

In 1938, Paramount bought the screen rights for $4,000, but studio executives soon came to believe that the novel was a hopeless project, and they fired the editor who purchased it. The book's editor then repurchased the rights from Paramount and sold them to MGM for $90,000. Believing that the studio responsible for the Andy Hardy series could not possibly do justice to *Tortilla Flat*, Steinbeck offered to buy back the rights, but the studio refused.

Steinbeck's instincts proved to be correct. Screenwriters John Lee Mahin and Benjamin Glazer took liberties with the novel, and in the process, changed the entire emphasis of the story. Extracting the episode with Sweets Ramirez, they made the love story the backbone of the film. In the novel, Danny's time with Sweets is brief, lasting little more than a chapter. After Danny returns home from the war, Sweets wants to be his lady because, according to the standards of Tortilla Flat, Danny is wealthy. She seduces him, but his friends quickly free him from her influence. The film (MGM, 1942) turns this brief encounter into an uplifting romance between Danny (John Garfield) and Sweets (Hedy Lamarr), ending not with Danny's death but with his marriage. Although Pilon (Spencer Tracy) is also in love with Sweets, he gives her up. Danny even gets a job in preparation for marriage, and the nuptials take place at film's close.

Frank Morgan as Pirate has the most charming scene in the film, lifted straight from the novel. Pirate takes a gold candle to give to the church and is followed there by his dogs, who break into the service, disrupting it. Then, leading them into the forest, he tells them about a saint, who appears to the dogs in a vision.

The film received generally good reviews. *Newsweek* said, "Probably nothing short of a documentary . . . could hope to catch all the earthy, amoral spirit of John Steinbeck's *Tortilla Flat*. . . . The result is an unusual film that creates a reasonable facsimile of the Steinbeck flavor." *Time* called the film "human and appealing," while *The New Yorker* found it "charming," and *Commonweal* thought it "intelligent." Only a few critics faulted the adaptation. The *New York Times*'s Bosley Crowther pointed out "a certain exaggerated piety," and Manny Farber, in *The New Republic*, objected to the film's sentimental and condescending attitude toward religion.

The next Steinbeck to be adapted for the screen was the patriotic novella, *The Moon Is Down*, written simultaneously as a play. Steinbeck conceived of the novel in 1941, prior to the United States' entry into the war, when he spoke to intelligence chief Col. William J. Donovan, and the two of them discussed the resistance movement in Eastern Europe. Donovan stressed the value of American writers in the war of propaganda, and with this kind of urging, Steinbeck soon began his participation by contributing to *Bombs Away*, a film designed to introduce the Army Air Corps to the American populace.

The Moon Is Down (20th Century-Fox, 1942) followed. It tells the story of a small village in Eastern Europe invaded by a "foreign army." Led by Colonel Lanser (Cedric Hardwicke), the invaders institute a new order, and try to enlist the aid of Mayor Orden (Henry Travers). When violence and sabotage escalate, Lanser resorts to harsher measures, which culminate with the arrest of Orden himself. As he awaits his execution, Orden tells his captor, "It is always the herd men who win battles and the free men who win wars. You will find that is so, sir."

Although the first reviews were mostly positive, some critics attacked Steinbeck for being too lenient toward the Nazis. Steinbeck's sin was that he had gone against official United States propaganda; Germans were to be portrayed as monsters, not men. In the *New York Times,* Bosley Crowther found, "[Nunnally Johnson] has wrung out such traces of defeatism as were apparent in the book and has sharpened with vivid incidents the horror of being enslaved."

Fox paid Steinbeck $300,000 for the screen rights, which turned out to be the most expensive part of the production. Thereafter to economize, the studio used no big-name stars, substituted the Welsh mining town from *How Green Was My Valley* for a Norwegian village, and shot the film in black and white.

Nunnally Johnson, who had written the screenplay for *The Grapes of Wrath*, also did the script for *The Moon Is Down*. He first consulted with Steinbeck, who told him, "Tamper with it." Johnson proceeded to open up the action, showing much that happened offstage in both the novel and play—the Nazi invasion, the massacre of Norwegian soldiers, the German brutality toward the villagers, the growing Norwegian resistance; yet, Johnson retained much of the original story and often used Steinbeck's dialogue verbatim. "There is no question," said Steinbeck later, "that pictures are a better medium for this story than the stage ever was."

Steinbeck followed *The Moon Is Down* with another World War Two effort, *Lifeboat* (20th Century-Fox, 1944), billed as "Alfred Hitchcock's *Lifeboat* by John Steinbeck." Hitchcock claimed that Steinbeck worked on the screenplay, but his treatment was incomplete, and the director brought in other writers, finally settling on Jo Swerling, who received sole screen credit. Some critics pointed out that the Nazi was the most admirable character in the film, but because it was—and still is—impossible to ascertain Steinbeck's contribution, the author came in for a relatively small share of blame.

Somewhat more typical of the author was *A Medal for Benny* (Paramount, 1945), based on an unpublished story by Steinbeck and Jack Wagner. The film's protagonists were the down-and-out *paisanos* in a small California town. Benny, the title character, has been run out of town long before the story opens, and the audience never sees him, but his character dominates the action. In many ways, he reminds us of Danny from *Tortilla Flat*. For all his pranks, fights, and love affairs, he has become a legend among his people just as Danny had. When Benny is killed in the war, the town wants to claim him once again. There are moments the film reminds us of Steinbeck, but without the availability of the source, and only Frank Butler's screenplay, it is once again difficult to pin down the author's contribution.

The next full-fledged Steinbeck adaptation was *The Pearl*, which first appeared as "The Pearl of the World" in *Woman's Home Companion* in December 1945. *The Pearl* (RKO, 1948) is an uncompromisingly ironic fable of a poor Mexican fisherman, Kino (Pedro Armendariz), who finds a fabulous pearl. The pearl quickly comes to symbolize freedom from poverty and a new beginning for him and his family. He envisions new clothes for his wife (Maria Elena Marques) and an education for his son. But the naïve Kino misunderstands the world around him, and instead of a better life and a more secure future, the pearl brings only misery and death. Men cheat him, beat him, murder his child, and finally turn Kino himself into a killer. In a final act of disgust, he throws the pearl back into the sea from whence it came.

As photographed by renowned cinematographer Gabriel Figueroa, the book translated into a series of beautiful images. From the opening shot of the crashing waves to the final one of Kino throwing the pearl back into that same violent sea, the film had a classic look that underscored the elemental violence of the story. Yet, some of the film's weakness lay in the photography, which was far too romantic and clean. The robed women and the white-clad men artfully posed along a curve of beach, the highly choreographed fiesta, the battle on the beach—were too deliberate and artificial. In addition, the peasants' clean and laundered look resembled Hollywood's picture of the Mexican peasants as seen through the eyes of Norman Rockwell.

Although Steinbeck himself had a hand in the script, which was also written by director Emilio Fernandez and Jack Wagner, some alterations were made in the story. Kino's older brother and a priest were both omitted. Two scenes not in the novel were inserted—a fiesta and a drinking sequence. In addition, the final fight scene, which in the novel took place in the high mountains, was shifted to a mangrove swamp and some foothills. Yet, despite these changes, the film managed to retain not only Steinbeck's central story but also much of his message of corruption and survival.

Although filmed in English, *The Pearl* was coproduced by two Mexican companies, and the cast was composed of Mexican actors. However, it proved too arty and ultimately too depressing for American audiences—reviewer Bosley Crowther said that it would leave the audience with "emotions exhausted"—and it died at the box office.

The problems of content also haunted the next adaptation of a Steinbeck novel. *The Red Pony* (1949) is really four short stories loosely connected, and only two of these involve a pony. In addition to the lack of a strong narrative, the stories present a rather grim psychological realism, making the task of turning such a novel into a box office success even more difficult.

The major studios passed on the project, but Republic, noted for its "B" Westerns and serials, stepped out of its normal role in order to make a prestige film and hired Steinbeck to write the screenplay. The studio also engaged Lewis Milestone to direct and Aaron Copland to compose the score, both having previously collaborated on the 1939 *Of Mice and Men*. Copland's score compares favorably with his *Rodeo* and *Billy the Kid* in capturing a feeling of Western Americana. *The Red Pony* also became the first Steinbeck adaptation to be filmed in color.

Steinbeck made several important concessions in writing the script. Three years before in MGM's film of *The Yearling*, the boy had been named Jody, and probably for that reason, Steinbeck changed his Jody Tiflin to Tom. Inexplicably, he also changed the names of the boy's parents from Carl and Ruth to Fred and Alice. In structuring the story, he combined "The Gift," "Leader of the People," and part of "The Promise," muting the harsh realities of the novel and giving the story a happier ending. The structure remained loose, and the result was a casual, rambling story that most audiences and reviewers found taxing. Only one scene, where Tom fights a vulture over the carcass of his dead pony, held any real excitement.

The film attempted to be "arty." In the scenes that open even before the credits, the camera travels across a dawn landscape while an omniscient narrator speaks. A furry white rabbit scurries along the ground beneath him. Suddenly, the owl swoops down and the death cries of the rabbit are heard as the camera watches the dogs react. This symbolism about nature in conflict is meant to be a commentary on the story, but it is too obvious and contrived. Even the fact that it has been so carefully filmed on a sound stage adds to the artificiality of the scene.

A few critics praised the film. *Newsweek* admired the "honest tenderness" of Steinbeck's screenplay while *Commonweal* found the story of Tom's growing maturity "fascinatingly told." However, these reviews were in the minority. The majority opinion was expressed by Bosley Crowther, who called the film "moody and depressing" and Robert Hatch, in *The New Republic*, who termed it "maudlin." Despite the care and concern that obviously went into the project, *The Red Pony*, with Myrna Loy and Robert Mitchum (as Billy Buck) in starring roles, was far too reverential and pretentious, and as such, far less a work of art than the book.

A TV production of *The Red Pony* (teleplay by Robert Totten and Ron Bishop, NBC Universal Television, 1973) avoided the pitfall of the film by abandoning the poetic approach in favor of a straight narrative of Jody (Clint Howard), his struggles with his ponies, and his attempts to understand his parents (Henry Fonda and Maureen O'Hara). However, the story inexplicably dropped the character of Billy Buck.

In the early fifties came *Viva, Zapata!* (20th Century-Fox, 1952) for which Steinbeck wrote the screenplay. Of necessity the script was episodic, but theme and characters were the glue that held it together. Using Edgcomb Pinchon's biography, *Zapata, the Unconquerable*, plus his own extensive research in Mexico, Steinbeck fashioned a script around the revolutionary career of Emiliano Zapata in the early part of this century. Uninterested in power for its own sake, Zapata is a man of the people, and it is to them he wants to turn over the power. "A strong man makes a weak people. Strong people don't need a strong man," he says.

The first reviews were generally good, but revisionist critics have pointed out that the film romanticized Zapata (played by Marlon Brando), who was much bloodier and probably more self-seeking than Steinbeck's creation. Such criticism missed the point. To Steinbeck, Zapata was a poetic and symbolic figure, an Everyman of the Mexican Revolution, a man who rose from the masses to lead his people.

Three years later, Elia Kazan, who had directed *Viva, Zapata!* once again turned to Steinbeck, this time for a film version of *East of Eden* (Warner Bros., 1955). It was written by Paul Osborn, who found the novel too long and unwieldy and used only the last third as the basis for his screenplay. In the process of cutting the book down to size, Osborn omitted some important characters, and in place of the deleted material, fleshed out the story of brothers Cal (James Dean) and Aron Trask (Richard Davalos) and their struggle for their father's love. Unless members of the audience had read the book, they were ignorant of a similar situation between the boys' father, Adam (Raymond Massey), and his brother, Charles. Also, the very center of the novel, Cathy's villainy—her destruction of the schoolteacher, the murder of her parents, her seduction of Charles on

Lobby card showing Jean Peters and Marlon Brando in *Viva Zapata!* (1952), based on an original John Steinbeck script.

the night of her wedding to Adam, her murder of Faye—is omitted.

However, the most damaging error was not one of omission but of commission. The character of Adam Trask was changed so much as to be unrecognizable as the one created by Steinbeck. In the novel, Adam was basically a warm man who repeated the error of his own father in loving one son more than the other. In his place, Osborn created an Old Testament patriarch, too stern and unbending to be sympathetic. When Adam has the stroke after hearing of Aron's death, the audience is unable to respond as readers did in the novel.

Despite these drawbacks, the film *East of Eden* has much to recommend it. James Dean in his starring debut (after a handful of tiny movie roles) gave a stunning performance as Cal Trask, establishing his screen persona that was to tab him a teenage idol and a cult figure that far outlasted his own life. If the Cal he created was not quite the Cal of Steinbeck, it was good enough to earn

him an Oscar nomination as Best Actor. Julie Harris as Abra came closest to realizing any of the Steinbeck characters, even if she did appear a little long in the tooth to be a teenager. Albert Dekker as Will Hamilton and Burl Ives as Sam the Sheriff were appropriately gruff and sympathetic, although their connections to the Trask family were far less clear in the film than in the novel. As Kate, Cal and Aron's abandoned mother, Jo Van Fleet was not the villain of the novel; nevertheless, she won an Academy Award as Best Supporting Actress. Through no fault of her own, she was simply not the Kate that Steinbeck created. If one has no knowledge of the novel and takes her performance strictly on merit, it is indeed a fine performance and worthy of such an award.

Most critics praised the film. Although she was critical of certain aspects, Pauline Kael called it "overwhelming." Gerald McDonald, writing in *Library Journal*, found it "one of the best films of this or any other year." However, the problem remains that *East of*

Eden is only a partial adaptation; too much of the missing story dilutes the complexities of characters and events.

East of Eden has been remade once (teleplay by Richard A. Shapiro, ABC, ABC Circle Films, 1981) as an eight-hour miniseries that attempted to cover the entire novel. For the most part, the characters emerged on the small screen just as Steinbeck imagined them. The script not only restored the importance of Adam Trask (Timothy Bottoms) and Cathy (Jane Seymour) but also included much of the author's symbolism and philosophy. All in all, this proved to be an excellent adaptation and a superior television production.

The 1950s saw one other film adaptation of a Steinbeck novel, *The Wayward Bus* (1947), which was the author's first one after World War Two and his first full-length novel since *The Grapes of Wrath* eight years earlier.

The book proved disappointing on many levels, but little blame can be placed on Steinbeck's shoulders for the film *The Wayward Bus* (20th Century-Fox, 1957). The studio hired William Saroyan to do the script, as a vehicle for Jayne Mansfield(!), and his first draft followed the novel closely, but Fox rejected his efforts and replaced Saroyan with Ivan Moffat, who proceeded to write a cliché-ridden potboiler that oversimplified the plot and concentrated on a wild ride full of floods and landslides. In the process, the complex characters turned into stereotypes, and happy endings became the order of the day. Instead of Steinbeck's ambiguous ending, the film had Juan find a repentant wife waiting for him at the end of the line.

The last Steinbeck adaptation to reach the screen was *Cannery Row* (MGM/United Artists, 1982), derived from two different novels: *Cannery Row* (1945), which introduces the inhabitants and sets up the events that lead to two disastrous parties for Doc, and *Sweet Thursday* (1954),* which has Doc fall in love with Suzy, a prostitute unsuited for her profession. Director David S. Ward, who also wrote the screenplay, opted to shoot the film on a sound stage, and because of this, it takes on a very stylized appearance. The shanties and deserted boilers that substitute for homes of the tenants of Cannery Row appear like the remnants of some future holocaust; yet they also appear warm and cozy, especially the one that Suzy moves into after she quits the bordello. As narrator John Huston intones: "Cannery Row has never been like anywhere else."

Huston's narration attempted to link a very episodic

*Sweet Thursday was the source for Rodgers and Hammerstein's 1955 Broadway musical, *Pipe Dream*.

Richard Davalos and James Dean as brothers Aaron and Cal Trask and Julie Harris as Abra in Steinbeck's *East of Eden* (1955).

story of mismatched lovers. As Doc (Nick Nolte) says to Suzy (Debra Winger, replacing Raquel Welch), "The only thing we have in common is that we're both wrong for each other." In the midst of their growing love occurs the frog hunting expedition and the party that wrecks Doc's laboratory, both incidents from *Cannery Row* in which Suzy is not a character. Added to the story was a scene in the bordello where Doc and Suzy dance the latest steps to big band numbers, and while the twirls and flips provided a few laughs, the scene was out of place.

Along with the narration, the love affair between Doc and Suzy holds the film together. As in the novel, Doc is basically a loner, a confirmed bachelor, who moves from misery to a resolution through love. Just avoiding the stereotypical, Suzy is the prostitute with the proverbial heart of gold; yet she is blessed with a quick mind and an independent spirit, the very attributes that appeal to Doc. The plot is therefore conventional: boy meets girl, boy rejects girl, boy wins girl back. In the end, both the novels and film are warm and sentimental fairy tales for grown-ups, and on this level, the film captured the spirit of the Steinbeck novels, especially *Sweet Thursday*.

A television production of Steinbeck's last novel, *The Winter of Our Discontent* (teleplay by Michael DeGuzman, CBS, Lorimar Productions, 1983), told the story of a grocery store clerk (Donald Sutherland) who dreams of buying back a store that had been in his family for generations and his corruption by the town banker. It was a weak novel that produced a weak film.

Television is also where Steinbeck's story, "The Harness," ended up as a 1971 TV movie, adapted by Leon Tokatyan and Edward Hume, with Lorne Greene as the star.

John Steinbeck has been well-served by the screen. The proof is evident in the classic and faithful adaptations of *Of Mice and Men*, *The Grapes of Wrath,* and *East of Eden*, and to a lesser degree, *The Moon Is Down* and *The Pearl*. While not classic films by any stretch of the imagination, *Tortilla Flat*, *The Red Pony,* and *Cannery Row* each possess some good moments. Only *The Wayward Bus* is a genuine failure, truncated so badly by studio interference, a poor script, inept direction, and infantile performances that all evidence of Steinbeck vanishes.

Steinbeck himself showed the greatest affinity for the movies, even proving that he understood the craft of screenwriting by adapting his own *Red Pony* and by creating an original, Academy Award–nominated screenplay for *Viva, Zapata!* Many of the qualities he used in writing these screenplays can be found in his fiction, dominated by believable characters and visual imagery, two ingredients easily translatable to the screen.

Nick Nolte as Doc tries to revive Sunshine Parker as The Seer while Frank McRae as Hazel grieves for his friend in Steinbeck's *Cannery Row* (1982).

Paul Muni (center) as Wang confronts the villagers in *The Good Earth* (1937).

EIGHT

OTHER SIGNIFICANT WRITERS OF THE THIRTIES

Nathanael West, Nelson Algren, William Saroyan,
John Marquand, John O'Hara, Erskine Caldwell,
Pearl Buck, Marjorie Kinnan Rawlings

From the thirties emerged a group of writers who either because of limitations within themselves or because of a relatively small output of works failed to match the stature of either John Steinbeck or James Cain. Yet each of these writers produced at least one important work that made its way to the screen.

One of the least prolific yet important writers of the thirties was Nathanael West (1904–40), who during his career produced only four novels and one play. He also worked in Hollywood, churning out a number of unimportant and mediocre screenplays for Universal, RKO, and Republic studios.

The first of his novels to reach the screen was *Miss Lonelyhearts* (1933), a study of a lovelorn columnist with a Christ complex. The first adaptation was a programmer, *Advice to the Lovelorn* (United Artists, 1933), a comedy-melodrama written by Leonard Praskins

that emasculated West's novel, even substituting a happy ending in which a fast-talking newspaperman (Lee Tracy) solves his own as well as everyone else's problems.

The novel returned as *Lonelyhearts* (United Artists, 1958), a more faithful adaptation produced and written by Dore Schary. Adam White (Montgomery Clift) is assigned the Miss Lonelyhearts column by his cynical editor, Shrike (Robert Ryan), who says, "I love to see youth betray their promises." Shrike pushes Adam to become more involved with those who write to him, finally persuading the journalist to go to bed with the pathetic Fay Doyle (Maureen Stapleton), the wife of a cripple. In the novel, this costs Miss Lonelyhearts his life, but in the film, Adam escapes the frenzied husband, although the experience has taught him that he has only enough love for girlfriend Justy (Dolores Hart). Together the two leave Shrike and Miss Lonelyhearts behind.

147

While the film remained faithful, West's novel was not cinematic, which was surprising coming from a man who wrote screenplays. But the truth of the matter was that West didn't like Hollywood and wasn't particularly interested in writing novels that would become films.

Another stab at *Miss Lonelyhearts* came on TV in 1983 with an *American Playhouse* production on PBS starring Eric Roberts.

In *The Day of the Locust* (1939), people are tricked and seduced by Hollywood, a theme that most Hollywood films about Hollywood avoided, but the movie (Paramount, 1975) had the guts to tackle the subject. Waldo Salt provided an excellent and faithful screenplay, and John Schlesinger directed with a cutting edge. The result was to slice up the myth of Hollywood success and expose the underbelly of a shallow society.

The film shifts its emphasis to concentrate more on Faye (Karen Black), an actress with little talent and no depth. Despite her transparency, she is loved by Tod (William Atherton), an art director, but she toys with his affections. After the death of her father (Burgess Meredith), she moves in with Homer (Donald Sutherland), an oafish accountant from Iowa, whom she and others constantly humiliate. Homer is further vexed by a nasty neighborhood child, ironically named Adore (Jackie Haley) and, finally devastated finding Faye making love with a stuntman, he runs to complain to his friend, Tod. At a premiere of a new film, Homer is once again confronted by Adore, and distraught by Faye's whoring, he explodes and stomps the boy to death. This precipitates a riot, and the angry mob literally tears Homer limb from limb.

Most of the characters who paraded back and forth across the screen were from West's novel, although the film invented Big Sister (Geraldine Page), an evangelist patterned after Aimee Semple McPherson. Despite the shift of emphasis, the film was remarkably true to its source, including West's pessimistic ending that captured the spirit and intent of a minor literary masterpiece.

Nelson Algren (né Nelson Ahlgren Abraham, 1909–81) was also a product of the thirties. For a time after graduating from the University of Illinois in 1931, he drifted around the country, riding the freights and taking odd jobs when he could find them. While the forties became the decade of his greatest productivity, his experiences bumming around during the Depression shaped his fiction. His most successful novel, *The Man With the Golden Arm* (1949), is a tale of morphine addict Frankie Machine, an ex-GI who deals cards at a local gambling house.

In the novel, the grittiness of Chicago life was an important ingredient, but Otto Preminger's film version (United Artists, 1955) opted for a slick script in which the windy city was only a faceless backdrop. While it courageously broke ground in its portrayal of drugs, thereby defying the Production Code, there were so many compromises in plot and characters that the overall effect is far less powerful than it might have been.

As the film opens, Frankie (Frank Sinatra) has just returned from Kentucky where he has taken the treatment and has supposedly kicked his addiction. He wants to begin life anew as a drummer in a band, but his shrewish, wheelchair-bound wife, Zosch (Eleanor Parker), uses his guilt over an auto accident to force him back to his job as a dealer in an illegal poker parlor. Only his girlfriend, Molly (Kim Novak), understands him and allows him to practice at her apartment. His drug pusher, Louie (Darren McGavin), keeps trying to get him back on smack, but Frankie resists the temptation until he overextends himself at his job, gets caught cheating, and sustains a terrible beating. In the meantime, Louie goes to his apartment, where he discovers that Zosch can walk, and to keep him quiet, she pushes him down the stairs, killing him.

When Frankie hears that he is wanted by the police, he realizes that he must cure himself cold turkey. After three days of this harrowing self-exorcism, Frankie returns to Zosch. In their confrontation, when he learns she's been faking being a cripple, Zosch sees police in the hallway and jumps out the window to her death, thus freeing Frankie to be with Molly.

The black and white photography gave the proceedings a gritty realism but the Walter Newman–Lewis Meltzer screenplay went soft, as so many Hollywood films did, and opted for a more or less happy ending. The whole scenario pointed to a dead end for Frankie (who in the book commits suicide) and Molly, but a last-minute dive by Zosch wrapped everything up in a neat package and allowed goodness and virtue to win.

Only one other Algren work made it to film, *A Walk on the Wild Side* (1956), a novel filled with dark humor and irony. The screenplay for *Walk on the Wild Side* (Columbia, 1962), however, went through the hands of a dozen or more writers, who removed all the power and black humor of Algren's novel. (John Fante and Edmund Norris ultimately got screen credit.) Dove Linkhorn (Laurence Harvey) comes from Texas to New Orleans searching for his true love, Hallie (Capucine), finding her working in a house of prostitution run by Jo (Barbara Stanwyck), who has her own interests in Hallie. Upset that Dove wants to whisk away her number one attraction, Jo has her goons beat him up and when Dove persists in hanging around, she orders his death. In the shootout, Hallie dies in Dove's arms.

Despite all the degradation and sexual perversions, little of Algren showed up on the screen. Algren himself

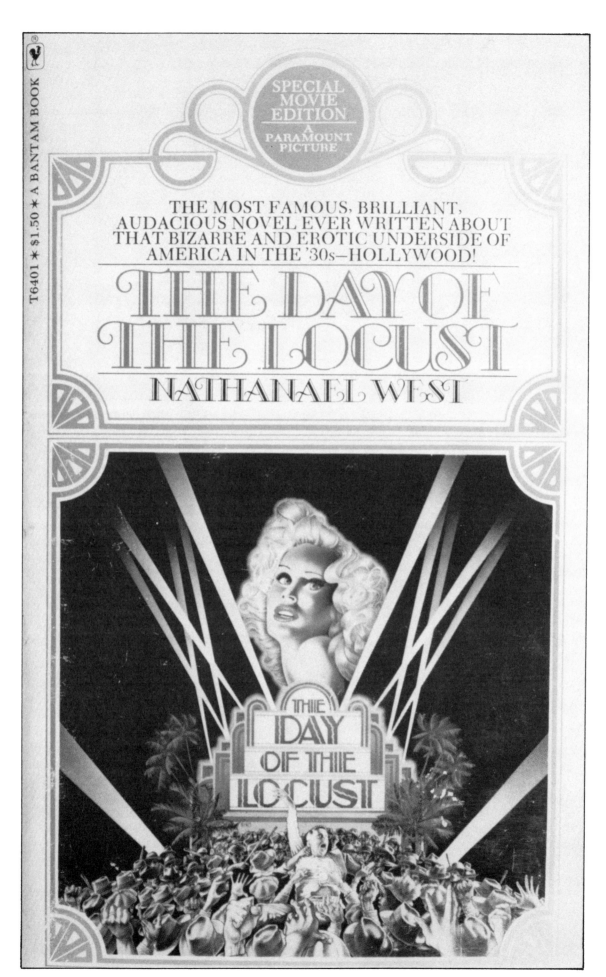

SPECIAL
MOVIE
EDITION

A
PARAMOUNT
PICTURE

THE MOST FAMOUS, BRILLIANT,
AUDACIOUS NOVEL EVER WRITTEN ABOUT
THAT BIZARRE AND EROTIC UNDERSIDE OF
AMERICA IN THE '30s—HOLLYWOOD!

THE DAY OF THE LOCUST

NATHANAEL WEST

THE
DAY
OF THE
LOCUST

"Special Movie Edition" paperback cover for the 1975 film tie-in of Nathanael West's *The Day of the Locust*.

Sally Blane and Lee Tracy show off their engagement ring to Jean Adair in *Advice to the Lovelorn* (1933), a very loose adaptation of Nathanael West's *Miss Lonelyhearts*.

Frank Sinatra as Frankie Machine dealing cards in a big game in *The Man With the Golden Arm* (1955).

Lobby card for *Lonelyhearts* (1959) picturing Montgomery Clift as Adam White, aka Miss Lonelyhearts, the advice columnist, adapted from the novel *Miss Lonelyhearts* by Nathanael West, though uncredited in the advertising.

Capucine as Hallie receives the advances of Laurence Harvey as Dave Linkhorn in Nelson Algren's *Walk on the Wild Side* (1962).

these peculiarities and even falls for one of Joe's stratagems, hiring Harry (Paul Draper) as a part-time dancer in the bar. One of the place's many denizens is Kitty Duval (Jeanne Cagney), a down-on-her-luck streetwalker, whom Joe eventually fixes up with Tom. For most of the story, Joe just sits, but when a small-time hood (Tom Powers) threatens to upset the structured world of the bar, Joe not only gets out of his chair but administers him a sound thrashing and restores tranquility to his turf.

Originally the script had called for the hood to die offscreen just as in the play, but preview audiences refused to accept this resolution, and the ending was reshot to include the confrontation. Despite this, Saroyan liked the film, telling Cagney that he had made "one of the most original and entertaining movies" he (Saroyan) had ever seen. While critics responded favorably, the public didn't, and the *The Time of Your Life* became the rare Cagney film to lose money. (When *The Time of Your Life* was produced on television in 1958 on *Playhouse 90*, Jackie Gleason starred.)

Fascinated by Saroyan and his play, Louis B. Mayer asked the author to write a story for his studio, and the result was Saroyan's first novel, *The Human Comedy* (1943). The nostalgic and sentimental story centers around fourteen-year-old Homer Macauley of Ithaca, California, during World War Two, but the high schooler's experiences and those of his friends, relatives, and acquaintances possess a certain universality.

The Human Comedy (MGM, 1943) proved on screen to be an almost exact translation (by Howard Estabrook) of the book. Homer (Mickey Rooney) is a telegraph

was philosophical about what Hollywood had done to his novels, comparing the experience to a baseball game. "Either you win or lose," he said. "You come to bat in the last of the ninth with one out. . . . You hit into a double play, that's all."

William Saroyan (1908–81), on the other hand, was quite prolific, turning out over fifty works during his lifetime. Surprisingly, only one play and one novel made it to the screen. His most sustained work was *The Time of Your Life* (1939), which had a very successful Broadway run and won the Pulitzer Prize. James Cagney purchased the rights for his and brother William's production company, and later met with Saroyan to discuss the property, but otherwise the author had no input.

Yet the film *The Time of Your Life* (United Artists, 1948) proved extremely faithful to the play, an almost line-by-line translation. Joe (James Cagney) is a barroom philosopher who drinks expensive champagne, listens to old records, and uses his friend Tom (Wayne Morris) as his errand boy. Nick the bartender (William Bendix), although a little perturbed at Joe's antics, puts up with

Gale Page and James Cagney in *The Time of Your Life* (1947).

151

John Craven as Tobey George comes to Ithaca and is greeted by
Mickey Rooney as Homer Macauley in *The Human Comedy* (1943).

Van Heflin as Bill King, Robert Young as Harry, and Hedy Lamarr as Marvin
Myles celebrate in *H. M. Pulham, Esq.* (1940).

messenger, making his daily rounds after school to
deliver notices of local boys who have been killed in the
war. His younger brother, Ulysses (Jackie "Butch"
Jenkins), inadvertently talks Homer out of running away
because his job has become so painful. Because his
father is dead and his older brother, Marcus (Van
Johnson), is away at the war, Homer feels a responsibility
as head of the family.

Like the novel, the film sees Homer's experiences as
universal—his nightshift at the office delivering tele-
grams; pondering the nature of the world with Mr.
Grogan (Frank Morgan), the alcoholic telegraph operator;
running track at school; receiving the news of his brother
Marcus's death. It is this last sequence wherein the basic
weakness of both the novel and film lies. As Homer goes
home to inform the family, he meets Tobey George
(John Craven) outside his house. Tobey, who has no
family, served with Marcus and fell in love with Marcus's stories of his family and Ithaca, and, by long
distance, with Marcus's sister, Mary (Donna Reed).
Homer invites Tobey in, assuring him that, without a
family of his own, he will be a welcomed replacement
for the dead Marcus. Tobey assures the Macauleys that
Marcus is not dead, that he can never die as long as they
hold him in their hearts.

This ending fails to allow the family to internalize the
death of Marcus. However, this is not the only problem.
The novel and the film both lack a definite structure.
Events do not logically flow one from the other but
rather what happens at the beginning could just as easily
happen in the middle and vice-versa. Added to these are
moments of artificiality where lines and scenes fail to
ring true. But these two works of art, the novel and the
film, possess moments of power where scenes have the
ring of truth and reach deeply to touch the heart.*

The 1930s also witnessed the rise to prominence of
John Marquand, John O'Hara, Pearl Buck, and Erskine
Caldwell. While their renown continued well into the
forties and even later, by the sixties they had fallen from
critical acclaim. Today only a few of their most popular
works are still in print, and of the films made from their
works, only a few have survived the judgment of time.

By 1937, John Marquand (1893–1959) had already
published close to a hundred short stories and seven
novels, including two about the Oriental adventurer-
detective, Mr. Moto, made into a popular "B" series
with Peter Lorre. His first to reach the screen was the less
than imposing *H. M. Pulham, Esquire* (1941). Despite
mixed reviews, the book was an immediate best-seller
and made many of the "ten best" lists for 1941.

*The 1959 *DuPont Show of the Month* television version, adapted by
S. Lee Pogostin, starred Jo Van Fleet, Russell Collins, and Michael J.
Pollard.

Ronald Colman (second left) as stuffy George Apley with Richard Ney
and Peggy Cummins as his children, John and Eleanor, and Richard
Haydn (right) as Horatio Willing in *The Late George Apley* (1947),
based on the Marquand novel and the play he later wrote with George
S. Kaufman.

The film *H. M. Pulham, Esq.* (MGM, 1941) is a rather long, bittersweet tale of a love lost, regained, and lost again. Harry Pulham (Robert Young) is a product of Boston society who, in his youth, went off to New York where he had an affair with Marvin Myles (Hedy Lamarr), a would-be model from Iowa. Her rather strange accent is explained away by the fact that she grew up in Europe with her parents. The affair ends badly when Pulham's Brahmin father (Charles Coburn) refused to give his sanction to his son's marriage. Pulham weds socially correct Kay Motford (Ruth Hussey) instead, but twenty years later, Marvin, now an ad executive, returns to reignite the flame. Soon they both realize that they can't recapture the past, and the two part once again, this time for good. Pulham returns to his wife, who has been waiting patiently for her husband to come to his senses.

Shortly after MGM purchased the rights to the novel and assigned King Vidor to direct, Marquand sent him a list of suggestions for background details of Boston life. Somewhat impressed, Vidor summoned Marquand to Hollywood to help with the script (eventually credited to Vidor and Elizabeth Hill). Marquand stayed a month, just long enough to see who would be cast in the major roles and to discover in what ways the story would be changed; but the alterations in plot and character did not bother Marquand as much as many of the minor details—Pulham's dog should have been a fat cocker instead of the Sealyham; Robert Young as Harry Pulham should have been clean shaven instead of mustached; the Harvard students should not have been wearing the big H's on their sweaters—"We were all carefully dressed in Brooks Brothers suits," Marquand said.

After the success of *H. M. Pulham, Esquire* as both a novel and film, David O. Selznick purchased the rights to *So Little Time* (1943), but the low-keyed, static book proved too difficult to adapt, and he traded the rights to MGM for *The Paradine Case*. MGM could do no better with Marquand's book, and a script was never developed.

The same fate seemed to await *The Late George Apley* (1937) in which a dull and pretentious fictional biographer presents a series of letters, some of which were written by the late George Apley and others written to him. By the time the novel is complete, the reader has a sense of Apley's life.

A play of *The Late George Apley* by George S. Kaufman and Marquand reached Broadway in 1944 and ran through the next season. It was a comedy that concentrated on one year in Apley's life. Based on the moderate financial success of the novel (which won the Pulitzer Prize) and the far greater success of the play, Hollywood bought the rights three years later, and *The Late George Apley* (20th Century-Fox, 1947) became a film bearing little resemblance to its predecessors.

Van Heflin as Tom Brett is consoled by Barbara Stanwyck as Polly Fulton in *B. F.'s Daughter* (1948).

Kirk Douglas as Maj. Gen. Melville Goodwin watches with wry amusement while Susan Hayward as Dottie Peale displays his pistol in *Top Secret Affair* (aka *Their Secret Affair*, 1947), based on Marquand's *Melville Goodwin, U.S.A.*

153

Apley (Ronald Colman) is a turn-of-the-century Bostonian who believes his city is the hub of the universe and is shocked when son John (Richard Ney) falls in love with the wrong sort of girl. He forbids a marriage, an edict which his son docilely accepts. In the end, he will turn out like his father, a man to uphold Apley tradition and maintain the social order. His daughter, Eleanor (Peggy Cummins), falls for a Yale man who, although he quotes Apley's favorite author, Emerson, is also unsuitable. However, Apley finally relents when he sees the error of his ways. Other than wiping out most of the novel, the script by Philip Dunne reconceived the character of Apley as a man who changes from an uptight Boston Brahmin to a genial, understanding father. In doing so, the meaning of the title also changes; Apley does not die but has merely converted to sentimentality.

In *B. F.'s Daughter* (1946), Marquand wrote his first novel with a woman protagonist. The book's sprawling structure was not easily adaptable, and by the time it reached the screen, *B. F.'s Daughter* (MGM, 1948) had been modified by writer Luther Davis to the point of being unrecognizable. Polly Fulton (Barbara Stanwyck) meets and marries an ultra-liberal but penniless college professor, Thomas Brett (Van Heflin), who is unaware that she is the daughter of B. F. Fulton (Charles Coburn), an industrialist who stands for everything Brett despises. When Brett learns that Polly has used her father's wealth to open doors, his love turns to loathing, and he leaves her. It is only when the war comes and Brett is in uniform that Polly tells him that she needs him. With that, he forgives her, and they are reunited.

For reasons of censorship, much of the discreet sex was deleted. For a brief time. Polly believes that Brett is fooling around with his secretary. When Polly meets her face to face, however, she sees that the secretary wears a leg brace. Obviously under such circumstances there could be no truth in Polly's suspicions. Marquand found wry amusement in these changes, consoling himself with the $90,000 he had been paid for the property.

At the outbreak of the Korean War, Marquand, believing the time was right for a military novel, published *Melville Goodwin, U.S.A.* (1951). Originally the property had been purchased for a Bogart-Bacall film, but the script ultimately was rewritten (by Roland Kibbee and Allan Scott) as a light comedy, *Top Secret Affair* (Warner Bros., 1957), that dispensed with most of the novel. Dottie Peale (Susan Hayward) runs a magazine that is out to discredit General Melville Goodwin (Kirk Douglas) so that he will be denied a political post in favor of a friend of hers. This leads to a Senate investigation, but the more important result is that Dottie and Melville discover that they love one another.

In *Top Secret Affair*, the real Melville Goodwin disappeared altogether, which shouldn't have come as

any surprise to the author. Hollywood never properly adapted even one of Marquand's novels. The reason is easy to understand. They were too sprawling, and the plotting was a complicated series of character studies that moved too slowly for the big screen. Scriptwriters took only bits and pieces, pasting them together into some sort of coherent stories that the public could accept.

Two Marquand novels that thus far have gone unfilmed but were produced live on television in the late 1950s, both with adaptations by Frank Gilroy, were *Sincerely, Willis Wayde* (1955) and *Point of No Return* (1949). Walter Abel and Sarah Churchill starred in the former; Charlton Heston and Hope Lange in the latter.

Like John Marquand, John O'Hara explored the lifestyles of the rich and near rich, although he was much more likely to indulge himself in examining the seamy side of such lives. He already had one successful novel, *Appointment at Samarra* (1934), when he wrote *Butterfield 8* (1935), which was based on the real case of the promiscuous Starr Faithfull, whose body was washed up on the Long Island shore in 1931.

By the time *Butterfield 8* (MGM, 1960) reached the screen, O'Hara had already served time working on a few Hollywood scripts that included *Cass Timberlane*. His studio experience should have prepared him for the worst, but even he was shocked at what was done to *Butterfield 8*. The script by Charles Schnee and John Michael Hayes strayed so far from its source and was such a piece of trash that critics en masse castigated the film, although most reserved some praise for Elizabeth Taylor's performance as Gloria. Taylor herself thought it was the most pornographic script she had ever read. "It's in bad taste. Everyone in it is crazy, mixed-up, sick," she said. She demanded extensive revisions before finally coming to terms with the studio.

The whole thirties atmosphere of the novel disappears under the freewheeling screenplay that updates the material to the present. A model by day, call girl by night, Gloria Wandrous (Taylor) finally discovers Mr. Right, socialite Weston Liggett (Laurence Harvey); but alas, he is married. Undaunted, she pursues him anyway. The affair ends badly when Gloria, believing that Liggett is incapable of leaving his wife, Emily (Dina Merrill), drives her car over a cliff, thus providing an easy out for the screenwriters.

Other characters such as the mayor who abuses Gloria and the professor who seduces her are gone, and with them, any clarification as to why Gloria is the way she is. Another character, Steve Carpenter (Eddie Fisher), was created at the insistence of Taylor who wanted her husband of the moment to have a part in the film. The character of Emily Liggett is so self-sacrificing as to be totally unbelievable, forgiving her philandering husband

over and over. At one party, she sees Gloria with her (Emily's) fur coat, supposedly stolen, and barely reacts. One might get the mistaken impression that she was on heavy doses of Valium. The film was pure Hollywood schmaltz with little connection to the O'Hara novella, but earned Taylor an Oscar as Best Actress.

In 1938, O'Hara began publishing in *The New Yorker* the "Pal Joey" stories, which were a series of letters from Joey Evans to his friend Ted. Joey is a dancer who prides himself on his appeal to woman, but he is powerless to control his own life.

Two years later, *Pal Joey* was published as a novel and also became a Broadway musical with the script by O'Hara and a score by Lorenz Hart and Richard Rodgers. The film version (Columbia, 1957) was based more on the play than the book, but because of censorship restrictions, there were major changes. The language was cleaned up and the sexual situations toned down. However, the most radical change came in the character of footloose Joey (Frank Sinatra). As the film opens, he arrives in San Francisco—rather than the Chicago of the novel—where he gets a job in a nightclub as a singer—rather than a dancer (Gene Kelly had the title role on stage). He is quickly scoring with all the girls in the chorus with the exception of Linda (Kim Novak). When Joey and his group perform at a posh party, he recognizes the hostess as Vera (Rita Hayworth), an ex-stripper. Now wealthy and worldly wise, Vera offers to set up Joey with his own club, but she insists that he drop

Linda, for whom he has fallen. In an unselfish act, he rejects Vera, saying that if he has the talent, he'll make it sooner or later without her help.

The story, through Dorothy Kingsley's screenplay, lost much of its bite and satiric content by going soft with the character of Joey, but the overt sex was actually quite daring. Critics were especially kind to Sinatra, who captured the language and feel of Joey, and when O'Hara was asked in an interview what he thought of the star, he said, "I didn't have to see Sinatra's performance. I invented him."

In *Ten North Frederick* (1955), which won the National Book Award, O'Hara showed the disintegration of a family from within, and like the novel, the film version (20th Century-Fox, 1958), adapted by Philip Dunne, opens in 1945 with the funeral of Joe Chapin (Gary Cooper), then retreats into a flashback. Joe is a wealthy lawyer who is comfortable with his life, but his shrewish spouse, Edith (Geraldine Fitzgerald), wants more, and tries to push Joe into the political arena. In the meantime, Edith alienates daughter Ann (Diane Varsi), who runs off to live in New York. Joe goes after her, and he meets her beautiful roommate, Kate Drummond (Suzy Parker), with whom he has a brief affair before ending it, recognizing the incompatibility of their respective ages. His daughter is shocked at the affair, and only when Joe discovers that he is dying of cancer does his son, Joby (Ray Stricklyn), bring Ann home so she and her father can be reconciled. Then, at the funeral, Joby tells his

155

mother what a selfish, heartless bitch she has been and walks out.

O'Hara had two problems with the screen adaptation. First, he didn't like the setting changed from Pennsylvania to some anonymous piece of American real estate. Also, he felt that the daughter's lover, Charley Bongiorno (Stuart Whitman), was a miscalculation. Despite these weaknesses, O'Hara said, "I have seen *Ten North Frederick* and am more than pleased with it."

Certainly O'Hara's most ambitious novel was *From the Terrace* (1958), almost nine hundred pages in length, a fictional biography of the scion of a Pennsylvania steel mill owner. Producer Jerry Wald bought the rights with the intent to make a series of films out of the massive novel, but only *From the Terrace* (20th Century-Fox, 1960) emerged.

As written by Ernest Lehman, the script ignores most of the novel for a far more traditional and clichéd story of love, money, and sex—not necessarily in that order. Alfred Eaton (Paul Newman), a navy pilot who returns from the war seeking some solace from his wealthy family, is quickly disgusted by his cold father (Leon Ames) and his drunken mother (Myrna Loy). Moving to New York, he meets Mary St. John (Joanne Woodward), a socialite whom he woos and marries, but when he becomes involved in his Wall Street investment firm, he begins to ignore her. This sends her into the arms of an old flame. On a trip out west, Alfred meets Natalie (Ina Balin), with whom he has a fling. The affair is discovered by one of his cohorts at the firm, who threatens to tell the prudish management unless Alfred helps him with an illegal deal. Rather than compromise his values, Alfred admits all to the board, resigns, and heads off to paradise with Natalie.

Much of the novel's sexual explicitness was lost in

Lobby card for *10 North Frederick* (1958) tries to give the appearance of action in a film devoid of any.

156

Frank Sinatra in one of his lavish musical numbers in *Pal Joey* (1957).

Bradford Dillman as Sidney Tate and Suzanne Pleshette as Grace Caldwell play a couple with more than a couple of problems in O'Hara's *A Rage to Live* (1965).

transition to the screen due to Production Code restrictions, but that wasn't the real problem with this film. Three years earlier, director Mark Robson had a hit with *Peyton Place*, an intelligent adaptation of a sleazy novel, and he hoped to repeat that success here. But O'Hara's book, while full of sexual tension and high finance, had a sprawling structure that wasn't movie material. Before writing the script, Lehman tried to get some input from O'Hara, but the author showed little enthusiasm for the project, so this left Lehman to his own devices.

O'Hara saw only about thirty minutes of the finished product and was appalled. Although he liked Joanne Woodward as Mary St. John, he thought Paul Newman totally miscast as Alfred Eaton. He also hated the way Lehman updated the novel, and he was further angered by comments from director Robson, who claimed that the film included values that the novel did not possess.

"He [Robson] ducks the basic problems, takes the easy way, and right away the cheapness shows," said O'Hara. Most critics tended to agree with him.

O'Hara considered *Ten North Frederick* and *From the Terrace* as part of a trilogy of novels about Pennsylvania. The first was *A Rage to Live* (1949). The novel suffered structural problems, but whatever drawbacks it may have had, the film *A Rage to Live* (United Artists, 1965) was a pathetic attempt to transfer the book to screen. Grace (Suzanne Pleshette) is a young, wealthy nymphomaniac who has numerous affairs with the men at her country club, which finally causes her old mom to pass on from a heart attack. When she meets Sidney Tate (Bradford Dillman), she falls in love and makes an honest attempt to walk the straight and narrow, but her libido won't let her, and unable to face his wife's infidelities, Tate leaves her.

O'Hara's feelings about the film—if, indeed, he saw it at all—are unclear, but he could not have been happy. *A Rage to Live* was not the best O'Hara, but at least the characters were alive and breathing; the film, as written by John T. Kelley, turned them into cardboard. The

157

story became a soap opera without interest. For the most part, that was how all the adaptations of O'Hara fared.

Equally as prolific as Marquand or O'Hara, Pearl Buck (1892–1973) has fallen just as far out of favor as her two male counterparts. The majority of her fiction was set in mainland China where she lived until her mid-twenties, and while her works reeked of authenticity, she often relied too heavily on melodrama to accomplish her purposes. Only her Pulitzer Prize-winning *The Good Earth* (1932) retains much of its power, carrying the reader through several generations of the Wang clan.

The story was dramatized briefly on Broadway in late 1932, and Irving Thalberg saw a performance and envisioned the story as an epic. When he approached Louis B. Mayer at MGM with his idea, Mayer asked, "Who wants to see a picture about Chinese farmers?" As it turned out, quite a few people did.

In *The Good Earth* (MGM, 1937), many sequences from Pearl Buck's novel showed up on the screen— Wang (Paul Muni) appearing at the manor house to claim his bride, O-Lan (Luise Rainer, in an Oscar-winning performance); their working the farm; the famine that drives them south; the looting of the palace house; Wang's rise to prosperity and his taking of a second wife; his neglect of O-Lan; and, his discovery of the romance between the second wife and his son. In addition, the screenwriters (Talbot Jennings, Tess Slesinger, and Claudine West) invented a terrifying locust attack that sweeps down on Wang and his family, threatening to destroy their crops and ruin their prosperity. When O-Lan dies, Wang comes to realize that it was she who was the cause of his success. Standing next to the tree that she planted on their wedding night, he cries out, "O-Lan, you are the earth!"

The *New York Times* called *The Good Earth* on its premiere "one of the finest things Hollywood has done this season or any other." Otis Ferguson, writing in *The New Republic*, pointed out how Hollywood could easily have turned out a star vehicle of unparalleled crassness. "And yet the treatment of the book's large simplicities," he said, "runs across the screen for nearly two hours and a half and turns out to be among the grandest things done in picturization."

Pearl Buck didn't reach the screen again for seven years. In 1942, she wrote *Dragon Seed*, a piece of patriotic propaganda, which became a best-seller, prompting MGM to buy the rights. The reviewer for *Time* called *Dragon Seed* (MGM, 1944) "a kind of slant-eyed *North Star*." Family patriarch Ling Tan (Walter Huston), elder in a small Chinese village in the late thirties, does not put much stock in the Japanese threat, but when the enemy gets close, his son, Lao Er (Turhan Bey), and his son's wife, Jade (Katharine Hepburn), flee

to the interior where they plan to set up munitions factories. There Jade encounters Wu Lien (Akim Tamiroff), a wealthy merchant who is spying for the Japanese. At a banquet given by Wu Lien, Jade poisons the food, killing several of the enemy. Wu Lien is arrested and executed for the deed. Soon after, Jade and her husband return to their village, where they discover Ling Tan ready to fight.

As some critics pointed out, despite the predominantly Caucasian cast, the acting was of a genuinely high caliber, and the script by Marguerite Roberts and Jane Murfin, while probably twenty minutes too long, had its share of humor and pathos. However, much of Pearl Buck's novel was either omitted or restructured. In the novel, Ling Tan realizes the Japanese threat much earlier than in the film, and becomes one of the key members of the Chinese resistance in his area. While the character of Jade is very similar to that of Mayli, the highly melodramatic events between Lao San, a minor role in the film played by Hurd Hatfield, and Mayli disappeared under a complete rewrite. Despite all these changes, the film had a remarkable sense of style, highlighted by the fine camera work of Sidney Wagner, that somehow managed to retain the spirit of the novel.

In the same year that Pearl Buck wrote *Dragon Seed*, she also agreed to write a novel aimed strictly for film. The result was *China Sky* (RKO, 1945), a minor effort about an idealistic American doctor in war-torn China. It cast stalwart Randolph Scott with two women, Ruth Warrick and Ellen Drew, fighting for his affections. The film adaptation by Brenda Weisberg and Joseph Hoffman devoted far too much time to the love triangle at the expense of action.

In 1962, director Leo McCarey submitted an outline of a story and sometime later a completed script to Pearl Buck from which she went on to write an original paperback novel, *Satan Never Sleeps*. The film, starring William Holden and Clifton Webb, was a rehash of *Going My Way* (without the humor and the heart), also directed by McCarey. The only difference was that *Satan Never Sleeps* (20th Century-Fox, 1962) was set in China. The author's participation was little more than the services of a hack.

Far more prolific than Pearl Buck was Erskine Caldwell (1903–87), who often created quite vivid characters among his rural settings. His sensational content pushed him perilously close to producing schlock literature, and it was his sensational content that attracted the attention of Hollywood.

Caldwell's most famous novel, *Tobacco Road* (1932), was an unflinching portrait of a Southern rural family, the Lesters, who live on land that no longer yields enough crop to support them. They have been starving for years, becoming callous in the process. Caldwell's combination of social realism and black humor made it to the Broadway stage in 1934, where the play had a very successful run.

Nunnally Johnson's screenplay for *Tobacco Road* (20th Century-Fox, 1941) eliminated most of the Caldwell story and most of the objectionable material from the play that could not pass the film censorship boards. Instead, Johnson concentrated on Jeeter Lester (Charley Grapewin), turning him into an amiable but amoral character who struggles to hold his farm and family together. No one in the film seems to want to work—they live by stealing from others and from each other—but for a short period of time the family rallies around a shiny new automobile that Dude, the son, destroys in one day. Although only twelve in the novel, the daughter, Ellie May (Gene Tierney), is quite a bit more mature in the film; and Jeeter never sells her, although her sexuality is an open invitation. Grandma (Zeffie Tilbury) doesn't get run over as she did in the novel but simply wanders off into the woods to die. In the end, Jeeter manages to get $100 to save his farm for one more month, but it is obvious that all his worrying and fretting over the farm is a useless gesture to a dead past.

Despite all these changes, *Tobacco Road* emerges as an engaging film in which John Ford, usually the staunch supporter of family and tradition, turns his values upside down and gives them a vigorous shake. Out pop the Lesters, and if they are not the same creation of Erskine Caldwell, their amoral conduct is as refreshingly original today as when the film first reached the screen. Caldwell himself especially liked the screenplay, but he was disturbed by studio interference. Later he said, "I was very unhappy about the inept ending that a producer at Fox had arbitrarily substituted for the realistic conclusion of the novel and play."

Caldwell returned to the same setting for his next novel, *God's Little Acre* (1933). The book took twenty-five years to reach the screen, and when it did, *God's Little Acre* (United Artists, 1958) proved a more forthright and honest adaptation than anyone had a right to expect.

Ty Ty Walden (Robert Ryan) is a poor white Georgia farmer who is driven to search for a gold mine his grandfather once hinted was located on the family property. For fifteen years, he has been digging holes all over his farm with the help of his black friend, Uncle Felix (Rex Ingram). His youngest daughter, Darlin' Jill (Fay Spain), is being pursued by fat Pluto Swint (Buddy Hackett) but is finally seduced by the albino Dave Dawson (Michael Landon), whom Ty Ty is using as a divining rod. Ty Ty's middle daughter, Griselda (Tina Louise), is having an affair with Bill Thompson (Aldo

Ray), who is married to her sister, Rosamond (Helen Westcott). Bill wants to reopen the cotton mill and bring prosperity back to the region, but before he can accomplish this, he is tragically shot and killed. Director Anthony Mann and screenwriter Philip Yordan treated Caldwell's characters with dignity and respect, even if they weren't part of the country club set. Of course there were changes as a sop to Hollywood's morality police, but on the whole, the novel's theme and spirit arrived almost intact.

The only other Caldwell work to reach the screen was *Claudelle Inglish* (1958), another exercise in rural rutting. The film version (Warner Bros., 1961) concentrates on the jilted Claudelle (Diane McBain), who tries to find solace in wantonness. As the *New York Times* observed, the film proved that "life can be hideous down on a Warner sound-stage farm."

Like Caldwell, Marjorie Kinnan Rawlings also wrote of the rural South, although her fiction tended to be much less earthy and far less controversial. Her most famous novel, *The Yearling* (1938), which won the Pulitzer Prize, took a twelve-year-old boy, Jody Baxter, for its protagonist, and the remarkable feature of his character is that he is neither idealized nor feminized; he is a well-rounded, believable boy who captures the reader's attention and interest.

Louis B. Mayer attempted to bring the novel to the screen in 1941 under Victor Fleming's direction, and dispatched him to Florida with Spencer Tracy and Anne Revere, and an adaptation by John Lee Mahin, but the production got mired down and subsequently was abandoned.

After the war, Mayer revived the property and *The Yearling* (MGM, 1946) was transferred to the screen almost intact under director Clarence Brown, with a script by Paul Osborn. The story centers around the fawn that Jody (Claude Jarman Jr.) receives as a gift from his father (Gregory Peck). The fawn destroys the corn corp, and the Baxters, backwoods farmers barely eking out a living from the land, come to realize that the animal must be disposed of if they are to live. Jody is forced to kill the fawn after his mother (Jane Wyman) has wounded it, and once he finishes the job, he runs away, hating his parents. He returns a few days later, realizing that their decision had been the only one possible. In his time in the woods alone, Jody has grown from a yearling to a man. What might have been a mawkish story emerged full of restraint and intelligence. To be sure, there are moments when an unseen heavenly choir sings, and Jody's hysterics at the end seem overlong—Rawlings showed more restraint in the novel—but those aside, the film is a faithful rendering of a family classic.

Capitalizing on the success of Rawlings's name, the

Katharine Hepburn as Jade, Walter Huston as Ling Tan, and Turhan Bey as Lao Er in Pearl Buck's *Dragon Seed* (1944).

Gene Tierney as Ellie May Lester in a romantic pose for the very unromantic *Tobacco Road* (1941), based on Erskine Caldwell's novel.

Buddy Hackett as Pluto closes his eyes to avoid a glimpse of Fay Spain as Darlin' Jill in *God's Little Acre* (1958).

Robert Ryan as Ty Ty has a word with God in Caldwell's *God's Little Acre* (1958).

Jane Wyman, Claude Jarman Jr., and Gregory Peck as the Baxters survey the damage done by the deer who is young Jody's pet in *The Yearling* (1946).

Jeanette MacDonald as the concert star seeking a new life, with Lassie as one of her costars in *The Sun Comes Up* (1948), loosely based on the Marjorie Kinnan Rawlings novel.

Dana Preu as the older woman and David Peck as the bounder who marries her for her money in *Gal Young Un* (1979), based on Rawlings's short story.

same studio came up with *The Sun Comes Up* (MGM, 1949), supposedly based on several of Rawlings's short stories, including "Mountain Prelude." Here a war widow, Helen Lorfield Winter (Jeanette MacDonald), who has also lost her son, retreats to the backwoods of Georgia where a boy from the local orphanage, Jerry (Claude Jarman Jr.), captures her heart. The mawkish story by William Ludwig and Margaret Fitts had little connection with Marjorie Kinnan Rawlings or her fiction. Actually it was turned into a Lassie movie, with Mac-Donald in her final role.

One of Marjorie Rawlings's most fully realized short stories is "Gal Young Un" (*Harper's,* June 1932), the plot of which is somewhat reminiscent of a Faulkner story. The independent feature *Gal Young Un* (Nuñez Films, 1979), produced, written, directed and photographed by Victor Nuñez, translated the story faithfully to the screen. Mattie Syles (Dana Preu) marries Trax (David Peck), a man fifteen years her junior, who

misuses her savings to set up an illegal still. He is often gone, and on one of his return trips, he brings along his mistress, Elly (J. Smith), a waif he picked up in southern Florida. Soon, Trax has discarded Elly in the same way he has discarded Mattie, and Mattie, finally asserting herself, destroys his still and runs him off. As she is about to run Elly off, too, she realizes the girl is a lost soul with no place to go and no one to turn to. Mattie's maternal instincts take over, and she allows Elly to became the child she never had.

Even though it is a low-budget affair, the film's period details proved first rate, as did the beautiful camera work and rich country music score. The acting by the three principals, all unknowns, is superb. But what allows this movie to rise above the merely pedestrian is its well conceived script. *Gal Young Un* is one of those rare instances where the short story provided enough meat for a completely realized film.

In 1928, Rawlings moved to Cross Creek in southern

162

Florida, and from her experiences there came *Cross Creek* (1942), a montage of various stories, anecdotes, and naturalist studies, all written in a plain but delightfully timeless style. When the autobiographical work reached the screen, *Cross Creek* (Universal, 1983) had taken on a far more definable structure. Marjorie Kinnan Rawlings (Mary Steenburgen) arrives at the backwoods Cross Creek to escape a failing marriage and to find time to write her great novel. There she meets an assortment of interesting people, including her maid, Geechee (Alfre Woodard), and the gruff but basically decent Marsh Turner (Rip Torn). She even finds romance in the person of Norton Baskin (Peter Coyote). While some of the incidents from the book show up, including a scene between a fawn and a girl which provides the inspiration for *The Yearling*, the script by Dalene Young is only loosely based on the Rawlings book. The incidents and story line have been jazzed up for public consumption.

Of these authors who have fallen from critical grace—Marquand, O'Hara, Buck, Caldwell, and Rawlings—it might seem surprising to some that not more films were adapted from their works. Yet, in each case, the authors seldom strayed from their locales: Marquand in Boston, O'Hara in the midwest, Buck in China, and Caldwell and Rawlings in the rural South. While they were all competent craftsmen and proficient storytellers, their material had little variation and their characters little emotional or psychological range. Although the screenwriters were forced by circumstances to play around with plots and characters, they still managed to produce from the bunch some good films and a classic or two.

Dana Hill as Ellie Turner in Marjorie Kinnan Rawlings's autobiographical *Cross Creek* (1983), in a scene which becomes the inspiration for Rawlings to write *The Yearling*.

Broderick Crawford as Willie Stark in Robert Penn Warren's *All the King's Men* (1949).

NINE

THE NEW BREED

Walter Van Tilburg Clark, Carson McCullers,
Truman Capote, Flannery O'Connor,
Robert Penn Warren, Vladimir Nabokov,
Shirley Jackson, Paul Bowles

The 1940s saw the first Western novel accepted as a classic among mainstream literature, Walter Van Tilburg Clark's *The Ox-Bow Incident* (1940). What begins as a standard horse opera ends as a study of human misery in which there are no heroes, and it took a heap of doing to convince a dubious Darryl F. Zanuck to make it.

The film version (20th Century-Fox, 1943), in Lamar Trotti's screenplay, compromised with the plot. The film opens with two cowboys, Gil Carter (Henry Fonda) and Art Croft (Henry [Harry] Morgan) riding into town and joining the posse when it's formed. They are not heroes, just ordinary men who assist in taking the law into their own hands. But unlike some of the posse members, the experience sobers them. Once the posse captures three accused horse thieves, Gil and old-timer Davies (Harry Davenport) take the lead in trying to stop their hanging without trial. They prove ineffectual, and the film remains as bleak and uncompromising as the novel.

The story catalogs a wide range of human faults—revenge, cruelty, ambivalence, moral weakness, irrationality—against which the forces of reason and justice prove powerless. As the events draw closer to their conclusion, the camera moves in on the faces, laying bare the emotions of the characters and drawing us deeper into the tragedy.

The film failed at the box office. During the war years, moviegoers wanted escapist fare, not a brooding, pessimistic Western. In addition, the uncomfortable message was at odds with accepted Western mythology. However, critics admired it, and today the film is as important and original as the day it was released, a timeless study of man's inhumanity to man.

More optimistic is *The Track of the Cat* (1949), Clark's story of a Nevada family, the Bridges, whose fate is enmeshed with that of a black mountain lion. As a film, *Track of the Cat* (Wayne-Fellows/Warner Bros.,

1954) is a static, ponderous affair. The problem is that the book is talky, a good deal of the action taking place in the kitchen of the house, and the brooding film followed suit. To further emphasize the bleak nature of the story, director William Wellman chose to film in color, but almost everything—the sets, the house, the horses, the clothes—are in black and white. Only the flesh tones of the characters, an occasional glimpse of blue sky, a yellow scarf worn by Gwen (Diana Lynn), and the brilliant red checkered mackinaw worn by Curt (Robert Mitchum) possess color.

A. I. Bezzerides's screenplay follows the book faithfully, including the symbolic overtones that the author so clearly intended. If anything, it even clarifies the feelings of Curt. When the big cat begins to kill the cattle, Curt sees it as a threat to his authority and becomes obsessed with its death, even at the expense of the life of his brother, Arthur (William Hopper). After Curt's death, Harold (Tab Hunter), the youngest brother, takes up the challenge and proves his manhood, killing the beast that has haunted the family. Throughout this film, including the climax, the cat is never seen. It is a dark, mysterious force that prowls outside waiting to destroy the family.

The forties also saw the emergence of Carson McCullers (1917–67), a Southern writer who explored the grotesque. She worked in films only once, helping to doctor the script for *Indiscretion of an American Wife* in the fifties on which her friend, Truman Capote, also worked.

Her first novel, *The Heart Is a Lonely Hunter* (1940), received a limited number of reviews upon publication, but most were highly enthusiastic. In his screenplay for the film version (Warner Bros., 1967), Thomas Ryan, a fellow Southerner, made several important changes. He dropped tomboy Mick's older brother and her two older sisters. In the novel, Portia spoke an exaggerated Aunt Jemima dialect full of "I were" and "They is," but Ryan makes her an articulate black militant who takes a job as a maid as a form of rebellion. Portia (played by Cicely Tyson) may have been the least believable character in the film, but the change here was probably motivated by the political climate of 1968 rather than some intrinsic literary merit.

In 1963 after Ryan had finished the script, Carson McCullers asked him to visit her. When he had read her his screen adaptation, she embraced him with tears in her eyes and told him, "If I had had you with me to help me write the book, then it really would be as good as some people think it is." In an interview with critic Rex Reed, she said that she believed that the script had much of the original feeling because Ryan was a fellow Southerner. "I wouldn't trust a Northern writer with it."

Many of the surface details of the novel made it into the film. John Singer (Alan Arkin) is the deaf-mute who moves to the Southern town to be near his friend, Antonapoulos (Chuck McCann), another deaf-mute who has been placed in a nearby institution. He rents a room from a family who needs the money, and they move their daughter Mick (Sondra Locke) out of her quarters. At first resentful, she gradually befriends Singer. Later, after learning that her father has become a permanent cripple and that she will have to go to work in order to help support the family, Mick turns on Singer. At the same time, Singer learns that his friend Dr. Copeland (Percy Rodrigues) is dying of cancer, and that Jake Blount (Stacy Keach), a semi-alcoholic drifter he has befriended, has died. These events coupled with other disappointments lead to his own suicide. At Singer's graveside, Mick comes to realize just how much the deaf man changed her life.

The film *Reflections in a Golden Eye* (Warner Bros., 1967), based on McCullers's 1941 novel, failed to engender any sympathy or interest in either the story or the characters. In his *Village Voice* review, Andrew Sarris noted that "what the late Carson McCullers was content to leave implicit on the printed page, John Huston, Chapman Mortimer, and Gladys Hill have chosen to make explicit on the screen." However, two scenes managed to capture some sense of the novel. The first is when Major Weldon Penderton (Marlon Brando) lectures a group of soldiers on the mystique of leadership, and the second is when he takes a whip to his amoral wife Leonora's (Elizabeth Taylor) horse that has just thrown him. Both show the hopeless frustration and pent-up rage within the man. These scenes, like the majority of the script, display an amazing surface fidelity to the source, retaining most of the events and characters from McCullers's short novel.

Before he began the film, director John Huston dropped by to see the author and left a copy of the script for her perusal. Not long afterward, she wrote him a note telling how profoundly grateful she was for the fine job he and his screenwriters had done in re-creating her work, but while the story worked fairly well in written form, it did not work well on the screen. Critic John Simon in *The New Leader* said that the author created "an atmosphere redolent with morbid fascination," but called the film "pedestrian, crass, and uninvolving to the point of repellence."

McCullers's third novel, *The Member of the Wedding* (1946), was rather thin in plot but strong in characterization. Once again she turned to the world of an adolescent girl to tell the story of Frankie Adams, a gawky, motherless tomboy whose only companions are the family cook, Berenice Sadie Brown, and a six-year-old neighbor boy, John Henry West, who dies of meningitis before the story is over. McCullers successfully adapted her own novel into a Broadway play that ran for

Dana Andrews, Paul E. Burns, and Henry Fonda in a publicity shot for *The Ox-Bow Incident* (1943).

Ethel Waters as Berenice Sadie Brown watches a happy Julie Harris as twelve-year-old Frankie Adams in *The Member of the Wedding* (1953).

Robert Mitchum and Tab Hunter as brothers and Carl Switzer as Joe Sam, a hundred-year-old Indian, in *Track of the Cat* (1954).

fourteen-and-a-half months and then sold the rights to Stanley Kramer for $75,000 plus 10 percent of the profits.

In the film *Member of the Wedding* (Columbia, 1952), adapted by Edna and Edward Anhalt, Frankie Adams (Julie Harris, re-creating her Broadway role) is a twelve-year old girl approaching adolescence who dreams of being in her older brother's wedding. Dejected that she is not allowed to go on the honeymoon, she runs away, but

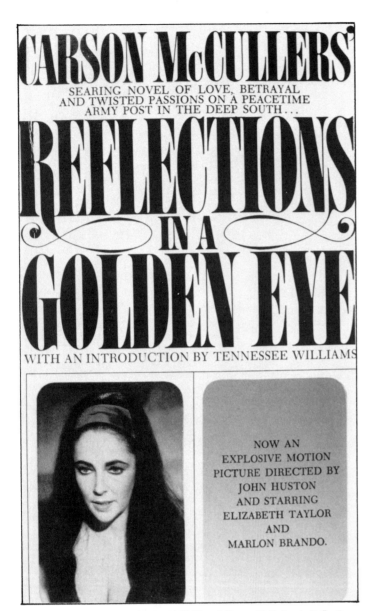

Paperback tie-in for the 1967 film of Carson McCullers's *Reflections in a Golden Eye*.

after an encounter with a drunken soldier in which she almost loses her virginity, she returns home, only to receive news that her young cousin John (Brandon de Wilde) has died. After a passage of time, she enters upon the dating stage of teenhood.

Julie Harris was twenty-seven at the time of the film, and her performance made her a screen star. Two years later she would play opposite James Dean in *East of Eden*. Still, it must be admitted that her age, which had been less a factor on-stage because of the distance between her and the audience, was a handicap on the screen where the camera often locked in on her mature face and form, neither of which was that of a preteen.

It is possible that the model for John Henry West in *Member of the Wedding* was Carson McCullers's good friend, Truman Capote, whom she allowed to read the manuscript before she submitted it to the publishers. Two years before, in June 1945, her sister, Rita Smith, then fiction editor of *Mademoiselle*, had published Capote's first story, "Miriam."

Ten years after Truman Capote's (1924–84) first splash on the literary scene with *Other Voices, Other Rooms* came "Breakfast at Tiffany's," an extended piece of fiction that first appeared in *Esquire* in 1958. In it, a narrator tells the story of Holly Golightly, a demi-prostitute who insists on "a $50 powder room charge" from those she dates, yet is able to influence people long after she has disappeared from their lives.

Capote was outraged at what Hollywood did to *Breakfast at Tiffany's* (Paramount, 1961). "It was high treachery on the part of the producers. They didn't do a single thing they promised," he said. In the novel, the narrator was a successful writer, probably Capote himself, who was never romantically involved with Holly (Audrey Hepburn). The film substituted a character—a kept man named Paul Varjak (George Peppard)—for the narrator, then provided an obligatory Hollywood happy ending. "It was the most miscast film I've ever seen," said Capote. "It made me want to throw up."

In late 1959, Capote read a dozen or so paragraphs in the *New York Times* about a multiple murder in Kansas, and for the next six years devoted almost all his energies to researching and investigating the crime. The result was four long articles that appeared in *The New Yorker* in 1965 and in book form the following year as *In Cold Blood*. It told of the events surrounding the murders in Holcomb, Kansas, of Herbert W. Clutter, his wife, and their two children, and of the subsequent apprehension, conviction, and execution of their killers.

The film *In Cold Blood* (Columbia, 1967) omitted most of the life of the Clutters and the Kansas atmosphere. The first thirty-five minutes concentrates on the lives of the two drifters, Hickock (Scott Wilson) and Smith (Robert Blake), and gets them to the scene of the crime.

Robert Blake and Scott Wilson as killers Perry Smith and Dick Hickok in Truman Capote's *In Cold Blood* (1967).

There is a sudden rip in the narrative as the maid enters the house the next day and discovers the bodies. The killers flee to Mexico as the police begin their investigation but return to the States where they are caught and arrested in Las Vegas. Not until they are taken back to Kansas and Smith confesses does the audience witness the grisly murders. There is a barely sketched-in trial, and their execution is a ritualistic death by hanging.

Like the book, the climax is the murder of the Clutter family. The arrogant Hickock and Smith burst into the house, believing that they have come only to rob, but when there is no expected loot, they explode in fury, slaughtering the family. While showing all the slow and terrifying buildup to the maniacal mayhem, writer-director Richard Brooks avoided the actual shooting and knifing of the victims, preferring the roar of a shotgun and blood splattering on the wall, yet the scene possesses a horrifying nightmare-like reality, thanks to Conrad Hall's black-and-white photography.

Unlike the novel, there is little poetry in this docudrama. However, the film reflected the novel especially well in the performances that illuminated the two killers. Actors Scott Wilson and Robert Blake captured disturbing dimensions to the tensions, torments, and conceits of these petty killers. In the scenes involving their plans to rob the Clutters, the murder of the family, and their own executions, the film comes closest to reproducing the essence of the book.

After *In Cold Blood*, Capote never again produced a major literary work. His literary reputation rests on a collection or two of short stories, three short novels, and one nonfiction novel. In addition to this is his other work in films. With director John Huston, he cowrote the script for *Beat the Devil* and, as mentioned earlier, was one of the cowriters on *Indiscretion of an American Wife*. He also cowrote the film *The Innocents* and wrote a draft for *The Great Gatsby* that was rejected by Paramount. In *Murder by Death*, a spoof of the detective genre, he even appeared as an actor. Capote once said, "I don't like doing scripts of my own work, I prefer doing scripts of other people's." Yet some of his best work to reach the screen was in *Truman Capote's Trilogy* (Allied Artists, 1969), which he cowrote with Eleanor Perry.

Truman Capote's Trilogy, like *O. Henry's Full House* (see Chapter Six), was an anthology composed of short stories—"Miriam," "Along the Path to Eden," and "A Christmas Memory." All three were originally intended for television, but only "A Christmas Memory" was actually broadcast, and then all three were reedited and briefly released to theaters. "Miriam" is the story of a nanny (Mildred Natwick) slowly losing her mind. "Along the Path to Eden" tells of a widow (Maureen Stapleton) who searches for a new husband among the men who visit their wives' graves in a cemetery. The last and the

Susan Dunfee and Mildred Natwick in "Miriam," one segment of *Truman Capote's Trilogy* (1969).

Paperback tie-in for the 1961 film of Truman Capote's *Breakfast at Tiffany's* with Audrey Hepburn as Holly Golightly.

Maureen Stapleton and Martin Balsam in "Along the Paths to Eden," a segment of *Truman Capote's Trilogy* (1969).

Truman Capote in a rare acting role as Lionel Twain, with Richard Narita, Peter Sellers, and Eileen Brennan in Neil Simon's *Murder By Death* (1976).

Brad Dourif as Hazel Motes, the mad preacher, in Flannery O'Connor's *Wise Blood* (1979).

best, "A Christmas Memory," narrated by Capote himself, looks back to a time when he was a young boy (Donnie Melvin), examining his relationship with a much older distant cousin (Geraldine Page) and their last Christmas together.

Best known for her short stories during her brief writing career, Georgia native (Mary) Flannery O'Connor (1925–64) also wrote two novels, the first of which was *Wise Blood* (1952). Much of the story and almost all of the characters from the novel showed up in the film version (New Line, 1979). Because of the cinematic insuitability of the material, the movie could easily have been a failure, but director John Huston and screenwriters Benedict and Michael Fitzgerald created a quirky, self-contained world in which the bizarre characters are believable and the events, even when motivations are sometimes unclear, are compelling.

Returning home from the war, Hazel Motes (Brad Dourif) takes up street preaching. "I'm a member and preacher to that church," he says, "where the blind don't see and the lame don't walk and what's dead stays that way." His Jesus is the Jesus of his grandfather (John Huston), an unloving hellfire-and-brimstone preacher. Too wrapped up in himself, Hazel fails to organize his church, and fast-talking promoter Hoover Shoates (Ned Beatty) steps in to fill the void. Hazel also hooks up with a supposedly blind preacher (William Hickey) who convinces Hazel to blind himself in order to learn the truth. When Hazel's middle-aged landlady (Mary Nell Santacroce) falls in love with him, she keeps him a virtual prisoner, although she, too, fails to understand him. When she finds that he has wrapped barbed wire around his chest to mortify his flesh, she scolds him. "People have quit doing it," she says. Hazel answers, "They ain't quit doing it as long as I'm doing it."

Robert Penn Warren (1905–89) had already written two historical novels, a number of short stories, a biography of John Brown, and several collections of poetry before publishing *All the King's Men* (1946), which earned him his first Pulitzer Prize. Based loosely on the career of Huey Long of Louisiana, the novel is narrated by Jack Burden, who has allied himself with Willie Stark, the governor of some unnamed Southern state. In telling the story of Stark, Burden also tells his own story. It opens with Stark, already governor, and Jack riding along one of the highways that Stark has built throughout the state. Then in a series of flashbacks, Jack works his way to the present where he finishes with Stark's assassination and the events of his own life that follow. Stark begins as a voice of the people, but by the end, power has corrupted him. As he dies, he tells Jack, "It might have been all different, Jack. You got to believe that."

In writer-director Robert Rossen's film *All the King's*

Clark Gable as Hamish Bond and Yvonne DeCarlo as the octoroon, Amanda Starr in a romantic pose for *Band of Angels* (1957), and later Patric Knowles as dastardly Charles de Marigny tries to silence her.

Men (Columbia, 1949), while the narrator continues to be Jack Burden (John Ireland), the emphasis has shifted, and it becomes more the story of Willie Stark (Broderick Crawford). Once the novel begins, the reader witnesses only what Jack witnesses, since there are no events except what he sees and understands; but the film shifts viewpoints so that some of the things the audience sees, Jack does not. Warren's novel had a quasi-religious, introspective center, but in shifting the narrative focus, Rossen has turned the story into one of the American political system gone wrong. At one point, the camera locks in on a close-up of the state motto above the capitol entrance—"The Will of the People Is the Will of the State." At the same time, the hicks, among whom Willie once counted himself, flood the city to ensure Willie's autocratic rule.

The film drops the last forty pages of the novel and concludes with the assassination of Willie. If there is any doubt that this is Willie's story, the final image should dispel it. After being shot, he slumps against a pillar of the capitol building. "It could've been the whole world," he mutters to Jack. "The whole world."

Robert Penn Warren called the film "extraordinarily good," and said, "I can praise it, because it seems to me that when a movie is made from a novel, the novel is merely raw material, the movie is a new creation, and the novelist can properly attract neither praise nor blame for it. The movie, as a matter of fact, does not 'mean' what I think my book meant."*

*A two-part 1958 television adaptation of *All the King's Men*, written by Don Mankiewicz and directed by Sidney Lumet, starred Neville Brand as Willie Stark and Maureen Stapleton as Sadie Burke.

171

Sue Lyon in the title role is approached by James Mason as Humbert Humbert in *Lolita* (1962).

For his next novel, *Band of Angels* (1955), set in nineteenth-century Kentucky, Warren chose to deal with the South, slavery, and the coming of the Civil War. The story is told through the eyes of Amantha Starr, the daughter of a Kentucky planter and a Negro slave, who grows up believing she is white.

Some critics greeted Warren's book with enthusiasm while others thought it tailored to quick profits from Hollywood. Defending the novel, Warren pointed out that if the book reads like melodrama, it is because of its faithfulness to history. "History," he said, "is not melodrama, even if it usually reads like that."

Whatever weaknesses the novel may have, the film *Band of Angels* (Warner Bros., 1957) magnifies them into major calamities by emphasizing and adding to the melodramatic qualities of the story. As the movie opens, Hamish Bond (Clark Gable), a slave trader turned plantation owner, attends a slave auction in New Orleans where he buys beautiful octoroon Amantha Starr (Yvonne de Carlo). As a sop to his conscience, Bond has already educated one Negro slave, Rau-Ru (Sidney Poitier), and given him a place of importance on his plantation. Now

he installs Amantha in his household and treats her as a lady. Romance blossoms between Bond and Amantha. When the war breaks out, Rau-Ru runs off and joins the Union forces, but once New Orleans is taken, he returns to his former benefactor intent on turning him in. He relents, and instead, helps Bond and Amantha to escape.

The film never attempts to see the events through Amantha's eyes, and much of the intensity and reflective nature of the novel is lost. Even the racial conflict is only a minor subplot reminiscent of *Show Boat*. Also, all of Amantha's early life has vanished, and Hamish Bond has been turned into a romantic creature along the lines of Rhett Butler as the producers and writers (John Twist, Ivan Goff, and Ben Roberts) opted for a poor man's *Gone With the Wind*.

One of the most unusual American writers is Vladimir Nabokov (1899–1977), who was born in Russia and educated in England. He immigrated to the United States in 1940 where he became a citizen five years later. Until 1938, he wrote his novels in Russian, but in 1941 he turned to English, and began to produce highly-acclaimed fiction and poetry. His best-known work became the

172

very controversial *Lolita* (1955), the story of middle-aged Humbert Humbert, who has an obsession for young girls, which he has hidden under a series of unhappy affairs with older women.

After selling his property to films, Nabokov was hired to adapt his own screenplay, and his first drafts were not only very long but very unwieldly. After numerous rewrites, he pared down the story to just over two-and-a-half hours. Much of the story remains—probably too much—but the real problem of the darkly comic *Lolita* (MGM, 1960), directed by Stanley Kubrick, lies in changing the age of Lolita (Sue Lyon) from twelve to fifteen. By making her just a bit older, much of the bite of the story was taken away. Also, Humbert (James Mason) has no obsession with young girls in general—only with this young girl in particular.

The story opens with Humbert shooting Clare Quilty (Peter Sellers) and then moves into an extended flashback. As in the novel, Humbert marries Charlotte (Shelley Winters) to be near her nymphet daughter, Lolita. He writes in his diary his real feelings about mother and daughter, even contemplating killing Charlotte to get to Lolita. This proves unnecessary when Charlotte reads his diary and rushes out into the street, where she is hit by a car. Humbert becomes Lolita's guardian, but Quilty is also after her. When Humbert takes her on a cross-country trip, Quilty follows, steals the girl away, and Humbert doesn't hear from her for two years, at which time she writes and tells him that she left Quilty because he wanted her to do strange things; she also asks for money. Humbert goes to see Lolita and finds her married to a day laborer, pregnant, and unhappy. At this point he rushes out to confront Quilty. The epilogue confirms the fact that Humbert dies of a heart attack while awaiting trial.

Many people found the novel shocking, but the film proved to be very mild, with the most erotic scene being a pedicure given by Humbert to Lolita. The adaptation came in for its share of negative criticism. Stanley Kauffmann in *The New Republic* said of the Nabokov screenplay, "There are flashes in it of the original. . . . But instead of a prodigious madman's flaming autobiography in love, we get in sum a rather soggy odyssey of a rueful, obsessed mature man, a diluted *Blue Angel* with a teenage temptress instead of a tart." Nabokov himself said, "My first reaction to the picture was a mixture of aggravation, regret, and reluctant pleasure."

Although recognized widely for her short stories, especially the oft-anthologized "The Lottery," Shirley Jackson (1919–65) began her career writing novels, the first of which appeared in the late 1940s. Her third, *The Bird's Nest* (1954), was the story of a woman, Elizabeth,

who suffered multiple personalities, four of them, dominated by one called Lizzie. The novel, adapted to the screen by Mel Dinelli, became *Lizzie* (MGM, 1957) and pared down the multiple personalities to three. A kindly neighbor (Hugo Haas, who also directed) and an alcoholic aunt (Joan Blondell) finally drag Lizzie (Eleanor Parker) off to a psychiatrist (Richard Boone) who, through various treatments including shock therapy, rids her of the added baggage.

An incomplete woman is also the center of Jackson's best-known novel, *The Haunting of Hill House* (1959), which became *The Haunting* (MGM, 1962). Despite the changes in the plot, especially the relationship between Eleanor (Julie Harris) and Theodora (Claire Bloom), the basic idea of a woman searching for love and finding it in the guise of a haunted house remained. Director Robert Wise opted to play the familiar "old dark house" story without blood and gore, just as had Shirley Jackson in

Joan Blondell as the boozy mother and Eleanor Parker as the daughter with multiple personalities in *Lizzie* (1957), based on *The Bird's Nest* by Shirley Jackson.

Julie Harris, Richard Johnson, and, in the background, Russ Tamblyn and Claire Bloom
in *The Haunting* (1963), an adaptation of *The Haunting of Hill House*.

her novel, and the suspense is masterful, building frame by frame, in Nelson Gidding's screenplay.

With the publication of *The Sheltering Sky* (1949), author Paul Bowles (1910–90) was praised for his portrayal of a modern married couple afflicted with ennui and malaise. In a sense, his novel was also a nightmare extension of Twain's *Innocents Abroad* in which the author dropped his travelers, Port and his wife, Kit, in Northern Africa where they are searching for some sort of romantic catastrophe. There was little physical action as interior monologues and philosophizing carried the tale along.

When director Bernardo Bertolucci came to the task of making a film of *The Sheltering Sky* (Warner Bros., 1990), he said, "Instead of using language and psychology, I wanted to be more physical." As a result, Bertolucci and cowriter Mark Peploe captured much of Bowles's novel with images rather than dialogue. The desert is the prevailing image. Insects are everywhere,

and breakfast is served with a can of DDT. When Kit (Debra Winger) isn't sleeping with an upper-class companion (Campbell Scott), she is complaining about the heat, and Kit's husband, Port (John Malkovich), comes down with a case of typhoid fever that he endures in a sea of sweat.

What seems profound and meaningful in the novel seems pretentious and absurd on the screen. During the last half of the movie, there is very little dialogue by anyone except for the Tuareg nomads who speak Tamashek. The desert with all its profound images becomes the spokesperson for Kit, who has hitched a fateful camel ride, leaving Port behind. Unfortunately the images do not explain the motivations of the characters.

The 1940s saw the rise of writers who experimented with style and content. Although these authors occasionally proved successful with the public, Hollywood often used their material without fully understanding it. Yet, surprisingly, some good films and some true classics emerged from the adaptations of these authors. Director John Huston, who made *Reflections in a Golden Eye*, also made an exceedingly honest and faithful adaptation of Flannery O'Connor's *Wise Blood*. Carson McCullers's *Member of the Wedding* received an excellent adaptation, and *The Heart Is a Lonely Hunter*, while not a complete film, had some good moments. Capote's *In Cold Blood* became a chillingly faithful film that captured many of the subtleties, although little of the poetry, of the nonfiction novel. Robert Penn Warren's *All the*

King's Men, while considerably abbreviated for the screen, has become a true classic from the studio system. Vladimir Nabokov's *Lolita* was truncated by the author himself, but still managed to create some impressive moments, mostly on the strength of the performances. *The Haunting*, based on Shirley Jackson's *Haunting of Hill House*, translated into a superb ghost story that was as eerie as the novel. Thus the forties proved a fruitful period for the development of American fiction and fertile ground for Hollywood to explore.

Debra Winger and John Malkovich as Kit and Port Moresby in *The Sheltering Sky* (1990).

Writer and director Norman Mailer on the set of his *Tough Guys Don't Dance* (1987).

TEN

WRITERS FROM THE WAR

Irwin Shaw, James Michener, Norman Mailer, James Jones,
Herman Wouk, Thomas Heggen, Joseph Heller

James Michener once said, "World War Two and the airplane opened the horizons and Americans suddenly wanted to read about the rest of the world. I came along and wrote books that satisfied the reading experience." The same could be said for a number of writers who emerged from World War Two. Not only did their works find immediate favor with the public, who were anxious to read about the war, but also with filmmakers, who were anxious to cash in on their successes. Once established, the majority of these writers went on to other topics, but in most cases, it was their war fiction for which they are best remembered and which Hollywood most actively sought.

Irwin Shaw (1913–84) began his writing career in 1936, and throughout the remainder of his life, he would turn out not only novels, short stories, and plays but also screenplays such as *The Talk of the Town, Commandos Strike at Dawn,* and *Desire Under the Elms,* adapting Eugene O'Neill. In all, he had fifteen separate efforts reach the screen, and in one case, *In the French Style,* he adapted his own material.

Shaw's own work did not come to the screen until 1941 with an adaptation of his 1939 play, *The Gentle People,* which emphasized the plight of little people preyed upon by gangsters. The film adaptation, *Out of the Fog* (Warner Bros., 1941), however, concentrated upon a domestic triangle. The story was played seriously until the end when Jonah (Thomas Mitchell) sets up Goff (John Garfield) for the payoff, which got a somewhat lighthearted approach. Overall the film was a competent but hardly outstanding adaptation by Robert Rossen, Jerry Wald, and Richard Macauley of Shaw's play.

In March 1954, "Tip on a Dead Jockey" appeared in *The New Yorker,* and in many ways it was reminiscent of Hemingway's stories of Americans in Europe. Metro-Goldwyn-Mayer bought the rights and hired Charles Lederer to do the script, which turned *Tip on a Dead Jockey* (MGM, 1957) into hokey melodrama with Robert Taylor, having little to do with Shaw's story except the catchy title.

In 1942, Shaw enlisted in the armed forces, serving in Africa, France, England, and Germany. When the war

Eddie Albert as George Watkins, John Garfield as Harold Goff, and Ida Lupino as Stella Goodwin in *Out of the Fog* (1941), an adaptation of the Irwin Shaw play *The Gentle People*.

ended, he began work on his first and most famous novel, *The Young Lions* (1948). After his agent sold the film rights for $100,000, a tidy sum for 1954, Shaw began writing the screenplay, but director Edward Dmytryk felt that his script was hopelessly talky and disorganized. Dmytryk brought in Edward Anhalt, who emphasized the larger issues of the war. At the insistence of Marlon Brando, Anhalt also changed the character of Christian Diestl, the idealistic German officer, who Brando believed should be a young man gradually growing disillusioned with Nazism rather than the ruthless killing machine he becomes in the novel. Dmytryk agreed, feeling that showing good Germans as well as bad Germans was a "better lesson" than showing that all Germans had been turned into animals by war.

When Shaw, who was making daily visits to the set, discovered the liberties that the director and actor were taking with his novel, he was furious and almost came to blows with Brando, who told Shaw that the writer didn't understand the character. "It's my character, I gave birth to him. I created him," Shaw shouted.

The film *The Young Lions* (20th Century-Fox, 1958) remained fairly close to the novel in plot, but of course, the fundamental change involved the character of Diestl. The film makes no discernible difference between Diestl the Nazi and the Americans Michael Whiteacre (Dean Martin) and Noah Ackerman (Montgomery Clift). The

New York Times' Bosley Crowther pointed out how Brando had subverted Shaw's character and suggested that the film "was not so much anti-Nazi as it is vaguely and loosely anti-war."

In defense of his interpretation, Brando claimed that Shaw had written the novel very close to the end of the war when feelings still ran high against the German people, and that given the chance to update the material, Shaw himself would have made Diestl more sympathetic. Shaw denied the claim, saying if he could rewrite the book, he would present Diestl in exactly the same way. One other important change involved Ackerman, who in the novel is killed by Diestl but in the film is allowed to survive.

When Irwin Shaw saw the film in Paris, he had mixed feelings. He liked the Clift performance, but he couldn't judge Brando's because he was so angry at the actor. Shaw also felt that every idea he had so carefully woven into the novel had been neatly excised by director Dmytryk and screenwriter Anhalt. However, the combination of the novel's reputation and the three big stars brought in the paying public and had a marvelous effect on the paperback tie-in, which did please Shaw.

As the decade of the sixties opened, Shaw published *Two Weeks in Another Town* (1960), a novel of Hollywood in Europe. MGM purchased the film rights for $150,000 plus a share of the profits. Shaw hoped that he would be able to write the screenplay but producer John Houseman chose Charles Schnee, with whom he had previously worked on *The Bad and the Beautiful* a decade earlier.

In *Two Weeks in Another Town* (MGM, 1962), Jack Andrus (Kirk Douglas) is a washed-up actor who goes to Rome to work for an over-the-hill director (Edward G. Robinson), and while there, he wallows in self pity and false sentimentality until he is revitalized by a new success. Bosley Crowther wrote that the script was "aimless and arbitrary."

At the same time that *Two Weeks in Another Town* was opening to less-than-kind reviews, Shaw was adapting two of his own short stories, "A Year to Learn the Language" and "In the French Style," into a screenplay that would become *In the French Style* (Columbia, 1963) with Jean Seberg. After a London preview where the critics were especially kind, Shaw had high hopes that this film would prove a commercial success back in the States. He was disappointed. Judith Crist, in the *New York Herald Tribune*, accused the film of an "overall triteness." Even more scathing was the review in *Time*,

which said that Shaw's script "tells a story that has been told, and told more excitingly, a hundred times before." The film turned a small profit and then disappeared.

Another of Shaw's Americans-in-Europe stories, "Then There Were Three" became simply *Three* (United Artists, 1969). In most respects the film, written by director James Salter, remained true to the story, but a serious problem lay in the casting of Charlotte Rampling, who was simply too withdrawn to convey the free-spirited Marty of Shaw's story.

Shaw's *Rich Man, Poor Man* (teleplay by Dean E. Riesner, ABC, Universal Television, 1976), which chronicled the lives of the Jordache brothers (Peter Strauss and Nick Nolte), became a twelve-hour miniseries, one of the first of its kind. Although it played rather loose with the plot of the original 1969 novel, actually dropping the important character the Jordache sister, it was a rich, smoothly done production with good and believable characters. (The sister was reinstated in the 1979 television sequel, *Beggarman, Thief*.)

To date James Michener (1907[?]–) has produced over a dozen fictional works, an equal number of

The soon-to-be-dead jockey (Jimmy Murphy) explains to Robert Taylor and Dorothy Malone as Lloyd and Phyllis Tredman how he'll win the big race in *Tip on a Dead Jockey* (1957). Behind the jockey are Marcel Dalio (left), Jack Lord, and Gia Scala.

Sophia Loren as Anna and Anthony Perkins as Eben Cabot in *Desire Under the Elms* (1958), Irwin Shaw's screen adaptation of Eugene O'Neill's play.

nonfictional ones, and more than a hundred magazine articles. While he has not received the critical attention of other major authors, his works have found favor with the public, which buys his novels with such rapidity that a new book by Michener is often a best-seller before it hits the stores.

In 1942, Michener volunteered for duty in the navy, and his first assignment was in the South Pacific. As the war wound down, he began writing a series of short stories that became *Tales of the South Pacific* (1947), a Pulitzer Prize winner. Because the book is endowed with a unified setting and recurring characters, many critics as well as Michener himself considered it a novel.

Joshua Logan, who directed the Rodgers and Hammerstein musical adaptation of it on Broadway, was brought to Hollywood to direct the film *South Pacific* (20th Century-Fox, 1958), which may have been a mistake since his stage technique failed to allow for much subtlety. Although the screenplay by Paul Osborn remained faithful to the stage hit, it rearranged the events and added one scene concerning Luther Billis (Ray Walston). Two stories are told simultaneously. First is that of Lieutenant Cable (John Kerr), who has a star-crossed romance with Liat (France Nuyen), a beautiful native girl. The second concerns the love affair between Nellie Forbush (Mitzi Gaynor) and Emile De Becque (Rossano Brazzi), a May-December romance that includes elements of miscegenation, since the French planter has several children by a native woman, now dead.

To many of those familiar with the Broadway musical,

Marlon Brando as the idealistic Christian Diestl in *The Young Lions* (1958).

Philippe Forquet visits Jean Seberg in *In the French Style* (1963), an adaptation of Irwin Shaw's short story.

Robie Porter, Charlotte Rampling, and Sam Waterston make up the ménage à trois in *Three* (1969), based on Shaw's "Then There Were Three."

Nick Nolte, Herbert Jefferson Jr., and Kay Lenz in the television miniseries of Irwin Shaw's *Rich Man, Poor Man* (1976).

the film, although very popular, seemed like second-rate entertainment, and many critics were quick to compare the two. While Osborn's script was generally overlooked, the direction of Logan—and especially his flamboyant use of color filters—was singled out for attack as was his rather awkward use of close-ups on the large Todd-AO screen. However, there was still the music, songs like "Some Enchanted Evening," "I'm Gonna Wash That Man Right Out of My Hair," "There is Nothing Like a Dame," "Younger Than Springtime," "Bali Ha'i," and "You've Got to Be Carefully Taught." One song originally cut from the stage version, "My Girl Back Home," was restored for the film.

In 1949, *Holiday* magazine asked Michener to return to the South Seas for a series of feature articles on places like Fiji, Guadalcanal, and Rubaul. For every nonfiction piece Michener wrote, he also wrote a fictional one, and the result was *Return to Paradise* (1951). Most reviewers

181

Gary Cooper as Morgan watches with consternation as his Polynesian daughter (Moira MacDonald) takes up with the young American flyer in *Return to Paradise* (1953), based on James Michener's "Mr. Morgan."

loved the nonfiction but agreed with Robert Payne writing in *Saturday Review of Literature*, who called the stories "bunk." Two of them were adapted into films.

"Mr. Morgan" became *Return to Paradise* (United Artists, 1953), which, while it did use many Samoans to give the film some semblance of authenticity, inserted far too many native dances as filler. Adapted by Charles Kaufman and directed by Mark Robson, it also offered some nice scenery and a rather good performance by Gary Cooper who, in his rather lackadaisical acting style, fit the character of Morgan, the American Wanderer.

A novelette, "Until They Sail," was the second story from *Return to Paradise* adapted for the screen. The plot concentrated on the four Neville daughters—Anne, Barbara, Delia, and Evelyn—of New Zealand who, after their father is killed early in the war, make out as best they can, especially with the available men in their lives.

Playwright Robert Anderson wrote the script for *Until They Sail* (MGM, 1957), and much of the Michener plot made it to the screen. Robert Wise directed in a restrained and unspectacular manner, much as Michener wrote the story. Although the narrative was often slow, the film was a heartfelt and honest examination of the effects of loneliness inflicted by war, and while the plot and some of the dialogue were Michener's, the introspective nature of the script was Anderson's. Generally speaking, the script fleshed out characters who in the story were rather thin. Also, Michener's ending was

William Holden as the downed pilot and Mickey Rooney as the helicopter jockey who tries to rescue him run from North Korean bullets in *The Bridges at Toko-Ri* (1954).

(From left) Van Johnson, Walter Pidgeon, Dewey Martin, Louis Calhern (as James Michener), Frank Lovejoy, and Keenan Wynn in Michener's *Men of the Fighting Lady* (1954).

somewhat ambivalent, but the film proved to be more specific on this issue, allowing the romantic couple to join before fade out. Overall, it presented a solid story that worked much better on the screen than in the book.

In 1953, Michener wrote a nonfiction piece, "The Forgotten Heroes of Korea," for the *Saturday Evening Post*. Metro-Goldwyn-Mayer purchased the story and used it to form part of the basis for *Men of the Fighting Lady* (MGM, 1954). Michener himself was a character in the film, played by Louis Calhern. It is to him that the stories are all told by crew members of a U.S. aircraft carrier, and he, in turn, relates them to the audience.

While working on this project, Michener witnessed the desperate and futile attempt to rescue a young airman downed behind enemy lines, which served as a basis for a novel, *The Bridges at Toko-Ri* (1953). *Life* called the novel a masterpiece, printing excerpts in July of 1953. Negative reviews in *The New Yorker* and *The New Republic* failed to quench the public thirst for the book, which quickly became a best-seller. Paramount purchased the rights, obtained a script by Valentine Davies, who retained most of Michener's jingoistic philosophy, and put Mark Robson in the director's chair for *The Bridges at Toko-Ri* (Paramount, 1955).

The film has plenty of action, opening with a successful rescue and closing with an unsuccessful one. Also, aerial footage of bombing raids and dogfights is thrown in for good measure. There is also much philosophizing, especially about war and its importance as a national policy.

While airborne, the film is fine, but when it goes groundside to lock in on the story of Lt. Harry Brubaker (William Holden) and his struggles with life and wife, Nancy (Grace Kelly), it becomes rather pedestrian, a problem that originates in the source material rather than the screenplay. Scriptwriter Davies did all he could to make the story exciting, but there are no emotional pyrotechnics to match the aerial ones.

Michener's time exploring the Korean War and its effects on pilots also resulted in *Sayonara* (1954), an interracial love story that mirrors the author's love of Japan. Even before Michener had begun to write the novel, David O. Selznick contacted him, inquiring whether the author thought it would be adaptable to film. Against his agent's wishes, Michener sent a synopsis to Selznick, who wanted to buy the book for his wife, Jennifer Jones. Through a complicated series of dealings, the rights to the novel finally wound up in the hands of Joshua Logan.

The novel's plea for racial tolerance was the cornerstone of *Sayonara* (Warner Bros., 1957), and the original script concluded as did the novel with Major Lloyd Gruver (Marlon Brando) in the United States and his Japanese lover, Hana-ogi, in Japan; but Brando insisted on an ending where the lovers are united in order to show that racial prejudice could be overcome. Director Logan agreed to the change, and Brando then began a complete rewrite of the script, only a few lines of which reached the screen. Otherwise, the film followed both Michener's plot and his theme with surprising fidelity. In some ways the film surpassed the novel. The beautiful Japanese settings provided visuals that the book could not duplicate, and since the Japanese culture was so foreign to American audiences, this proved to be a decided advantage.

In addition, the Paul Osborn script added nuances that the novel lacked, especially in the character of Gruver. In the novel he was a warlike Westerner intent upon stemming the Communist tide, much like Brubaker in *The Bridges at Toko-Ri*, but the script turned him into a good-humored, impish Southerner under his hard-as-nails West Point exterior. Therefore, being a Southerner in the 1950s, his prejudices extend deeper and are more complex than the Gruver of the novel. Perhaps today the moral stance of the film may appear quaint and a bit dated—if that is possible with any work of art that deals with so important a theme as racial prejudice—but when it was released in 1957, there were ten thousand servicemen who had married Japanese women, an act that the American military establishment and the Japanese government both frowned on. Perhaps the novel and film in some small way helped to ease the pain and suffering these couples experienced.

In 1959, the territory of Hawaii became a state. In the same year, Michener published *Hawaii,* not a historical novel in the traditional sense, because not a single actual name or event is given, but one that chronicles the birth and growth of the islands.

For *Hawaii* (United Artists, 1966), Dalton Trumbo and Daniel Taradash were assigned screenwriting duties, and they concentrated on the part of the massive novel that dealt with the early nineteenth century New England missionaries who came to the islands to save the heathens but wound up almost exterminating them. The theme of the movie, directed by George Roy Hill, thus becomes the destruction of the Hawaiian people and culture.

The story opens in 1819. Abner Hale (Max Von Sydow) is a young divinity graduate from Yale who plans to go to Hawaii to convert the natives. He believes that first he must find a wife and shyly proposes to Jerusha Bromley (Julie Andrews), who is in love with Rafer Hoxworth (Richard Harris), a sea captain from whom she has not heard in the three years he's been away. Lacking any better alternatives, Jerusha accepts Abner's proposal, and the couple sets sail around the storm-tossed Cape Horn for Hawaii. Once at their destination, Hale is appalled at the native customs, especially their "indecent" attire, where the women go bare-breasted, and incest between brother and sister is commonplace.

Unexpectedly, Rafer Hoxworth shows up and tries to persuade Jerusha to go off with him, but she refuses. Once he departs, her life returns to normal. Jerusha ultimately has three sons and never ceases trying to soften Abner's heart and convictions. Other sailors arrive, followed by settlers and merchants, and the native population begins dying of various imported diseases. The years pass, and Hoxworth returns once again. When he discovers that Jerusha is dead, he slaps Abner around, and Abner keeps turning the other cheek. More years pass, and Abner is informed by his superiors that his services are no longer required. He sends his sons off to England for a proper education but remains in the islands, where he believes that he can still do the Lord's work.

Critic Pauline Kael called Abner Hale "the most unlikely hero who ever dominated an expensive American movie" His domineering Calvinistic beliefs make him a thoroughly unappealing character, although not an evil one. He is too insensitive to see his insistence on following fundamentalist thought affects the islanders, his wife, and even himself. He is even a racist who believes not only in the superiority of his God but also the superiority of his skin, and he is much the same at the end as he was at the beginning.

The Hawaiians (United Artists, 1970) was also made

from *Hawaii*. The story picks up two generations later with Whip Hoxworth (Charlton Heston), the grandson of Rafer, who comes to the Islands with his sister-in-law, Purity (Geraldine Chaplin), and brother Micah (John Phillip Law) to establish a successful plantation. *The Hawaiians*, directed by Tom Gries from James R. Webb's adaptation of the last hundred pages or so of Michener's novel, received generally unfavorable reviews, but it did complete the story begun in *Hawaii*, bringing into focus Michener's belief that the strength of the Islands comes from the intermingling of the races.

To date, the last work of Michener's to reach the big screen is *Caravans* (1963). The film version (Universal, 1978) adapted by Nancy Voyles Crawford, Thomas A. McMahon, and Lorraine Williams, was a joint American-Iranian effort that follows the novel rather closely. An American consular employee (Michael Sarrazin) is sent into the desert to find a U.S. Senator's headstrong daughter (Jennifer O'Neill) who has run off from her Iranian husband to live with a sheik (Anthony Quinn)

Max Von Sydow as stern Abner Hale making a fire-and-brimstone sermon in James Michener's *Hawaii* (1966).

Insert card for James Michener's *Sayonara* (1957) showing Miiko Taka as Hana-ogi and Marlon Brando as Major Lloyd Gruver.

who leads a band of desert nomads. It was neither a very good book nor a very good movie.

Two sprawling Michener novels made it to television. *Centennial* (teleplay by numerous writers, NBC, Universal Television, 1978–79) was a twenty-six-hour opus that attempted to span an entire fictional history of Colorado. Since it was so long and disjointed, parts were often better than the whole. Especially interesting were the early sections dealing with McKeag (Richard Chamberlain) and Pasquinel (Robert Conrad). *Space* (teleplay

Charlton Heston as Whip Hoxworth attempts to settle a dispute at the leper colony in *The Hawaiians* (1970), a sequel taking place two generations after *Hawaii*.

Robert Conrad as Pasquinel, the French-Canadian trapper, in the massive television miniseries of *Centennial* (1978–79).

Jennifer O'Neill as an American senator's free-thinking daughter and Anthony Quinn as an Arab chieftain with whom she runs off in Michener's *Caravans* (1978).

186

by Stirling Silliphant and Dick Berg, CBS, Paramount Pictures Television, 1985) was a fictional examination of America's space program from World War Two to the early 1970s.

Where James Michener is a romantic, Norman Mailer (1923–   ) is a realist. His 1948 novel, *The Naked and the Dead*, which achieved a remarkable critical and popular success, follows a fourteen-man World War Two infantry platoon on a small Japanese-held island in the South Pacific. Writing in an omniscient voice, Mailer refused to allow his readers to get close to his characters. After spending lengthy time with Lieutenant Hearn, the author kills him off with one sentence: "A half hour later, Hearn was killed by a machine-gun bullet which passed through his chest."

Originating from such an important novel, the film version (RKO, 1958), directed by Raoul Walsh, proved a major disappointment. Because of contemporary standards, screenwriters Denis and Terry Sanders were forced to tone down much of the brutality and language

Barbara Nichols receives the close attention of Aldo Ray in *The Naked and the Dead* (1958), based on Norman Mailer's novel.

Stuart Whitman shows Janet Leigh what will happen to her if she is setting him up, as Barry Sullivan (center) looks on in Mailer's *An American Dream* (1966).

William Devane played Warden and Natalie Wood was Karen in television's *From Here to Eternity* (1979).

of the novel, but they did include flashbacks into the lives of various members of the platoon, invented scenes of sweethearts, wives, and family. Among these flashbacks are various comic sequences that seem hopelessly out of place in a grim film about the realities of war. The producers also threw in a striptease by burlesque queen Lili St. Cyr, which does little to forward the dramatic action.

The platoon is made up of men from various walks of life: Roth (Joey Bishop), the wry, stereotypical, comic Jew; Wilson (L. Q. Jones), the hillbilly who makes "Jungle Juice" for the platoon; Red (Robert Gist), the laconic loner; Martinez (Henry Amargo), the Indian scout; Ridges (James Best), the Southern religious boy; and Gallagher (Richard Jaeckel), the youngster saddened by the loss of his wife. The by-the-book commanding officer is General Cummings (Raymond Massey), who believes in the theory that the best leader is the one most hated by his men. The field equivalent of Cummings is sadistic, battle-hardened Sergeant Croft (Aldo Ray), who pries gold teeth from the dead Japanese, kills prisoners, and shoots helpless birds. Lieutenant Hearn (Cliff Robertson) tries to curb Croft's worst excesses and also tries to prove Cummings wrong by being a benevolent leader. The film concludes with a final speech by Hearn to Cummings extolling the indestructible spirit of man.

"*The Naked and the Dead* was one of the worst movies ever made," said Mailer. "If it had been just a little worse than that it would have come out the other end and been extraordinarily funny, a sort of pioneer classic of pop art. . . . It just expired in its own glop." Yet, Mailer realized the pragmatic benefits of selling his work to the film industry. "A novelist or playwright sells his work to Hollywood," he wrote, "not in order that his work shall survive the translation, but to purchase time for himself."

Mailer's next book, *An American Dream* (1965), was a radical departure. Its protagonist, Stephen Rojack, murders his deranged wife and casts off his old identities of professor, war-hero, author, and socialite. He then goes through a struggle of rebirth becoming a new intellectual, one attuned to his nonrational being.

The book proved too cerebral for Hollywood, which turned *An American Dream* (Warner Bros., 1966) into a prolonged chase. The watered-down film, with Stuart Whitman as Rojack, was burdened by a script by Mann Rubin that made the dialogue sound little better than a sophomoric attempt at philosophy. The *New York Times*'s, Howard Thompson began his review by saying, "With four months still to go, the year's worst movie may well turn out to be *An American Dream*, a tired, jaded, mire-splattered old turkey." Pauline Kael thought that *An American Dream*, directed by William Conrad, was for the connoisseurs of the tawdry.

Mailer himself entered into the realm of filmmaking with *Wild 90* (Supreme Mix, 1967), which he wrote, produced, and directed. He followed this maiden effort with two more improvisational works, *Beyond the Law* (Grove Press/Evergreen, 1968) and *Maidstone* (Supreme Mix, 1970)—which Vincent Canby of the *New York Times* called an "ego trip."

Mailer's next film project was built around his own novel, *Tough Guys Don't Dance* (1984), a complex, metaphysical murder mystery full of violence and philosophy. When Mailer came to film the novel (Cannon, 1987), he abandoned his former cinema verité style and replaced it with a more traditional form of storytelling. This time he was working from a prepared script. The novel had taken two months to write, and the screenplay took six more. It was filmed in Provincetown on Cape Cod with Ryan O'Neal in the lead. Whatever faults this black comedy might have, Mailer couldn't blame them on the system. The author was in charge from beginning to end.

When Mailer's film, which he described as "a murder mystery, a suspense tale, a film of horror, and a comedy of manners," was shown at the Cannes Film Festival, it was greeted with jeers and laughter. Perhaps it tried to be too many things, and in doing so, failed to do any one properly. The story sets up like a mystery, but the mystery is neither very mysterious nor very important. The suspense is present but never very involving. The horror is weak, the comedy often unintentional.

Mailer's Pulitzer Prize-winning 1979 nonfiction account of the career of convicted murderer Gary Gilmore, *The Executioner's Song* (teleplay by Norman Mailer, NBC, Lawrence Schiller Productions, 1982), made it to television as a two-part film. Tommy Lee Jones gave an Emmy-winning performance as Gilmore. Mailer's script followed his own narrative with fidelity, and the documentary-like approach worked well with the material. Of all of Mailer's work to be filmed, this may well be the best.

Like Mailer, James Jones (1921–77) based his first

Burt Lancaster as Sgt. Milt Warden and Deborah Kerr as Karen Holmes, his C.O.'s wife, in the famous beach scene in James Jones's *From Here to Eternity* (1953).

189

Frank Sinatra as Dave Hirsh and Shirley MacLaine as Ginny Moorehead in *Some Came Running* (1959).

Paperback cover for the tie-in with the 1964 film of *The Thin Red Line*.

novel, *From Here to Eternity* (1951), on his army experiences. Hollywood mogul Harry Cohn hired Jones to write a treatment that would avoid problems of language and sex, problems that would arouse the ire of the Breen Office, Hollywood's successor to the Hays Office. Jones so truncated and bastardized his own book that even Cohn couldn't accept the results.

Cohn turned over scriptwriting chores for *From Here to Eternity* (Columbia, 1953) to Daniel Taradash. The studio wanted the military's cooperation, and Taradash realized that the army would have trouble accepting the stockade scene in which Maggio (Frank Sinatra) is brutally tortured and beaten. He suggested the scene be dropped, that Maggio's death would be enough. He also had Robert E. Lee Prewitt (Montgomery Clift) play taps after the death of Maggio. In the novel, the martinet Captain Holmes (Philip Ober) not only escapes punishment but is promoted. Taradash also knew this had to be changed if the army was to accept the script.

In the novel, Lorene (Donna Reed) is a prostitute, but the film makes her a dance hall hostess, although looking deep enough, the viewer can understand the dark side to her job. Even though there was no real connection between the love stories of Prewitt and Lorene and top-kick Milt Warden (Burt Lancaster) and Karen Holmes (Deborah Kerr), the C.O.'s wanton wife, Taradash interlaced the action, which included the two women meeting and speaking at the end without knowing one another.

Montgomery Clift consulted with the author about his performance as Prewitt, rehearsing each scene with a dog-eared copy of the novel beside him, and Jones often visited with director Fred Zinnemann to offer technical advice about the prewar army. Early on, Jones had expressed doubts about the film, but the care lavished on it by all concerned, including Harry Cohn, caused the author to reevaluate his feelings. He thought the film "an immensely fine one" and especially liked the performances of Clift and Sinatra, his two drinking buddies.

The reviews were overwhelmingly good. The *New York Times* said, "Out of *From Here to Eternity*, a novel whose anger and compassion stirred a post-war reading public as few such works have, Columbia and a company of sensitive hands have forged a film almost as towering and persuasive as its source." The movie won Oscars as Best Picture and for Fred Zinnemann's direction, for Daniel Taradash's screenplay, and for Frank Sinatra and Donna Reed's performances.

A television miniseries of *From Here to Eternity* (teleplay by Don McGuire and Harold Gast, NBC, Columbia Pictures Television, 1979) starred William Devane and Natalie Wood as Milt Warden and Karen Holmes. It attempted to cover the entire story, and while it may have lacked the power of the original, it did manage to restore much of the sexual content. A brief series followed.

Jones's next novel was the massive *Some Came Running* (1957), which ran in its first edition over twelve hundred pages. Despite his rather downbeat ending, Jones thought of his novel as a comic story of modern love, but critics panned it unmercifully. However, the public liked it, and an abridged paperback edition sold over a million copies. MGM bought the rights and then set John Patrick and Arthur Sheekman to reducing the lengthy novel into a coherent screenplay of just over two hours. While director Vincente Minnelli did the best he could with the material in *Some Came Running* (MGM, 1958), obtaining some splendid performances from the cast (Frank Sinatra, Shirley MacLaine, Dean Martin, et al.) who brought some life to Jones's characters, the structure was weak, and the melodramatic ending seemed an easy way to resolve the story. James Jones saw the film at an army base near Paris, and to one friend he wrote, ". . . with their usual acumen, the Hollywood people have one by one, and piece by piece, accurately and fully reversed and subverted every single point I was trying to say about America and Americans." In a letter to fellow author William Styron, he warned, "For God's sake, don't go and see *Some Came Running*."

Later, James Jones landed a job working on *The Longest Day* (20th Century-Fox, 1962) for Darryl F. Zanuck. Although his effort was limited to changing dialogue, Jones was frustrated because even mild words like "damn" and "hell" were forbidden and the censorship office was concerned that there was too much killing in the film. Outraged, he wrote to Zanuck. "What did they think Omaha was, if not a 'bloodbath'?" he asked.

Jones, who had been wounded by shrapnel at Guadalcanal, knew the horrors of fighting first hand, and recalling these experiences, he wrote *The Thin Red Line* (1962), a book that he hoped would debunk the myth about the glory of war. The notices were generally favorable, including in the *New York Times Book Review* where Maxwell Geismer gave it front page coverage and said that Jones once again "proves his talent and his integrity."

Jones sold the rights to Hollywood for $40,000 and also wrote a screenplay, which was scrapped in favor of one by Bernard Gordon. The script concentrated on the conflict between Private Doll (Keir Dullea), who at first wants only to survive but soon learns to take a sadistic pleasure in war, and Sergeant Welsh (Jack Warden), who is an older version of the man Doll will become. Whole scenes of the novel are compacted, and the narrative technique that Jones used to explore the minds of so many different characters is dropped in favor of a more melodramatic approach. However, within its limits, the story captures the mayhem and brutality of war. When Jones saw the film, he said that like most out of Hollywood, it violated the spirit of the book, but in its own way, he thought it a very good war movie.

Like most major fiction writers to emerge during the 1940s and early 1950s, Herman Wouk (1915–) found work at one time or another in Hollywood, and also like most of these artists, he was more interested in his personal work than in providing scenarios and scripts for Hollywood.

The same year James Jones published *From Here to Eternity*, Wouk published *The Caine Mutiny* (1951). In 1942, Wouk had enlisted in the navy and served three years on a minesweeper in the Pacific, and from these experiences came the material for his novel. The book won the Pulitzer Prize for literature and the Columbia University Medal of Excellence, remaining on the *New York Times* best-seller list for over two-and-a-half years. Part of the novel was also made into the landmark 1953 Broadway play, *The Caine Mutiny Court-Martial*.

Such success could not be ignored by Hollywood, and Columbia paid $60,000 for the screen rights. When producer Stanley Kramer tried to enlist the aid of the U.S. Navy, he ran into opposition because that service, protesting that it had never had a mutiny in its ranks, refused to help. Kramer went straight to the Secretary of the Navy and the Chief of Naval Operations, where he obtained the use of three destroyers, three tenders, aircraft carriers, and two thousand marines. Despite Kramer's success with the navy, studio head Harry Cohn put certain restrictions upon the project, limiting the

Humphrey Bogart as Captain Phillip Queeg tries to prove a point to Van Johnson as Lieutenant Steve Maryk in this lobby card scene from *The Caine Mutiny* (1954).

shooting schedule to fifty-four days and a budget of only $2 million.

In order to meet Cohn's condition that the film run no longer than two hours, the original Stanley Roberts script of 190 pages had to be trimmed to 150. Michael Blankfort then wrote additional dialogue. Unfortunately, the writers chose to retain the unnecessary love story between Ensign Willie Keith (Robert Francis) and May Wynn (May Wynn, who took her professional screen name from her character), which only padded a story already full of incident. Whenever the love affair intrudes, the genuine drama takes a hiatus. More incidents on the ship or in the courtroom would have proven far more meaningful. However, this seems a minor quibble with a truly outstanding film, one in which the disintegration of Captain Queeg (Humphrey Bogart) has become a classic scene in American films. Like Queeg in the novel, the one in the film begins as a man the audience despises but ends as a figure it has come to pity.

The original Broadway play, dealing solely with the court-martial sequence, the heart of Wouk's novel, was produced for American television in 1955 as an hourlong drama on *Ford Theater*, and three years later, another production was staged in Great Britain by the BBC. In 1988, Robert Altman directed a television movie version, unique in its staging from first scene to

Gene Kelly as Noel Airman and Natalie Wood in the title role in Herman Wouk's *Marjorie Morningstar* (1958).

192

last (slightly opened up from the play) in "real time" with an ensemble cast.

Before *Caine*, Columbia Pictures had lost money on ten straight films, but an $11 million gross made up all those losses and then some. However, the adaptation of Wouk's next novel, *Marjorie Morningstar* (1955), was not so fortunate.

At first glance the novel seems to be a predictable soap opera, but a closer examination shows an honest and interesting study of customs and traditions. Once again Wouk wrote a story of maturation. This one follows a young Jewish girl who lives in New York and engages in many relationships that help her reach womanhood and understand her heritage.

The Everett Freeman screenplay for *Marjorie Morningstar* (Warner Bros., 1958) deviated considerably from the book. First, it concentrated upon the show business angle of the story, which was hardly Wouk's intent. Next, where the book delved quite deeply into the religious background of the principals, the film only sketches them in. At her brother's bar mitzvah, Marjorie (Natalie Wood) questions the stern values of her father, but there is little real religious conflict within the framework of the story. Just as in the novel, Marjorie changes her last name from Morgenstern to Morningstar to disguise her ethnic background.

The ending was pure Hollywood schmaltz and not part of Wouk's story. The novel had no neat, tidy conclusion that suggested that Marjorie would live happily ever after. While the whole Jewish experience was played down in the film, Claire Trevor and Everett Slone as Marjorie's upper-middle-class parents managed to convey ethnic qualities without ever relying on burlesque or caricature. Some of the scenes in the Catskills also carry a Jewish flavor. However, the film erred in casting Russian-French Wood and the much older Irish Gene Kelly as Jewish lovers, and in Kelly's case, his connection with musicals was so ingrained that the audience had trouble accepting him as Noel Airman, a Broadway failure.

Wouk's next novel was *Youngblood Hawke* (1962), the story of a talented Southern writer who struggles to succeed in a world full of publishers, theatrical agents, and tax collectors leagued against him. *New York Times* critic Howard Thompson said of the move *Youngblood Hawke* (Warner Bros., 1964), "Mr. Wouk's story of a turbulent young novelist-genius has become as thin and glossy as wax paper." Delmer Daves, who produced, adapted, and directed the film, turned Wouk's obviously serious study of a writer's woes into a soap opera wherein Hawke (James Franciscus), a truck driver from Kentucky turned novelist in New York, finds fame and fortune, succumbs to greed, and finally, when hospitalized with pneumonia, realizes that his place is really with pretty editor Jeanne Green (Suzanne Pleshette) rather than his married socialite mistress, Frieda Winter (Genevieve Page).

Wouk's massive *Winds of War* (teleplay by numerous writers, ABC, Paramount Pictures Television, 1983) and its even more massive sequel *War and Remembrance* (teleplay by numerous writers, ABC, Paramount Pictures Television, 1988) were both multipart miniseries that attempted to capture the entire history of World War Two through the lives of an American military family. The very length of this endeavor assured unevenness, yet in sheer magnitude, this is one of the most impressive presentations ever attempted by television.

Before he committed suicide, Thomas Heggen (1919–49) wrote only one novel, *Mister Roberts*, and collaborated with Joshua Logan on a very successful 1947 stage version of the same work. Logan and Frank S. Nugent wrote the screenplay for *Mister Roberts* (Warner Bros., 1955), which, for the most part was a strict translation of the play which had followed the main events of the novel with fidelity. Without opening the action to any great extent, the screenplay followed the story of Mister Roberts (Henry Fonda), a disillusioned naval officer, and his struggle against the tyrannical captain (James

Robert Mitchum's "Pug" Henry dominates the artwork for the climax of ABC-TV's massive production of *The Winds of War* (1982).

194

Henry Fonda in the title role,
William Powell as Doc, and
Jack Lemmon as Pulver in
Mister Roberts (1955).

Cagney), with the admiration of young Ensign Pulver
(Jack Lemmon) and philosophical Doc (William Powell). There are a few sight gags added, including one
where a motorcycle goes off a pier. During the final
editing, the scene was deleted, but Jack Warner forced it
to be reinstated. The stage play had some language the
film could not use, but these were minor omissions. In
spite of these changes, *Mister Roberts* became a true
American classic, in large part due to the original novel
which provided the structure and characters. In his
review, *The New York Times*'s, A. H. Weiler remarked,
"Like its predecessors, this version of *Mister Roberts* is a
strikingly superior entertainment. . . . To Mister Roberts
and all hands involved in one of the season's greatest
pleasures: 'Well done!' "

Enamored over the success of *Mister Roberts*, the
studio belatedly produced a sequel, *Ensign Pulver*
(Warner Bros., 1964), a slapstick comedy with Pulver
(Robert Walker Jr.) once again at odds with the Captain
(Burl Ives) while Doc (Walter Matthau) is pulled along
for the ride. It had little connection to the original
Heggen novel or play.

Joseph Heller (1923–) was forty when he published
Catch-22 (1961), his hilariously macabre novel based on
the author's experiences as a bombardier in World War
Two. As an all-star film, *Catch-22* (Paramount, 1970)
made an attempt to duplicate the convoluted structure of
the novel, and as Vincent Canby wrote in the *New York
Times*, "I'm not sure that anyone who has not read the

Burl Ives as the Captain and Robert Walker Jr. as Pulver in *Ensign
Pulver* (1964), a sequel concocted from *Mister Roberts*.

195

novel will make complete sense out of the movie's narrative line." It was the character of Yossarian (Alan Arkin) and his monomaniacal intensity to survive that provided the film with whatever continuity it possessed. Yossarian is a neurotic, but not of the ordinary garden type; rather, he is a man in continual panic, fearful that everyone wants him dead—the Germans, General Dreedle (Orson Welles), Nurse Duckett (Paula Prentiss), Nately's whore (Gina Rovere)—in fact, anyone connected with the war. He is convinced that the whole world is crazy. It is the special achievement of Heller's novel and director Mike Nichols's film, based on Buck Henry's adaptation, that Yossarian's paranoia emerges as something so reasonable, so moving, and so funny.

Joseph Heller himself thought that Nichols did a fine job. "It is really Nichols's conception of a film taken from material in *Catch-22*," he said, "and I think it would have been an atrocious film if he'd tried any other thing." However, Heller still believed the book was better. "I can't think of any film ever adapted from any work of literature that I or other people feel has any quality to it that even approaches the original work of literature that was its source."

The writers who emerged from World War Two stretched the boundaries of American literature. This is especially true of Norman Mailer and James Jones, both of whom explored a new realism full violence and sex, and Joseph Heller who went beyond realism to present the war in terms of black comedy. However, with the exception of Jones's *From Here to Eternity*, the film versions of these authors' works usually failed to match the perception and honesty of the works themselves.

Jack Gilford as Doc Daneeka explains the famous *Catch-22* to Alan Arkin as Yossarian in Joseph Heller's *Catch-22* (1970).

Paul Newman as Butch, Katharine Ross as Etta Place, and Robert Redford as Sundance in *Butch Cassidy and the Sundance Kid* (1969), a William Goldman original.

ELEVEN

THE FABULOUS FIFTIES

William Styron, Bernard Malamud, William Goldman,
John Barth, James Agee, Philip Roth, John Updike

The 1950s saw the emergence of the Virginia-born William Styron (1925–   ), whose first novel, *Lie Down in Darkness* (1951), full of stream-of-consciousness narration, showed the influence of William Faulkner. With later novels he carved out his own territory. For *The Confessions of Nat Turner* (1967), he won the Pulitzer Prize, but his crowning achievement may very well be *Sophie's Choice* (1979), the intricate story that examined the complex nature of evil and guilt through the experiences a young Polish woman who survived Auschwitz.

Alan J. Pakula wrote the screenplay and directed *Sophie's Choice* (Universal, 1982), an unusually faithful adaptation. The story opens in the late 1940s when Stingo (Peter MacNicol) moves into a Brooklyn boarding house and becomes involved with two of its tenants: Sophie (Meryl Streep, in an Oscar-winning performance), a survivor of Nazi concentration camps; and her lover, Nathan (Kevin Kline), who lies about being a research chemist. Early on, the relationship appears sedate and average, except for a darkly comic and

foreboding scene where Sophie and Nathan are talking to Stingo at the same time, each so loud as to drown out the other. It soon becomes clear that Nathan is unbalanced, and Stingo has trouble understanding why Sophie has chosen to be with him. Through a series of flashbacks, we are given the reason. In the concentration camp, Sophie had to make a choice, forced upon her by a sadistic guard. She was allowed to choose which child she could keep with her; the other was taken away to its death.

At this point, the film makes the only serious departure from the novel, in which Sophie gives up her son, the older of the two children, because she believes he might be able to survive longer, and her guilt is so enormous that her later attachment to Nathan makes sense. Nathan is Jewish, and it was the Jews who died in concentration camps, just as her son died. However, the film reverses the choice. In the flashback where she is forced to make the choice, she keeps her son and sends her daughter away.

After this miscalculation, the film returns to the basic

197

Kevin Kline as Nathan, Meryl Streep as Sophie, and Peter MacNicol as Stingo ride the magic carpet at Coney Island in *Sophie's Choice* (1982).

Alan Bates as Yakov gets rough treatment at the hands of Oliver MacGreevy and George Murcell in *The Fixer* (1968).

plot of the novel for its conclusion. Stingo, fascinated by Sophie, convinces her to leave Nathan, and they have a brief affair. But Stingo does not understand the depths of Sophie's guilt, and she returns to Nathan. When Stingo goes looking for her, he finds both Sophie and Nathan dead, victims of a double suicide.

The change in Sophie's choice did not seem to bother William Styron. "I thought the film was a remarkably faithful adaptation of the book," he said. "The message of the book was retained. Of course, it could not contain any of the purely philosophical points that were made, but I thought it did an awfully good job of capturing the basic outline."

Although Bernard Malamud (1914–86) usually wrote of the Jewish experience, his first novel *The Natural* (1952) was a combination symbolic quest for the Grail and a baseball story. It took thirty years for Malamud's novel to reach the screen (Tri-Star, 1984), a big-budget commercial entertainment that forsook the author's brooding morality tale and substituted a story that was meant to warm the heart. The film was a beautiful fantasy that often captured the poetic mystique of America's pastime, yet a few surface details are the only connection with Malamud's novel.

Director Barry Levinson tried hard to canonize Robert Redford as Roy Hobbs, often finding him with a back light that cast a halo around his blond, tousled hair. And the dark side of Roy—his taunting of Bump, his denial of Iris, his accepting the bribe—have been dropped in

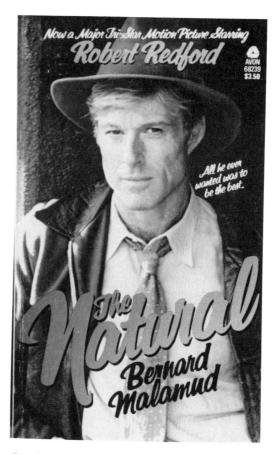

Paperback cover for Bernard Malamud's *The Natural* (1984), showing Robert Redford as baseball star Roy Hobbs.

Glenn Close as Iris in *The Natural* (1984).

199

favor of presenting an all-American in deed as well as in spirit. As a film, *The Natural* works quite well and is often rather moving, but it is an unqualified failure as an adaptation (by Roger Towne and Phil Dusenberry) of Malamud's novel.

Malamud's most acclaimed novel, *The Fixer* (1966), won both the Pulitzer Prize and the National Book Award. As a film (MGM, 1968), it fared less well. The very theme of Bok (Alan Bates) being persecuted for being Jewish turned away those looking for entertainment—a few minutes of happiness followed by two hours of unrelenting torturing and suffering was too much to take for the average filmgoer. In addition, the unresonating truisms—"I am a man"—sounded trite and stilted without Malamud's prose surrounding it. Combined with this was the problem that the book filled in many details of Bok's life, but screenwriter Dalton Trumbo and director John Frankenheimer lost the details in compressing the story to a 132-minute running time. The audience ultimately knows nothing about Bok except that he did not confess and he did not die. He seems to have drawn courage only from the injustices done to him; his family and religious beliefs have little to do with his will to survive.

"I've only been a writer," William Goldman (1931–) once said. "My first novel was taken the summer I finished graduate school, so I've never known anything else." Beginning with *The Temple of Gold* in 1957, his work has touched five decades and included novels, plays, and criticism, and several dozen screenplays. His *Soldier in the Rain* (1960) emerged on the screen (Allied Artists, 1963) as a Blake Edwards film, adapted by Edwards and Maurice Richlin, with the odd starring combination of Steve McQueen and Jackie Gleason. It was his *No Way to Treat a Lady* (1964) that led to his first screenwriting job. Actor Cliff Robertson liked it well enough to offer Goldman the chance to write the script for *Charly*, based on Daniel Keyes's story, "Flowers for Algernon." Although his script wasn't used, it led to another assignment on the film *Masquerade* (United Artists, 1965), and Goldman went on to write screenplays based on the works of other writers such as Ross MacDonald, Donald Westlake, and Ira Levin, and in several cases he adapted his own material.

In *No Way to Treat a Lady*, Goldman wrote a detective novel that as a film (Paramount, 1968) captured the blackly comic tone of the book. Although murder and mental illness are seldom topics of humor, the two meshed extremely well, due in large part to John Gay's glib and funny script and the performance of Rod Steiger, who has his murderous character running through a gamut of disguises from an Irish priest to a homosexual hairdresser. During his last moments of madness, he

even throws in an imitation of W. C. Fields. While Goldman wrote an entertaining novel, there is no way his prose—or anybody else's, for that matter—could have captured the character that Steiger portrayed on the screen. It was too visual and too aural. It had to be seen and heard to be fully appreciated.

Financially, Goldman's most successful novel is *Marathon Man* (1974), a fast-paced modern thriller. When Paramount bought the rights to it, Goldman was

Rod Steiger as mad killer Christopher Gill attacks Lee Remick as the detective's girlfriend in *No Way to Treat a Lady* (1968).

200

hired to his do own screenplay but Robert Towne was brought in to rework the ending.

The film (Paramount, 1976) departed from the novel in two crucial areas. The way Goldman constructed the book, the reader sees a giant trap being set by crooks and former Nazis on three continents, all who are about to pounce on the defenseless marathon-runner-in-training, Babe (Dustin Hoffman). But instead of setting the situation as clearly as he had in the novel, Goldman—or perhaps director John Schlesinger—dissipated the suspense by cutting too quickly from one scene to another, which sacrifices some clarity. In addition, the original ending of the novel was far more violent. Although Goldman attempted to infuse some realistic touches, it was essentially a fantasy. "Goldman's imagination," wrote Pauline Kael in *The New Yorker*, "must have been fed by movies like *Lives of Bengal Lancer*, in which sticks were driven under Gary Cooper's fingernails and set on fire but he never betrayed his comrades-in-arms. *Marathon Man* has to have been conceived in this same boy's-book rites-of-manhood universe."

The buddy theme that Goldman pursued in much of his fiction and screenplays such as *Butch Cassidy and The Sundance Kid* (20th Century-Fox, 1969), was resurrected in *Magic* (1976), the first novel Goldman wrote under contract. Before this he claimed that he had always been afraid to write under a deadline, fearing that he

Dustin Hoffman as Babe Levy on the run in *The Marathon Man* (1976), and then facing Laurence Olivier as the vicious Szell.

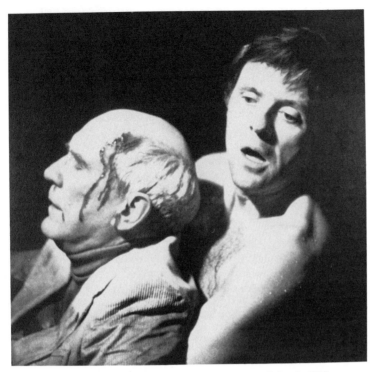

Anthony Hopkins as Corky with one of his victims in William Goldman's *Magic* (1978).

Mandy Patinkin as swashbuckling Inigo Montoya in *The Princess Bride* (1987).

Burt Reynolds as Nick Escalante has disposed of one of the bad guys in William Goldman's *Heat* (1987).

might come to dislike his book and want to quit. Perhaps his fears were not entirely unjustified because during the last parts of both the novel and the screenplay, the author seems almost indifferent to the fate of the characters.

In *Magic* (20th Century-Fox, 1978), the two buddies share the same schizophrenic mind of Corky (Anthony Hopkins), a ventriloquist. His alter ego is Fats, his dummy, who, as the story progresses, becomes the dominant personality. The main problem with both the book and script was finding a way to have the audience identify with Corky and not dismiss him as a psychopath. This was accomplished by showing a series of flashbacks that sketched out Corky's early career as he was learning his trade. Director Richard Attenborough also tended to play down the blood and gore that had been more pronounced in the novel and concentrated on the love story that ends in Corky's destruction. Unfortu-

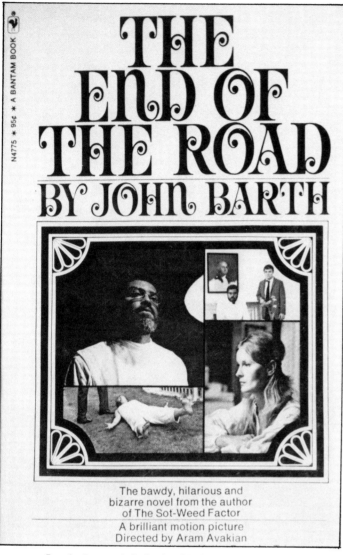

Paperback cover tie-in for the 1971 film of *End of the Road*.

Stacy Keach and Dorothy Tristan as a married couple with their kids in *End of the Road* (1970).

nately, the film scored well with neither critics nor the public. The story had been done before in 1929's *The Great Gabbo* and 1946's *Dead of Night* and twice as a segment of *The Twilight Zone* on TV, and *Magic* added nothing new.

Heat (1985) was the kind of thriller that Elmore Leonard might have written, the story of a Las Vegas gambler, bodyguard, and resourceful jack-of-all-trades who gets involved with Mafia hoods and bosses. Once again Goldman adapted his own novel, and with its potboiler plot, *Heat* (New Century-Vista, 1988) provided a vehicle for Burt Reynolds. Except for a fistfight between Reynolds and director Dick Richards, which happened behind the cameras, the film offers little excitement.

In 1973, Goldman wrote *The Princess Bride*, a novel he claimed was the S. Morgenstern's classic tale of true love and high adventure with all the boring parts cut out. Goldman opens with a long introduction explaining how he came to "abridge" the book, and then throughout the narrative he interjects comments about what he left out and why. Thus he set up the frame in which to encase the story of Wesley and Buttercup in the land of Florin, a medieval fantasyland that Disney might admire. Goldman quickly followed up the successful book with a screenplay, but for over ten years he peddled it around Hollywood with no luck. At last, however, his persistence paid off, and *The Princess Bride* (20th Century-Fox, 1987) made it to the screen under Rob Reiner's direction.

In his screenplay, Goldman made many changes in the plot. For one, the frame story was changed to a grandfather (Peter Falk) reading the S. Morgenstern's book to his sick ten-year-old grandson (Fred Savage), who would rather play video games than listen to a silly old story with kissing. "Back in my day, television was called books," says the old man, and then launches into the story, although not without occasional interruptions from the boy.

The Princess Bride was a fairy tale for grown-ups, a dazzling adventure that was a grand sendup of all those Errol Flynn swashbucklers, though without once resorting to camp. Also, Goldman's script never resorted to

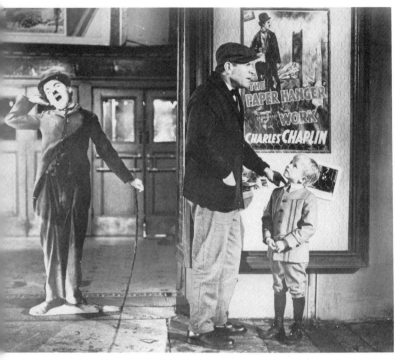

Robert Preston as the father with Michael Kearney as his son in *All the Way Home* (1963), an adaptation of *A Death in the Family*.

which included *The African Queen*, and fiction, which included his only full-length novel, *A Death in the Family* (1957), a series of prose poems, vignettes, and short stories molded into a multilayered work, but left unfinished at Agee's death.

The Pulitzer Prize novel was first adapted by Tad Mosel as a play in 1960 called *All the Way Home*, and then it became a film (Paramount, 1963). The screen adaptation by Philip Reisman Jr. followed the play more closely than the novel, concentrating on the family after the death of the loving father, Jay (Robert Preston). The mother (Jean Simmons) is left to teach her young son to cope with life's tragedies as well as its joys. Gone is the often meaningless chatter that the family uses to avoid dealing with the tragedy. Gone, too, are the religious

citing past films as Spielberg often has, but rather he allowed the story itself to make its own comparisons. The changes that Goldman made never undercut his material, and if anything, he improved on the story, even altering the ending, which in the novel was rather ambiguous in "The Lady or the Tiger" way. All in all, it was a faithful adaptation, especially in tone and mood. The warmth and good feeling generated by the novel was also generated by the film, a rare achievement all the way around.

Although his literary output has been rather limited, John Barth (1930–) had *The End of the Road* (1958) make it to the screen. The novel was an intellectual exercise—and not a very cinematic one at that—of Jake Horner, a man incapable of making decisions because he understands that one choice is no more inherently valid or attractive than another. *The End of the Road* (Allied Artists, 1970) was beautifully photographed, and although the images were often very right—especially an afternoon spent on the unstable professor's (Stacy Keach) lawn having tea—the beauty and color seemed to detract from the gritty subject. In many ways, the film (directed by Aram Avakian) followed the plot of the novel but often exaggerated the events beyond what Barth intended.

Due to an untimely death, the literary output of James Agee (1909–55) was relatively slight. He wrote film criticism for *The Nation*, *Time*, and other publications, and after 1948, divided his time between film scripts,

Aline MacMahon as the grandmother and Jean Simmons as the mother in *All the Way Home* (1963).

conflicts which in the novel made up the central problem between the husband and wife. The brother-in-law's invective against God has been summarily excised. What is left is a heartfelt story of a family tragedy, but hardly an adaptation of *A Death in the Family*.

The 1950s also saw the emergence of Philip Roth, one of the triumvirate of Jewish-American writers that included Saul Bellow and Bernard Malamud. Roth's wry novella *Goodbye, Columbus* (1959), which won the National Book Award, is on the surface a simple tale of boy finds girl, boy loses girl; but underneath it is a more complex tale of conflicting cultures.

Like the novel, the film *Goodbye, Columbus* (Paramount, 1969) had very little plot to sustain it, although the script by Arnold Schulman stressed characterization.

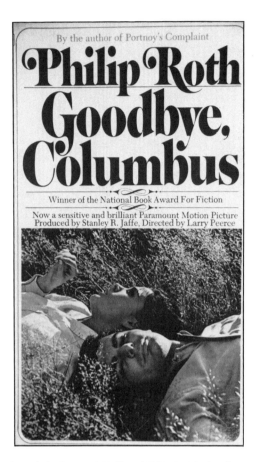

Paperback tie-in for the 1969 film of Philip Roth's *Goodbye, Columbus*.

It was also a rich and funny look at Jewish lifestyles in the fifties in the New York suburbs. But amid all the hoopla that attended this film, especially those critics who called it an honest adaptation, there were some glaring omissions, such as the constant anti-Semitic remarks by Jewish-American princess, Brenda (Ali McGraw), and her librarian boyfriend, Neil (Richard Benjamin). Also, in the novel, Brenda's sister-in-law, Harriet, is just a larger-breasted duplicate of Brenda, but in the film she is downright ugly. However, the most important change is in the character of Brenda. In the novel, she has a sense of guilt that ultimately subverts her emancipation. The film glosses over this as if it were not important. Thus, when Brenda and Neil go to a hotel in Boston, it is a dive rather than the nice upper-middle class establishment it should have been. In the end, the film makes it appear that Brenda awakens to a belated moral regeneration rather than surrenders to dehumanizing conventionality. It is these changes that doomed *Goodbye, Columbus* to a rather ordinary film that failed to convey the richness of Roth's novella.

Without a doubt, Roth's most controversial novel is

Richard Benjamin as Neil and Ali MacGraw as Brenda with Royce Wallace as their maid, Carlotta, in
Goodbye, Columbus (1969).

Portnoy's Complaint (1969), the story of a Jewish-American young man who is dominated by his mother and sex, not necessarily in that order. This was an amazingly complex work about a man and his culture, but the film version (Warner Bros., 1972), directed by noted screenwriter Ernest Lehman from his own adaptation, was an exercise in futility. The humor of the novel did not translate well. An early scene has a young woman relating her problems to Portnoy (Richard Benjamin), who is "Assistant Commissioner of Human Opportunity," and as she lodges her complaint, he mentally undresses her. The novel was narrated by Portnoy, and that helped the reader understand and accept him better, but the film has no such perspective. As a result, Portnoy appears crass and one-dimensional. His parents (Lee Grant and Jack Somack) are Jewish caricatures. Only "The Monkey" (Karen Black) seems real, mainly because she is less preoccupied with sex, accepting the act as part of life without guilt.

Hollis Alpert commented in *Saturday Review* that "a curious thing happens when the material of the novel is exposed to the bright, glaring colors of the screen. The people, the language, the incidents take on a vulgarity that may have been present in the literary version, but was hardly so obtrusive."

The same year that Roth published *Goodbye, Columbus*, John Updike (1932–), turned out his first novel, *The Poorhouse Fair* (1959). A year later, he published what was to become the first of a series of books, *Rabbit, Run* (1960), about Harry "Rabbit" Angstrom, a man whose nickname gives all the clues to his appearance, proclivities, and sexual appetite. In the film *Rabbit, Run* (Warner Bros., 1970), screenwriter Howard B. Krcitsek retained much of the plot but little of the tone and mood. The point of view of the novel was definitely Rabbit's (James Caan), but the film has none. It does have foul language and explicit sex curiously detached from the rest of the story, as if they were being used for shock value rather than as insights into character.

Updike's *Witches of Eastwick* (1984) received mixed reviews upon publication, in the main because many reviewers failed to take the novel seriously. As in much of Updike's fiction, extramarital affairs, small-town prudishness, and people searching for meaning to their lives are at the core of the work, but this time the author also incorporated witchcraft and devil worship.

Richard Benjamin as Portnoy in a session with his psychiatrist in *Portnoy's Complaint* (1972), and then having been pleasantly serviced by Karen Black.

Paperback tie-in for the 1970 movie of John Updike's *Rabbit, Run*.

James Caan as Rabbit and Carrie
Snodgress as his alcoholic wife in
Rabbit, Run (1970).

208

The Witches of Eastwick (Warner Bros., 1987) was so
far removed from its source that a stunned John Updike
commented that the movie was mainly about Jack
Nicholson's eyebrows. Where the book is ambivalent as
to whether the women really are witches, the film is
explicit, showing the effects of their incantations. This is
most clearly seen by comparing the two endings. The
novel concludes with Van Horne marrying and leaving
town; each of the divorcées then finds a respectable,
albeit boring, man of her own and returns to the
middle-class world of respectability. In the film, written
by Michael Christofer, the man-hungry women with
witch-like powers (Cher, Susan Sarandon, Michelle
Pfeiffer) take out their vengeance on the devilish Van
Horne (Nicholson) in a most spectacular manner that
incorporates all sorts of special effects. Where the book
relied on subtlety, the film relied on overstatement.

In the era when the screen began to experiment with
more freedom in which to express its art, the American
writer found his works more faithfully transferred to the
screen, but this new freedom did not insure quality.
Malamud's *The Fixer* was an overblown adaptation, and
The Natural, while an enjoyable film, was truncated so
badly that the dark and brooding novel disappeared;
Roth's *Portnoy's Complaint* was a sleazy, manipulative
effort; and Updike's *Rabbit, Run* was a weak screen
exercise that had trouble making the story or the characters come to life. Frankness and honesty did little to help
these films. On the other hand, without frankness, the
movie of Styron's *Sophie's Choice* would have been a
complete disaster, which was hardly the case. Goldman's *Marathon Man* and *The Princess Bride*, if not
great literature, were superior entertainment, due in large
part to the author's adaptation of his own works.

Academy Award winners Louise Fletcher as Nurse Ratchet and Jack Nicholson as McMurphy in *One Flew Over the Cuckoo's Nest* (1975).

TWELVE

THE SIXTIES AND BEYOND

Harper Lee, E. L. Doctorow, Larry McMurtry, Ken Kesey,
Jerzy Kosinski, Anne Tyler, Pat Conroy,
John Irving, Tom Wolfe

When it first appeared in 1960, *To Kill a Mockingbird* earned immediate critical acclaim for Harper Lee (1926–), a young woman from Monroesville, Alabama, who wrote the novel while working as a reservations clerk for an airline. Its message was a plea for racial tolerance and understanding at a time that the civil rights movement was polarizing blacks and whites throughout the South. In 1961, *Mockingbird* was awarded the Pulitzer Prize and the Brotherhood Award of the National Conference of Christians and Jews.

In the screenplay for *To Kill a Mockingbird* (Universal, 1962), Horton Foote captured all the characters and mood of the novel without sacrificing one important moment. The millions of loyal readers of the novel brought dangerously high expectations to the film, and they did not go away disappointed.

Like the novel, the film was praised for its stand on racism, but Foote and director Robert Mulligan saw that the enduring power of the story lay with the children coming to terms with life's ambiguities. Using an occasional voice-over narration, the film presents its story from the viewpoint of six-year-old Scout (Mary Badham), the tomboy daughter of Atticus Finch (Gregory Peck). Through her narrative, the viewer is allowed to see the struggle between good and evil in a small Alabama town during the Depression. In the midst of a slow, simple life, Scout and her ten-year-old brother, Jem (Philip Alford), weave a fantasy world that revolves around Boo Radley (Robert Duvall), the supposedly crazy son of mysterious neighbors.

The authority figure dominating this world is Atticus, a quiet small-town lawyer who is also a gentle but firm father. It is through Atticus that reality breaks through the children's make-believe world. By agreeing to defend a black man, Tom Robinson (Brock Peters), accused of raping a white girl, Atticus incurs the hostility of the white community. Scout and Jem soon discover their father's character as well as the implacable tyranny of societal codes. They watch as their father withstands threats and insults while he defends his client.

Paperback tie-in for the 1964 film of Harper Lee's *To Kill a Mockingbird*.

Under these circumstances, one of the most quietly powerful scenes in the film occurs. A lynch mob gathers at the jail, and Atticus stands in their way. Even though ordered to leave by his father, Jem remains by his side, and Scout, too young to understand the danger, chatters to a man whose son she knows at school. By humanizing the crowd, she disarms them, and the mob melts away.

During the trial itself, both children come to witness the moral courage of Atticus. They also learn the tangible reality of injustice. Atticus eloquently proves the innocence of Tom Robinson, yet Tom is convicted by the white jury. As Atticus leaves the courtroom, the black people in the gallery stand in silent respect. Soon after the close of the trial, Tom is killed when he supposedly attempts to escape.

This is a loving and faithful adaptation of Harper Lee's novel. Every detail, including the decision to use black and white photography, seems just right, yet the film is never calculating or contrived. Gregory Peck displays the proper amount of warmth and strength as Atticus, perhaps the best performance of his career—it won him the Academy Award. For the parts of Scout and Jem, director Robert Mulligan chose two Alabama youngsters without any prior acting credits, and Mary Badham's Scout stands as one of the most astonishing performances ever given by a child, constantly touching yet never saccharine. (She made only a handful of other appearances before leaving acting.) Philip Alford perfectly projects the growing seriousness of Jem. All the characters who walk across the screen seem as if they just stepped out of the novel, perfect embodiments of the Harper Lee creations.

Most reviewers concurred that this was a brilliant piece of filmmaking on all levels. If today the Tom Robinson story seems a bit too contrived and the ending too pat—after all, the sheriff allows Boo to go free and all accounts are settled—the fact remains that the film perfectly evokes the elusive world of children as they grow to realize the complexities of the adult world.

E. L. Doctorow (1931–) once said that he had no

Gregory Peck as lawyer Atticus Finch wipes spit away in *To Kill a Mockingbird* (1964).

Aldo Ray as the Man from Bodie takes a drink before beginning his killing spree in E. L.
Doctorow's *Welcome to Hard Times* (1967). Alan Baxter is standing in the doorway.

affinity for the Western genre, but in his job at the studios, he read countless Western screenplays and came to the conclusion that he could write just as well. The result was *Welcome to Hard Times* (1960), a symbolic exploration into the cyclic theory of history with the frontier town of Hard Times representing the rise and fall of civilizations, all done in the guise of a Western.

Even though the events strayed a bit from Doctorow, *Welcome to Hard Times* (MGM, 1967), scripted by director Burt Kennedy, retained the violent and harsh nature of the novel. The Man from Bodie (Aldo Ray) is a vicious bully who destroys the grimy town of Hard Times, and through the winter, Will Blue (Henry Fonda), the leading citizen who embodies the law, must live with his cowardice. When the badman returns, a crazed Molly Riordan (Janice Rule), humiliated by Bodie, forces Blue to face up to him, and in a desperate confrontation, the town burning around them, Blue kills his adversary.

Welcome to Hard Times is an attempt by writer-director Kennedy to stretch the limits of the Western genre, although the shootout between hero and villain is far too theatrical. Doctorow's ending in which Blue carries the badman to Molly so that she can exact her revenge is far more in keeping with the tone and mood of the story.

Doctorow's second novel, *The Book of Daniel* (1971), is a fictionalization of the Julius and Ethel Rosenberg case, although his story concentrates upon the children, orphaned by the execution of their parents. As adults, they must come to terms with their past. The son, Daniel, a graduate student at Columbia, narrates his attempts to formulate some sort of understanding of his relationship to his executed parents by writing their story, which, as the title suggests, is really his story.

Although many of the events of the novel show up in *Daniel* (Paramount, 1983), the film, directed by Sidney Lumet, is an overblown adaptation (by Doctorow himself) wherein Daniel Issacson (Timothy Hutton) stares off into space as he does a great deal of soul-searching over the guilt or innocence of his parents (Mandy Patinkin and Lindsay Crouse). Scenes through four decades are intercut throughout Daniel's story, allowing us to see the Issacsons from the time he is only a pudgy baby right through their trial and execution. But the past has alienated Daniel, who mistreats his wife (Ellen Barkin) and jeers at his mad sister's (Amanda Plummer) radical activism. He himself has retreated into the rigid, controlled academic world. It is his dislike of himself that triggers his flashbacks and forces him to hunt down the people involved in the case in an effort to discover the truth. Eventually Daniel comes to the conclusion that he can live with his past, and to show his spiritual rebirth, marches off with his wife and child to a protest rally.

The book plugged right into the same fears of victimization and persecution as the actual Rosenberg case, but the passion of the novel is noticeably absent in the film.

The book earned for Doctorow a Guggenheim Fellowship; the film earned only mediocre reviews.

Doctorow's most important novel is *Ragtime* (1975), a fictionalized account of the period just before World War One. Historical figures march in and out. Freud and Jung tour the tunnel of love on Coney Island; J. P. Morgan and Henry Ford discuss reincarnation. Intermixed with the historical fantasies are the stories of three fictional families—a family of blacks, a family of Jews, and the narrator's family—all of whom, like the historical figures, are carried along by economic and political forces beyond their control. The final section of the book concentrates upon Coalhouse Walker Jr., a black man who, because of injustices in the capitalist system, seizes the New York library of industrialist J. P. Morgan.

Henry Fonda as Blue is wounded but ready to fight on in *Welcome to Hard Times* (1967).

James Cagney as New York City Police Commissioner Rheinlander Waldo, a fictitious character, orders a sharpshooter to open fire on an unarmed black revolutionary in a climactic moment of Doctorow's *Ragtime* (1981).

Howard E. Rollins as Coalhouse Walker comforts Debbie Allen as his wife, Sarah, in *Ragtime* (1981).

Michael Weller's script zeroed in on the Coalhouse Walker section. *Ragtime* (Dino de Laurentiis/Paramount, 1981) opens with Coalhouse (Howard Rollins Jr.) playing ragtime composer Scott Joplin's music with newsreels—especially made for the film but utterly convincing in their black and white images—showing such personalities of the day as Teddy Roosevelt, Harry Houdini, and others. The scene shifts to upper-class New Rochelle where Father (James Olson), Mother (Mary Steenburgen), and Younger Brother (Brad Dourif) discover a black baby who has been deserted in their vegetable garden. They uncover the identity of the mother, Sarah (Debbie Allen), but she refuses to name the father. Several weeks later, Coalhouse, driving a shiny new Model T, arrives at the house where Mother is taking care of Sarah and announces that he plans to marry Sarah and make a proper home for her and the baby.

Before the wedding can take place, Coalhouse is goaded into a fight with racist firemen led by Chief Willie Conklin (Kenneth McMillan), who destroy Coalhouse's pristine roadster. In a misguided effort to help her husband seek redress, Sarah is killed trying to see the

Dustin Hoffman as gangster Dutch Schultz, Steven Hill as Otto, and Loren Dean in the title role in Doctorow's *Billy Bathgate* (1991).

President, who is speaking nearby. In retaliation, Coalhouse and several of his black friends—joined by idealistic Younger Brother, recruited because of his skill with explosives—take over the Morgan Library and threaten to blow it up unless Conklin is delivered to them.

Interspersed throughout the fictional story of Coalhouse are two real ones. The first involves showgirl Evelyn Nesbit (Elizabeth McGovern), whose jealous-crazed socialite husband, Harry K. Thaw (Robert Joy), shoots her former lover, noted architect Stanford White (Norman Mailer), at a posh New York supperclub. After the shooting, Younger Brother becomes involved (fictionally) with Evelyn, and while they are making love, two lawyers intrude and strike a deal over her dead husband's estate. The other story, severely truncated, relates the events surrounding Tateh (Mandy Patinkin), a humble Jewish immigrant, who rises from silhouette

maker to a famous film director. While *Ragtime* retained many of the vignettes from the novel, it missed the novel's sweep and power. Pauline Kael in *The New Yorker* wrote, "I don't know what people who haven't read it can make of the movie."

With *Billy Bathgate* (1989) Doctorow once again used historical figures—in this case real-life gangsters—as characters. Billy is a young teenager who wants to break into a life of crime, and while the book worked well on many levels, the film adaptation (Touchstone Pictures, 1991) by playwright Tom Stoppard, though remaining true to surface details, missed the penetrating insights of Billy (Loren Dean), who narrated the novel. The result was a rather cool, distant gangster film, dealing fictionally with the likes of Dutch Schultz (Dustin Hoffman), that failed to capture either the mood or tone of the novel.

Paul Newman as ne'er-do-well Hud Bannon and Melvyn Douglas as his rancher father in *Hud* (1962).

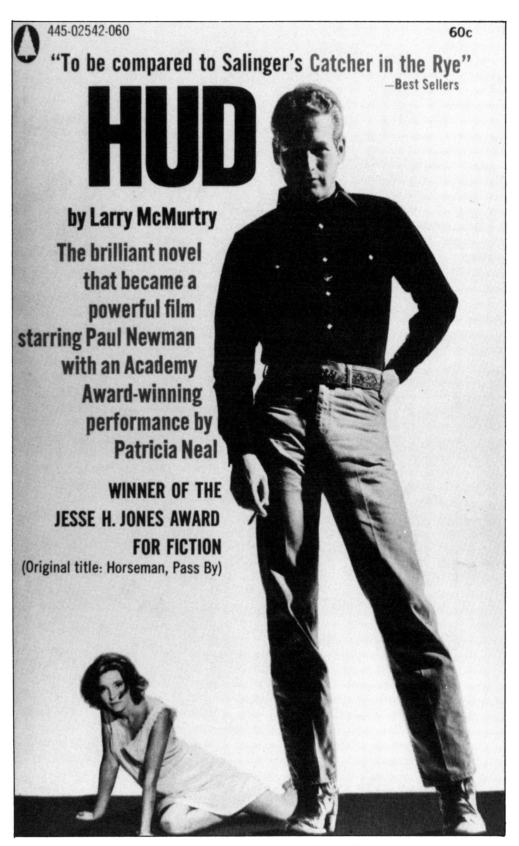

Paperback tie-in for the 1962 film of *Hud*, an adaptation of Larry McMurtry's *Horseman, Pass By*.

Jeff Bridges as Duane Jackson confronts Timothy Bottoms as Sonny in *The Last Picture Show* (1971).

Timothy Bottoms as the teenaged Sonny gives a present to Cloris Leachman as middle-aged Ruth Popper, the coach's wife, in *The Last Picture Show* (1971).

Descended from two generations of cattle ranchers, Larry McMurtry (1936–   ) is a regional writer whose novels reflect the values of the historical American West and the conflict of these values with the modern world. Of McMurtry's earlier novels, the best known is probably *Horseman Pass By* (1961), mainly because it became the basis of the film *Hud*. The story is told from the perspective of seventeen-year-old Lonnie Bannon. Homer Bannon, Lonnie's grandfather, represents the Old West values of courage and endurance. Homer's antagonist is his stepson, Hud Bannon, whose only values are those that involve profit. Caught between these two forces, Lonnie tries to forge his own values.

Hud (Paramount, 1963) was advertised as a character with a "barbed-wire soul." He drinks too much, drives too fast, and plays around with married women. Hud (Paul Newman) even tries to seduce Alma (Patricia Neal), the slatternly Bannon housekeeper, who lashes out at him for being a "cold-blooded bastard." She is not the only one who thinks badly of Hud. His aging father Homer (Melvyn Douglas) claims that he has always hated Hud for "not giving a damn."

Diseased cattle are discovered on the ranch, and Hud tries to sell the herd before word of it becomes commonly known. His father prevents him and complies with the

In Larry McMurtry's *Texasville* (1990), the belated sequel to *The Last Picture Show*, Cybill Shepherd as Jacy Farrow and Jeff Bridges as Duane Jackson (in the top photo) and Eileen Brennan (center) as Genevieve Morgan and Cloris Leachman as Ruth Popper (in the bottom one) reprised their original roles.

Ben Johnson (left) as Sam the Lion talks the ways of the world with Timothy and Sam Bottoms in *The Last Picture Show* (1971).

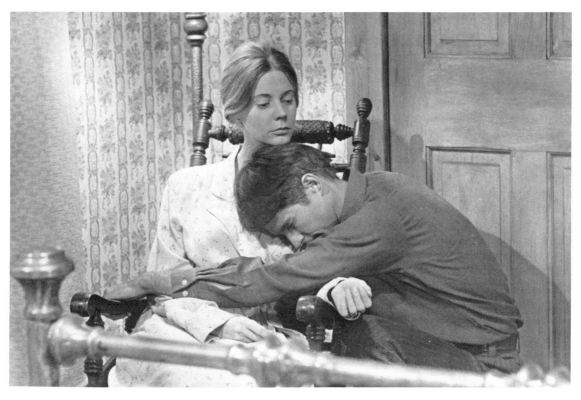

Blythe Danner as Molly and Anthony Perkins as Gid in *Lovin' Molly* (1973), an adaptation of McMurtry's *Leaving Cheyenne*.

Shirley MacLaine as Aurora Cunningham and Debra Winger as her pregnant daughter, Emma, in *Terms of Endearment* (1983).

government's regulations. When Homer dies of a stroke, young Lonnie (Brandon de Wilde), disillusioned, decides to leave the ranch. As he walks away, Hud shouts after him, "You'll find out the world is full of crap!"

The film, directed by Martin Ritt from a screenplay by Irving Ravetch and Harriett Frank Jr., makes one important change of emphasis. In the novel, there is never a time when the reader's sympathies lie with Hud. But in the film, Hud becomes the central character, and though we may condemn his actions, we cannot help but admire the son-of-a-bitch. Even at his most cruel moments, he somehow has us rooting for him rather than Homer.

In *Leaving Cheyenne* (1963), McMurtry allows each of his three main protagonists to narrate a section. On the screen, it became *Lovin' Molly* (Columbia, 1973), a title with a supposedly double meaning. Molly (Blythe Danner) marries one man but for the next forty years alternately beds Gid (Anthony Perkins) and Johnny (Beau Bridges). The loose structure turned the story (with a screenplay by Stephen Friedman) into a shambles, and Larry McMurtry castigated director Sidney Lumet in print, accusing him of having absolutely no feeling for the West.

McMurtry's third novel, *The Last Picture Show* (1966), examines life in a small Texas town patterned after Archer City, where the author is born. In planning the film version, director Peter Bogdanovich made several important decisions prior to shooting. First, he opted to go with a cast of no names. While many of the actors went on to successful film careers, they were relatively unknown at the time, and the introduction of fresh faces and the lack of stars added to the evocative feeling of small-town life. Second, to emphasize the bleakness, Bogdanovich chose to photograph the film in

Paul Newman, Henry Fonda, and Richard Jaeckel as a logging family on the outs with the community in *Sometimes a Great Notion* (aka *Never Give an Inch*, 1971).

Peter Sellers as Chauncey Gardiner indulging in his favorite pastime of television watching in *Being There* (1979).

he begins to learn the rules of mature love. But Sonny's head is turned by the fickle and callow Jacy Farrow (Cybill Shepherd), the school's homecoming queen whom he finds more alluring than the middle-aged Ruth. By this time, Sam has died, and his steadying influence is gone. In a barroom brawl, Duane, who also has a thing for Jacy, and is angry at Sonny for dating her, hits him with a beer bottle, blinding him in one eye. Now his physical blindness mirrors his intuitive blindness. At the end, Duane is in uniform and headed for Korea, and Sonny returns to Ruth Popper, who reluctantly agrees to resume their relationship.

At one point, Sam the Lion, surrogate father to both Sonny and Duane, reminisces to Sonny about a moment

high contrast black and white, which helped to give it a gritty, realistic feel. Finally, Bogdanovich chose Larry McMurtry to write the screenplay, and the author wisely made very few changes from his novel.

In *The Last Picture Show* (Columbia, 1971), set in 1951, Sonny Crawford (Timothy Bottoms) and best friend Duane Jackson (Jeff Bridges) divide their time between the pool hall, the movie theater, and the all-night cafe, all owned by Sam the Lion (Ben Johnson). Sonny develops a relationship with forty-year-old Ruth Popper (Cloris Leachman), the neglected wife of the football coach (Bill Thurman), and under her guidance,

224

from his youth when he and a woman went swimming in the nude. The woman turns out to be Lois Farrow (Ellen Burstyn), the mother of Jacy. She, too, clings to that moment with Sam. "I guess if it wasn't for Sam, I'd just about missed it, whatever it is," she tells Sonny.

This clinging to the past, this longing for something better, is part of the fantasy world of motion pictures themselves. Spencer Tracy tries to cope with Elizabeth Taylor in *Father of the Bride* while out in the audience Sonny and trampish Charlene Duggs (Sharon Taggert) grope at each other in the dark. When Sonny and Duane attend Sam the Lion's movie house just before it closes for the last time, they watch *Red River* in which the great herd that crosses the Texas prairies is a far cry from the

Peter Sellers lost in traffic in a climactic moment of *Being There* (1979).

few pitiful cattle that pass through their town of Texasville packed on the backs of trucks. The West of the imagination is a far cry from the dying town where tumbleweeds drift down the street full of buildings with boarded-up windows.

The visual style that helped to enrich the story must be credited to Bogdanovich, but it is Larry McMurtry's novel and his film script that captured and delineated character so perfectly. *The Last Picture Show* is a fine novel and the film a great adaptation.

McMurtry brought back his characters in *Texasville* (1987), a considerably more complex sequel. The film *Texasville* (Columbia, 1990), reuniting ten members of the original cast, was again directed by Bogdanovich, who this time wrote the script himself. The year is 1984, and the successful, graying Duane Jackson (Jeff Bridges), now a grandfather, owns a two-million-dollar house but the energy crisis is creating havoc with his finances. He is married to flashy, shop-till-you-drop Karla (Annie Potts), who is fed up with Duane's copious infidelities. Everybody in town, including Duane's son, Dickie (William McNamara), is sleeping around. Duane's best friend, Sonny Crawford (Timothy Bottoms), is a pathetic wreck; their high school buddy, the nervous banker, Lester Marlow (Randy Quaid), is afraid that he is about to be sent to jail; and to complicate matters even further, Jacy (Cybill Shepherd), after a minor career in the movies, has returned home a widow and reignites feelings in Duane he thought long dead. It may well be that neither the novel nor the film adds anything new to our understanding of the characters or situations explored so convincingly in *The Last Picture Show*, but the sad and funny *Texasville* is worth a read and a view.

In *Terms of Endearment* (1975), McMurtry concentrated upon Aurora Greenwood, a life-embracing widow from Boston who has settled in Houston. At times she verges on being intolerable as she corrects the grammar of her friends, exploits her suitors, and nags her daughter, Emma, but Aurora's love of life is infectious, and she emerges as a lovable if sometimes irritating character. The last quarter of the novel deals with the death of her daughter from cancer.

James L. Brooks wrote, produced, and directed the screenplay, concentrating on the relationship between Aurora (Shirley MacLaine) and Emma (Debra Winger), but he invented a quite different story to surround the main characters. The stodgy, seventy-year-old general in the novel becomes the fun-loving and much younger onetime astronaut, Garrett Breedlove (Jack Nicholson). Hector, with whom the married Emma has an affair, becomes the far more sympathetic Sam Burns (John Lithgow). What remains is a well-made, part comedy, part tearjerker distinguished by fine acting, but it is not the book that McMurtry wrote.

Kathleen Turner as Sarah Leary
announces to William Hurt as
her husband, Macon, that she
wants a divorce in *The
Accidental Tourist* (1988).

William Hurt as straight-laced Macon
Leary receives a lesson in dog training
from Geena Davis as kooky Muriel
Pritchett in *The Accidental Tourist*
(1988).

Almost three fourths of this film leans heavily toward the lighthearted, but once Emma's cancer is introduced rather abruptly, the mood takes a somber shift. The lack of foreshadowing seems to strike at the very foundations of dramatic unity, yet the turn of events retains a remarkable degree of reality. Certainly one of the triumphs of his screenplay was the creation of middle-aged, slightly paunchy Garrett Breedlove, who added a great deal of humor and warmth to the story. However, Brooks's real triumph was to remind us that our greatest gains come with risk and, sometimes, with loss.

Originally McMurtry wrote *Lonesome Dove* (1985) as a film script, but when it went unproduced, he turned the story into his most ambitious novel to date. Like the novel, which won the Pulitzer Prize, the eight-hour television production of *Lonesome Dove* (teleplay by Bill Wittliff, CBS, Cabin Fever Productions, 1991) tells the story of two old Texas Rangers, Woodrow Call (Tommy Lee Jones) and Gus McCrae (Robert Duvall), who drive a cattle herd from Texas to Montana. This production proved to be an almost literal translation of the novel, the only real difference lying in the relative importance of the black cowboy, Deets (Danny Glover), whose charac-

ter suffered some whittling down from novel to screen. Otherwise, this is superior entertainment.

Few authors have become as associated with a particular era as has Ken Kesey (1935–) with the hippie era, much of which is related to Kesey's own statements and to Tom Wolfe's book about Kesey, *The Electric Kool-Aid Acid Test* (1968). Also, Kesey's novel *One Flew Over the Cuckoo's Nest* (1962) became a favorite of the college crowd during the sixties.

The counterculture best-seller bombed as a 1963 Broadway play, despite having Kirk Douglas as its star, but as a film, *One Flew Over the Cuckoo's Nest* (United Artists, 1976), produced by Kirk's son, Michael, was a comic and unexpected hit. Czech director Milos Forman was an odd choice to helm the project, but his sense of black comedy merged effectively with a faithful script by Lawrence Hauben and Bo Goldman. The film made only a few minor changes, the biggest being that the stoic Chief (Will Sampson) no longer provides a drug-induced surrealistic narration. The plot and events have thus become far more structured and realistic.

The story remains basically identical to the book. McMurphy (Jack Nicholson), serving time for statutory

Jon Voight as Pat Conroy teaching his wards in Conroy's *Conrack* (1974).

227

Paperback tie-in with the 1979 film of *The Great Santini*.

suicide. McMurphy explodes, but guards subdue him and take him away. Later, when he is brought back to his bed, McMurphy, the Chief discovers, has been destroyed by the system—they have given him a frontal lobotomy. Enraged, the Chief rips the water fountain out of the floor and tosses it through the window, making good his long-dreamed-of escape.

Much of the poetic paranoia of the novel that made the book a leading contender for the Bible of the counter-culture has been dropped. McMurphy is no longer a Christ-like symbol but rather a symbol of freedom. This important mutation failed to hurt the film—on the contrary, it made it stronger by failing to link it so inextricably with the 1960s. Critics hailed the film, and even those who had some reservations, such as Pauline Kael in *The New Yorker*, thought it an outstanding effort. "*One Flew Over the Cuckoo's Nest* is a powerful, smashingly effective movie," she wrote. It won the Academy Award as Best Picture of the Year, with Oscars for director Forman, stars Nicholson and Fletcher, and writers Hauben and Goldman.

Kesey next wrote *Sometimes a Great Notion* (1964), a

Robert Duvall as Bull Meechum in *The Great Santini* (aka *The Ace*, 1979).

rape, is committed to the State Mental Hospital, where he encounters Nurse Rachet (Louise Fletcher) running a sterilized and impersonal ward with an iron hand. His antics soon awaken dormant feelings among the patients. He organizes a basketball game; when Nurse Rachet refuses to allow the ward to watch television, McMurphy provides a running commentary on an imaginary World Series game in front of a blank TV screen; he steals a bus and takes his fellow patients on a unsupervised fishing excursion; he slips playing cards of nude women into the deck; and finally, late one night, he brings two hookers into the ward.

It is this last act that precipitates the tragedy. When the next morning Nurse Rachet discovers the women, she bullies child-like Billy (Brad Dourif) into committing

228

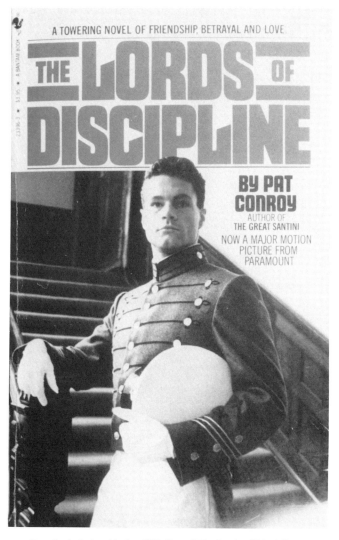

Paperback tie-in with the 1982 film of *The Lords of Discipline*.

an autobiographical nightmare of that period in his life. He followed this success with a number of powerful and unconventional novels of which one, *Being There* (1971), Kosinski's indictment of the mass media, was adapted for the screen by Kosinski himself and directed by Hal Ashby.

Being There (Lorimar/United Artists, 1979) is the story of Chance (Peter Sellers), a mentally retarded illiterate who has lived in a house with an old man for as long as he can remember, gardening and watching television. When the old man dies, Chance is thrust into a hostile environment, where he is hit by a limousine in which is Eve Rand (Shirley MacLaine), the wife of a rich and powerful financier (Melvyn Douglas). Fearing a lawsuit, Eve takes Chance home where his naïve honesty seduces everyone, including her husband. When Chance answers deep, philosophical questions in terms of gardening, which is all he knows, the Rands believe he is answering in symbolic logic, and are amazed at his intelligence. Soon he is appearing on television. He is an immediate hit with the public, and by story's end, he has met the President of the United States (Jack Warden) and is being considered as a running mate in the next election.

As a protagonist, Chance, because he is mentally retarded, shows no growth; neither does anyone else in the film. Yet, the power of the story and the characters is undeniable. Just as he did in the novel, Chance dominates

far more ambitious but ultimately less successful novel than *Cuckoo's Nest*. As a film, *Sometimes a Great Notion* (Universal, 1971), also known later as *Never Give an Inch*, was a rather old-fashioned story of Henry Stamper (Henry Fonda), patriarch of a family of loggers who defy the unions and keep their business open during a strike. One of the sons, Hank (Paul Newman), has stayed home to help run the business, and another, Lee (Michael Sarrazin), returns to get over a bad year. Although certain individual scenes often work quite well, the story, adapted from Kesey by John Gay, was murky from beginning to end.

Where Ken Kesey wrote in a surreal prose that often sounded drug-induced, Jerzy Kosinski (1933–91) wrote in a surreal prose that was experience-induced. Kosinski was a native of Poland who suffered through World War Two, and his first novel, *The Painted Bird* (1965), was

David Keith (right) tries to give some good advice to a plebe (athlete turned actor Mark Breland) under pressure in *The Lords of Discipline* (1982).

Nick Nolte as Tom Wingo and Barbra Streisand as Susan Lowenstein, his sister's (and then his) psychiatrist with whom he falls in love in *The Prince of Tides* (1991).

events, but he dominates because he spouts clichés and homilies he has heard from television. He doesn't have an original thought in his head, but people believe he does, and television makes him a celebrity and ultimately propels him toward the White House. And the President has a heart problem that he has not shared with even his closest advisors. It is a frighteningly caustic story disguised as comedy.

Anne Tyler (1941–) already had nine novels behind her when *The Accidental Tourist* (1985) appeared. This unsentimental, gently comic, and poignant novel for which she won the National Book Critics Circle Book Award told of Macon Leary, a middle-aged man who, after the death of his twelve-year-old son and an unwanted divorce, trades his well-ordered life for the surprises in a bittersweet romance with a much younger woman.

Director Lawrence Kasden wrote six drafts of *The Accidental Tourist* (Warner Bros., 1988) before feeling confident enough to send a copy to the author. She so admired it that when Kasden came to Baltimore to scout locations, she chauffeured him around pointing out various locales where the events of the novel took place.

Much of the humor of the book remained, especially the scene in which the Learys play their favorite card game, Vaccination, which is so complicated that only the Learys can understand the rules.

Although he omitted some characters and telescoped some events, Kasden remained true to both the plot and spirit of the novel. He expanded the role of the wife (Kathleen Turner), making her even more hollow than in the book, and managed in the character of the veterinarian's assistant, Muriel (Geena Davis), to capture all the quirky innocence and vivacity that attracted Macon. One of the strengths of this film also lies in the understated performance of William Hurt, who so deftly captured Macon Leary, allowing us to see into the interior of a man too frightened by the world to show his feelings but through Muriel, able to open up to life.

Like Larry McMurtry, Pat Conroy (1945–) is also a regional writer, usually setting his novels in South Carolina. Also, like McMurtry, Conroy has begun to be recognized by critics and public alike as an important American novelist who uses regionalism as a way to examine universal values and ideas.

Robin Williams as T. S. Garp surveying their new house with Mary Beth Hurt as his wife, Helen, in *The World According to Garp* (1982).

Conroy's first novel, *The Great Santini* (1976), was also replete with autobiographical incidents. Born of a marine father from Chicago and a Southern belle from Georgia, Conroy turned his family into the characters of Colonel Bull Meechum, a hard-nosed military officer, and his wife, Lillian.

Two standout episodes from the book are also standout episodes in the film *The Great Santini* (Orion/Warner Bros., 1979), adapted and directed by Lewis John Carlino. The first is the basketball game between Bull (Robert Duvall) and his son Ben (Michael O'Keefe). The game is rough and dirty, the epitome of Bull's attitude toward winning. Lillian (Blythe Danner) and the kids

Paperback tie-in with the 1982 film of *The World According to Garp*.

After graduating from The Citadel, Conroy became a high school teacher, taking a job for a year on one of the remote islands of the South Carolina coast. From this experience came *The Water Is Wide* (1972), an autobiographical recounting of that year. Conroy battles the ignorance of the school bureaucracy and the illiteracy of the young black children.

Hollywood was quick to see the possibilities, and the result was *Conrack* (20th Century-Fox, 1974), by the same team which worked on fellow author McMurtry's *Hud*, director Martin Ritt and screenwriters Irving Ravetch and Harriet Frank Jr. Conroy (Jon Voight) arrives on the island to discover most of the children are illiterate, and like a latter-day Mr. Chips, sets out to impart education to these unfortunate children whose inability to pronounce his name accounts for the title. He introduces them to a world that includes, among other things, classical music and baseball, neither of which they have ever experienced. At first the children and parents fight him and his methods, but gradually they are won over by his sweetness and dedication. However, a villain lurks in the wings. Skeffington (Hume Cronyn), a conservative, old-style state official who believes in the three R's, manages to get Conroy fired. As Conroy departs the island, he leaves behind the hope that he has made some lasting difference in the lives of the inhabitants.

231

cheer for Ben. As the game winds toward its conclusion, Ben baits Bull. "Do you know, Dad, that not one of us has ever beaten you in a single game?" And then with a quick move, Ben drives in for a lay-up and the winning basket. But Bull can't live with losing, and he abruptly changes the rules by insisting his son win by two baskets. Lillian protests, and he screams at her and the other kids. Then, as Ben walks into the house, he bounces the ball off his son's head, taunting him. "Come on, sissy. Is that tears in your eyes?" he asks. Later, as Ben and his mother watch Bull continue to shoot baskets in the pouring rain, Lillian tries to explain her husband's actions. "You've got a strange father, Ben, but in his own way, that's him down there saying, 'I'm sorry, Ben. I was wrong.'" Bull has become the vanquished, a situation that he may abhor but that he must come to accept.

In the novel, Ben was shorter than his father by several inches, but he had youth on his side. In the film, the two antagonists are much more closely matched, thus to some degree cheapening the victory. Also, in the novel, once the game is over and Lillian protests, Bull kicks his wife in the behind as a way to get her to shut up. This extra little bit of family abuse was omitted from the film.

The other scene, taken almost verbatim from the novel, is Bull's begrudging acknowledgment of the passing of the old order. On Ben's eighteenth birthday, Bull gives him his World War Two flight jacket. His gift represents genuine respect and love for his oldest son. It is the closest the fighter pilot can come to saying, "I love you." During the course of events, Ben gradually comes to understand his father, and through understanding, to respect and love him.

The central character of Conroy's second novel, *The Lords of Discipline* (1980), is Will McLean, a cadet at a Southern military school who acts very much like a slightly older Ben Meechum. As in the novel, the film version (Paramount, 1983) opens in 1964 during Will's senior year. The Institute is about to get its first black cadet, Pearce (Mark Breland), and the commander (Robert Prosky) assigns Will McLean (David Keith) to make sure that nothing happens to him. On his own, Will also takes responsibility for looking after Poteete (Malcolm Danare), a fat slop of a cadet who is seen by his fellows as a whining crybaby. It is while he is trying to protect these two cadets that Will learns of the Ten, a secret society that protects the purity of the corps. The Ten drives Poteete to suicide and tries to drive Pearce from the school.

A little over halfway through the novel, Will reflects upon his own first year as a cadet, when power itself was an attractive aphrodisiac, when the link between power and sex was so clearly evident. But this whole year is

missing from the film, as is also a love affair between Will and a local girl. The film concentrates upon Will's battle with the secret organization as he attempts to discover the identity of the man behind it.

Within the confines of plot, the film was reasonably faithful, although there was no way that the screen could adequately reproduce Conroy's rich style. In an effort to stay as close as possible to the first-person narrative, the audience saw and heard only what Will saw and heard. However, in the novel, Will was of Irish descent and far too sensitive to play Southern military man with any enthusiasm. Screenwriters Thomas Pope and Lloyd Fonvielle turned him into a Southerner who never questions his personal fitness for military life or Southern values until Pearce arrives. The problem with the film, directed by Franc Roddam, was that so much of the story—fully one-half of the novel—was entirely omitted, and therefore, much of Will's motivation is obscure and obtuse.

Conroy's most ambitious work certainly is *The Prince*

The eccentric Berry family in *The Hotel New Hampshire* (1984). Back row: Beau Bridges (left), Jodie Foster, and Rob Lowe; front row: Wallace Shawn and Jennifer Dundas.

Melanie Griffith as Maria Ruskin and Tom Hanks as her lover, Sherman McCoy, in *The Bonfire of the Vanities* (1990).

of Tides (1987), a marvelous story of a man coming to grips with his past. The film version (Columbia, 1991), with Conroy collaborating on the screenplay with Becky Johnston, retained many of the surface details of the novel, but cut down the role of the brother, the Prince of Tides, to concentrate upon the coach, Tom Wingo (Nick Nolte), especially his love affair with the psychiatrist, Susan Lowenstein (Barbra Streisand). The film, directed by Streisand, tried to make up for Conroy's rich prose by stunning photography, but the complexity of the narrative simply did not translate well to the screen, despite the hard efforts of all concerned.

Postwar novels have often been a mixture of the bizarre and the commonplace, and no author so successfully wedded these two elements as John Irving (1942–) in his most successful work, *The World According to Garp* (1978). Despite the rather grim plot outline, the novel is often hilarious. When it came to the screen, *The World According to Garp* (Warner Bros., 1982) followed

the book with amazing fidelity. Even the sexual content that twenty years before could never have been included now appeared intact.

The film makes only one rather important detour. At the end of the novel, Garp (Robin Williams) is shot and killed by a radical feminist. The film also has him shot by the feminist, but the final scene shows him being flown away in a helicopter with his wife (Mary Beth Hurt), and a doctor who tells her that he will live. This didn't seem to hurt things much, and John Irving, who had a small part as a wrestling referee, was around to supervise things. As the *New York Times* said, "Like the best film adaptations, *Garp* is essentially faithful to the novel on which it is based, even when it isn't following the book literally."

Irving's only other work to reach the screen to date is *The Hotel New Hampshire* (1981). As a film (Orion, 1984), directed by Tony Richardson, who also wrote the screenplay, it played fast and loose with the novel, dropping the names of some of the characters and calling them "Father" and "Mother," much as Doctorow did in

233

Bruce Willis as American journalist Peter Fallow and Morgan Freeman as Judge Kovitsky in *The Bonfire of the Vanities* (1990). In Wolfe's book, the journalist was British and the judge a white Jew (initially to have been played by Alan Arkin).

Ragtime. Also in the 1981 novel, one of the characters is Susie the Bear, a young American woman who wears a bear suit as a protection from reality. Inexplicably, the film turns Susie (Nastassia Kinski) into a European, although her phobia remains intact. Much of the early section of the novel disappears, and while the story opens and closes in the States, the family's tenure in Vienna has become the centerpiece. However, the film, with Jodie Foster as Franny, Rob Lowe as John, and Beau Bridges as Win Berry, did retain a semblance of the novel's fairy-tale atmosphere.

During the early 1960s, Tom Wolfe (1931–) was the leading exponent of the New Journalism, a method of telling a nonfiction story in fictional terms—in other words, the nonfiction novel, which Truman Capote claimed to have invented when he wrote *In Cold Blood*. Wolfe's *Right Stuff* (1979) was such a work.

The screenplay by Philip Kaufman, who also directed,

234

Paperback tie-in with the 1983 film of *The Right Stuff*.

was, like Wolfe's book, a reenactment of the early years of the space program. In a sense, the book and film both see the aerial pioneer as the lone Westerner, taking him beyond the sound barrier where he earns his spurs in space. To Wolfe and Kaufman, "the right stuff" is measured in how much physical courage a man shows, and no one shows this more than test pilot Chuck Yeager (Sam Shepard), who breaks the sound barrier while burdened with deep bruises and a couple of broken ribs.

Kaufman plays around with chronological events. The film ends with Yeager walking away from the crash of his NF-104, when in actuality this happened some months before the last solo flight in NASA's Mercury program. And, too, tall, slim playwright Sam Shepard is rather miscast as the short, squarely-built Chuck Yeager. Aside from such changes, the film is a remarkably faithful adaptation, if not in the strict sense of events, certainly in characters and tone. Throughout, Kaufman maintains a knowing hipness that comes right from the pages of the book. At times this hipness may extend to broad comedy—especially funny is the scene in which Lyndon Johnson (Donald Moffat) is trying to converse with Wernher von Braun (Scott Beach) but can't understand a word the man is saying—and other times the film utilizes unexpected irony—at a bar, Yeager is apparently picking up a girl with some very racy talk, but she turns out to be his wife (Barbara Hershey).

The astronauts themselves emerge as remarkably rounded characters. On the first orbital flight, Gus Grissom (Fred Ward) displays all "the right stuff" until his capsule lands in the ocean, the hatch blows and the capsule sinks. Grissom is indirectly blamed for the failure and is resentful when he receives less than a hero's welcome. John Glenn (Ed Harris), the one man among the Mercury group who fitted *Life* magazine's image of an American astronaut as a clean-living patriot, rebels against the news media. On the eve of his departure into space, Glenn tells his wife, who is embarrassed by her stuttering, that she doesn't have to let anyone into her house, including the President of the United States.

With his next book, Tom Wolfe forsook the New Journalism to write a darkly comic novel, *The Bonfire of the Vanities* (1988), the story of Sherman McCoy, a top bond trader on Wall Street, who, while out with his mistress, is involved in a hit and run accident for which he is not responsible but which ultimately rips apart the fabric of his life. The novel was a complex, multilayered work that explored the social strata of New York City from the wealthy world inhabited by McCoy to the impoverished world of the black community. Yet no one came away unscathed as Wolfe laid bare the pretensions and hypocrisies of each group, including his own world of journalism.

At whom the disastrous film *The Bonfire of the*

Vanities (Warner Bros., 1990) was aimed is anybody's guess. If it were aimed at the readers of the novel, it was a major miscalculation. Most readers were outraged at the changes, which undercut much of what the novel had to say.

Sherman McCoy (Tom Hanks), a self-styled Master of the Universe among Wall Street bond salesmen, takes a wrong turn into the South Bronx while driving his mistress, Maria (Melanie Griffith), home. Believing they are threatened by two black youths, they accidentally injure one of the kids, but because theirs is a clandestine affair, they fail to report the incident to the police. Once the press, exemplified by Fallow (Bruce Willis)— changed from a hack British journalist in the novel to a hack American journalist—gets hold of the story, justice is put aside at the expense of class and racial politics. Soon McCoy's life is in ruins, destroyed by junk

journalism and junk politics.

In the novel, McCoy eventually comes to a self-realization of what he has turned into and what the world has done to him, and throwing aside the last vestiges of his illusions, he turns on his tormentors. He wins, but his victory is a pyrrhic one. Not only has he lost everything, but the establishment continues to pursue the case even after the charges against him have been thrown out by the court. The film, adapted by Michael Christofer, forgoes this moment and substitutes broad comedy without moral weight. In the end, the judge (Morgan Freeman)—black here but a white Jew in the novel—makes a Capra-like speech in which he admonishes the people to remember what their grandmothers taught them, which manages to make a travesty of Wolfe's tough-minded cynicism.

Writers from the 1960s and beyond have fared rather well in having their works adapted for the movies. Doctorow's *Ragtime*, despite the difficulties in translation, is an intriguing film. McMurtry's *Last Picture Show, Hud*, and *Terms of Endearment* each won praise from critics and public alike. Tyler's *Accidental Tourist*, while taking its time developing its characters, paid dividends for those who saw it. Pat Conroy's *Conrack* is an entertaining film, albeit not a great one, while *The Great Santini* certainly deserves the status of minor screen classic. As a film, Irving's *World According to Garp* displayed a few problems, but overall captured the comic tone of the novel. Wolfe's *Right Stuff* emerged as a compelling nonfiction novel and a compelling movie. Thank goodness each of these films received better treatment than *The Bonfire of the Vanities*, a truly disappointing adaptation that missed all the subtleties of the novel.

The seven Mercury astronauts portrayed: (from left) Fred Ward as Gus Grissom, Dennis Quaid as Gordon Cooper, Scott Paulin as Deke Slayton, Ed Harris as John Glenn, Charles Frank as Scott Carpenter, Scott Glenn as Alan Shepard, and Lance Hendriksen as Wally Schirra in *The Right Stuff* (1983).

Warner Baxter as Jay Gatsby in the first version of *The Great Gatsby* (1926).

THIRTEEN

"OH, WOULDN'T THAT MAKE A GREAT FILM"

One evening after a bad day dealing with Marlon Brando on the set of *The Young Lions*, Irwin Shaw complained to Ernest Hemingway that Hollywood was ruining his novel. Hemingway told Shaw that he was a fool for not realizing what they were going to do to his book. In defense, Shaw replied, "I'm a writer for movies as well as for books." Hemingway told Shaw that he would have been a much better writer had he not written screenplays. Angered, Shaw took a poke at Hemingway, and the two had to be restrained by friends.

Shaw's excursions into the world of film, although more extensive than most American mainstream writers', were not unique. As motion pictures began to assume more and more importance in the lives of Americans, it was only natural for artists to be drawn into that world. Even before the 1920s, writers were becoming increasingly aware of the power and importance of film. Jack London tried his hand at writing scenarios and, a few years later, Booth Tarkington performed the same task. Damon Runyon turned to producing. Fitzgerald, Faulkner, and Steinbeck were at one time or another employed by Hollywood and put their abilities to writing

film scripts, a trend that escalated through the 1940s and beyond with writers sometimes adapting their own works. Throughout the forties and fifties, Irwin Shaw, Carson McCullers, Truman Capote, James Michener, James Jones, and Herman Wouk all, to one extent or another, worked in films. Even Joseph Heller wrote several screenplays under pseudonyms. In the case of Norman Mailer, he wrote, produced, directed, and even starred in his own productions.

But, as in the case of Shaw and Hemingway, there is still disagreement over how involved a writer should become in a film adaptation of his or her work. When Tom Wolfe sold *The Bonfire of the Vanities* to Hollywood, he took the money and ran, showing absolutely no interest in what they did to his novel. "I listen to what my wife and children say. I listen to my editor," said Wolfe. "I don't want the advice of a mob." He came under criticism from some like Spike Lee who thought that he should have shown more concern, but Wolfe explained further that after dedicating so much time to a book, he needed to move on to something new. He had exhausted the material. Although Larry McMurtry has adapted a number of his own works, he echoed Wolfe's feelings. "I just usually find I've exhausted my interest in a story after too much time," he said. Vladimir Nabokov added, "Turning one's novel into a movie script is rather like making a series of sketches or a painting that has long ago been finished and framed."

John Irving tried to adapt his first novel, *Setting Free the Bears* (1969), but the script was never produced. After that, he allowed others to adapt both *The World According to Garp* and *The Hotel New Hampshire*, films that were effective more in parts than as complete works of art. If he gave up control of the screenplays, he remained interested enough to keep some control. "Even if I don't want to do the screenplay," he said, "I steer the book into one director's hands, a director who cannot be replaced and who has final control."

Truman Capote once remarked that Hollywood experience had soured him. "I just despise it," he said. Yet even Capote produced *Truman Capote's Trilogy* in an effort to turn his written art into filmic art. Occasionally a writer might produce a novel with films in mind in order to make a quick buck, but in most cases, a writer's personal art is far more important than the money he or she might make from films. "I never write a piece of fiction with a film in mind," said John Irving.

But writers continue to sell their works to Hollywood, in many cases to buy time to write. Hollywood continues the practice of turning their works into something other than what the authors intended. Who could recognize Tom Wolfe's *Bonfire of the Vanities* from the film? It may be that a novel such as Wolfe's is simply not filmable, that the ironic and cynical tone of the book cannot make the transference to the screen. In that case, we may ask: Then why did Hollywood buy the book in the first place?

The *New York Times*, in reviewing the 1923 version of Sinclair Lewis's *Main Street*, provides an answer. "It would not really matter to many producers what was between the covers," said the critic, "so long as they could obtain possession of the title, a valuable box office asset." But in today's world where television, newspapers, and magazines churn out a plethora of reviews and articles on every new American film, the potential audience for such a film can learn about it long before it is even released. One that butchers a literary phenomenon like *The Bonfire of the Vanities* takes the chance of automatically killing itself at the box office with the very audience that it seeks to attract.

The viewing public can be thankful for one thing—that within the system that exploits artists, there have been a few people of consequence and conscience who have brought forth works of art. Occasionally these works of art have been adaptations. Among others, *The Haunting* (based on Shirley Jackson's *Haunting of Hill House*), *The Heiress* (based on James's *Washington Square*), *A Place in the Sun* (based on Theodore Dreiser's *An American Tragedy*), *The Grapes of Wrath*, *Of Mice and Men*, *The Last Picture Show*, and *Hud* have all become classics of the American screen just as they are classics of American fiction.

In a way, the problem with adaptations lies in the audience and its expectations. When we have read a book we particularly admire—or, in some rare instances, a book we love—we want to see the book come alive on the screen, to see our imaginations vindicated and realized. Too often films fail to do this. Even if a film is well conceived and executed, we leave the theater disappointed because there is no way it can live up to our imaginations. Perhaps John Irving put it into perspective when he said, "Some people read a book and say, 'Oh, wouldn't that make a great film.' I read a novel and I say, 'What a great novel.'"

Index

242

245